1993
- Nov-Dec
2006/

Summ 2016.

CW00486623

500
British Ghosts
and
Hauntings

500

British Ghosts and Hauntings

by
Sarah Hapgood

foulsham
LONDON • NEW YORK • TORONTO • SYDNEY

foulsham
Yeovil Road, Slough, Berkshire SL1 4JH

ISBN 0-572-01820-7

Photoset in Great Britain by Encounter Photosetting, Fleet, Hampshire
Printed in Great Britain by St. Edmundsbury Press, Bury St. Edmunds

Contents

5

CHESHIRE

CLEVELAND

CORNWALL

CUMBRIA

DERBYSHIRE

DEVON

8

DORSET

DURHAM

ESSEX

GLOUCESTER

LANCASHIRE

LEICESTER

LINCOLNSHIRE

LONDON

MERSEYSIDE

NORFOLK

NORTHAMPTONSHIRE

NORTHUMBERLAND

NOTTINGHAMSHIRE

OXFORDSHIRE

SHROPSHIRE

SURREY

Bletchingley Church   74
Carshalton House, Sutton   104
Clandon Park, West Clandon, Guildford   113
Farnham Church   146
Ham House, Richmond   164
Loseley House, Guildford   206
Polesden Lacey, Bookham   236
Puttenden Manor, Nr. Lingfield   243
St. Mary's Church, Reigate   260
Top Rank Bingo Hall, Sutton   296

EAST SUSSEX

Bateman's Burwash   53
Battle Abbey, Battle   54
Beachy Head, Eastbourne   55
Bodiam Castle, Nr. Robertsbridge   76
Brighton Royal Pavilion   89
Ditchling Beacon, Ditchling   133
Hastings Castle   171
Herstmonceux Castle, Hailsham   175
Michelham Priory, Upper Dicker   216
Pevensey Castle   233
St. Peter's Church, Preston Park, Brighton   262
Warbleton Priory Farm, Rushlake Green   312
Westham Church   317

WEST SUSSEX

Arundel Castle   44
Bramber Castle   84
Crab & Lobster Inn, Sidlesham   120
Kingley Vale, Stoughton   193
Uppark, South Harting   306

19

TYNE & WEAR

WARWICKSHIRE

WEST MIDLANDS

WILTSHIRE

NORTH YORKSHIRE

SOUTH YORKSHIRE

25

Foreword
by
Tom Perrott
Chairman of The Ghost Club

IT WAS with a feeling of very great pleasure that I accepted this invitation to write a foreword to what I feel will prove to be a most popular and often referred to book. For some considerable time, in a variety of ways, I have become aware of how great is the interest in ghosts. During the past year I have received well over a hundred letters from school-children living in all parts of the United Kingdom, who have chosen ghostly projects for some of their examinations and require further information about them. This I am only too willing to provide because some of these young and enthusiastic inquirers I could well be our psychical researchers of the future.

Again, for the last two years I have been fortunate enough to participate in a 'Ghostline Phone-In', as a member of an advisory panel, chosen by one of our national newspapers, to try and help people either claiming to be experiencing psychic problems in the present, or who are only too pleased to regale me with stories of confrontations with ghosts that might have happened to them in the past. On both occasions my colleagues and I have been inundated with calls from all parts of the country, which have kept us all occupied continuously from early in the morning until late in the evening. Many of these calls have been genuine 'calls from the heart', whilst those of a purely frivolous nature have been in a distinct minority. These examples would appear to indicate two things; the numbers of people who have a definite interest in apparitions, and the types of people who claim to have been most affected by them.

In addition I am constantly receiving calls from various branches of the media whose representatives wish to obtain details of sites said to be haunted, of which there are said to be several thousands in the United Kingdom alone. Last year, as a means of raising much needed funds, a national charity organised a number of sponsored nightly vigils in a selection of 'Haunted Houses' in all parts of the country, for which they consulted me for details of locations. It is this sort of enquiry that indicates to what extent this book could, perhaps, be utilized by providing relevant stories of ghostly happenings in specific areas.

I am also frequently asked to address various groups and organisations on the subject of 'Ghosts and Hauntings' and in the ensuing question time, am often asked "How did you become involved in this sort of thing in the first place ?" As an eventual member of the Folklore Society, I became interested in legends of hauntings at a very early age, and living in the country at that time, it was easy to approach members of the indigenous population and to hear from them accounts of old legends that had been passed down verbally from one generation to another. However one has to bear in mind that, as in the party game of 'Chinese Whispers', the latest version of a story offered, could well be deviated somewhat from the original.

In the course of my investigations I discovered that many of these old stories might well have been deliberate smoke-screens circulated by smugglers to scare local snoopers away from the scenes of their nefarious activities. What could provide a better storage space for illicit liquor and other contraband than a capacious 'haunted' crypt of an isolated church, or the roomy cellars of a 'haunted' vicarage or rectory situated in a lonely part of the country and occupied by an obliging and co-operative incumbent ? Some of these stories would appear to be of very ancient origin and could well be faint murmurs from the 'Dawn of our History' and the early days of our civilization as we know it. The Celts as a race, paid a great deal of respect to human heads and for the contents of intelligence that were believed to be contained within the skull. Accordingly the heads of both friends and enemies were often preserved for posterity after death. When barrows have been excavated the occupant has often been revealed peacefully recumbent with his severed head reposing between his legs. When people describe encounters with ghosts, they often claim that the apparition was headless. Could therefore this state of decapitation be a half-forgotten folk-memory of a form of ritual execution going back to Celtic times ? Another ancient belief which could well provide a basis for a commonly told 'ghost story' is that of the 'Wild Hunt'. The existence of this is to be found in both Germanic and Celtic folklore, and it tells of how a wild bunch of restless spirits of the dead would ride through the sky on their spectral horses, accompanied by their ghostly hounds, all baying and making unearthly noises. It was said in mediaeval times that witches would sometimes participate in the wild revelry, led by a pagan goddess, later to be demoted to the rank of Devil when Christianity became established. It was said that anyone who was unfortunate enough to hear the sounds of the Wild Hunt would not live for very long afterwards. This legend is to be found particularly in the West of England and it has been claimed that as late as the 1940's these horrifying and awesome sounds have been heard in the area, on the ancient feast day of Samhain, better known as 'All Hallows Eve'.

So much for certain aspects of our spectral antiquity, but when descending into modern times, we sometimes find that owners of certain licensed premises are not averse to spreading rumours of strange happenings taking place in the building when they find that their sales are plummeting. This does not mean to say that strange and inexplicable things *do* sometimes occur in some of these ancient houses, but not perhaps as frequently as is claimed. It would be well to state that the terms of reference of the Folklorist are to examine and record the traditional orally transmitted beliefs, practices and tales of people, and to record them as being a part of our heritage before they otherwise become either lost or forgotten. His function is not to establish the authenticity of these legendary happenings or indeed to rationalize upon them.

So much then for my initial approach to the subject of ghosts. At a later date I became aware of the fact that sometimes strange phenomena were said to manifest themselves at the present time and in an effort to learn more about these strange events, I became a member of the Society for Psychical Research, an organisation which was founded in 1882, to 'examine without prejudice or prepossession and in a scientific spirit those faculties of man, real or supposed, which appear to be inexplicable in terms of any generally recognized hypothesis'. In this capacity I have often had the opportunity to investigate cases of alleged hauntings, many of which have had natural causes, but a few of which have had to be discarded with the inevitable question mark against them.

With the absence of conclusive proof, where alleged phenomena are concerned, one can only advance one's own personal theories and as a result of this, one is likely to be accused, perhaps understandably, of "sitting on the fence", a position that I have occupied precariously for some considerable time.

In a world where strange and inexplicable things undoubtedly happen from time to time, but where many of them may be explained by the development of science in the future and as a direct result of research into such matters, it is as well to proverbially "keep one's weather eye open". In the light of this, I feel that I can do no better than to conclude by quoting an extract from a book written by the eminent parapsychologist Andrew Green, in which he writes: "It is essential for any investigator to adopt an open mind and to be prepared to sift and search and question everything. If you have any preconceived ideas about hauntings, re-consider their logicality. Never dismiss the possibility of the existence of apparitions for not only does this attitude resemble that of the proverbial ostrich, but it could result in some unpleasant experiences if you come face to face with a ghost."

Tom Perrott
London

Introduction

RECENTLY an American court decided that prospective buyers of a house were entitled to sue for the return of their £20,000 deposit, because they weren't aware that the building was haunted when they signed on the dotted line. An article in the *Liverpool Daily Post* on 8 August 1991 revealed that a similar law may be brought into effect in Britain soon, whereby all relevant information pertaining to a property MUST be disclosed to the buyer, and that includes the possibility of a ghost on the premises. Some people argue that a ghost can be a welcome addition to the household and may even help to push the value of the property up even further!

Great Britain has more ghosts per square mile than any other country in the world, a fact which makes many of us rather proud, but there is also a small band of dissenters who seem to have been getting rather a lot of attention in recent years. There has been an almost hysterical desire on their part to completely discredit anyone who has anything remotely to do with the field of the supernatural. I have no idea what motivates these confirmed sceptics and can only say that their narrowness of vision and negativity simply astonishes me.

What I have tried to do with this book is to provide a simple guide to the various haunted hotspots around the

British Isles that I have found of interest. With some 500 cases there are inevitably a wide variety of hauntings ranging from those that will stand up to further research, to those that have recently come to light and about which little is known at the present time, and those that are highly dubious but fascinating for the colourful legends and stories attached to them.

I do not claim to put any pretentious full stops on any arguments, sometimes I have given my opinion of a haunting, but I don't assume I have the one and only opinion on the subject. This book is merely intended as a guide for those showing a healthy and lighthearted interest in the supernatural. At this stage in the game it is enough to investigate, for we are still a very long way off obtaining scientific proof. The essence of psychic investigation is to keep an open mind (and a sense of humour) at all times – something the obsessive sceptics might do well to consider!

SARAH HAPGOOD
Wantage

A4
Between Chippenham and Bath, Wiltshire

LORRY-DRIVER Laurie Newman had a rather disturbing brush with the supernatural as he drove along this stretch of road at 2:30 one morning. He saw what appeared to be the figure of a nun walking beside the road, and slowed down to pull out and pass her. As he did so, the figure turned and sprang, grabbed the side of his cab, and leered through the side window. Laurie found he was looking into the face of a grinning skull.

A12
Between Lowestoft and Great Yarmouth, Suffolk

WHEN AT THE END of the 19th century a hunchback postman died, no one would have thought that this fairly innocuous event would lead to a spate of mysterious accidents on this road that have persisted for nearly a century. In 1960 a lorry-driver suddenly veered off the road into a tree and was killed outright. Twenty years later, a motorist had a similar accident.

Barely a year on, a cyclist inexplicably rode straight into

an oncoming car and on another occasion motorist Andrew Cutajar reported seeing an old man standing directly in his path. He drove straight through him and hit the kerb, while the old man calmly vanished. Former policeman Frank Colby saw the same hunchbacked figure cross the road and disappear. A psychic researcher stated that the problematic spectre was one William Balls, a hunchback postman, whose body was found frozen on the road during the winter of 1899.

A38
Barrow Gurney, Avon

A WOMAN IN a white coat has a habit of suddenly appearing and disappearing around here.

A38
Wellington, Somerset

UNLIKE THE aforementioned A38 phantom this particular one is fairly-well documented and several witnesses have given detailed accounts of his activities. He appears to be a very predictable ghost and his appearances are fairly routine. He usually carries a torch and flags down unsuspecting motorists.

In August 1970 he was reported in the *Western Morning News*. The story was that a lady travelling from Oake to Taunton late at night came across a middle-aged man in a raincoat. She narrowly avoided hitting him before he vanished. On another occasion lorry-driver Harold Unsworth was trundling along at 3:00 AM in the vicinity of the *Blackbird Inn*, which is about a mile from the *Heatherton Grange Hotel* where the ghost is normally sighted. Harold picked up a hitch-hiker who asked to be set-down at a bridge at Holcombe. Harold's passenger was a joyless soul who seemed to be a font of unwanted information regarding several accidents at the bridge.

A couple of days later, Harold saw the same man in exactly the same spot. Again, he asked to be dropped at the bridge at Holcombe. Harold saw him yet again a month later and the whole scenario became even more familiar, but when he saw him again in November 1968, three miles further on from the bridge, he felt that he couldn't bear to put up with the old misery again. He swerved to pass him and very nearly ran straight into him. Harold stopped and looked back to make sure he was alright. The man angrily shook his fist at him … and vanished.

A41
Chadwick End, Warwickshire

DURING THE 1960s some police officers were driving along this main road in the small hours when they saw several nuns out for a walk. The sisters' black habits made them rather difficult to see in the dark, so the policemen decided to stop and have a quiet word with them about the matter of pedestrian safety at night.

They followed the nuns into the grounds of Chadwick Manor and watched them vanish at the entrance of the house. The ghostly nuns were seen by other officers on the road about a mile south of the Manor. When the officers drove back to speak to the nuns they could find no trace of them.

A64
Between Pickering and York, North Yorkshire

THE GHOST on this particular stretch of road seems to be a very public-spirited spectre. The story behind her is that she was Nance, a farmer's daughter, who was once engaged to a mailcoach driver. For reasons best known to herself though, she decided to run off with another man. Her jilted lover later found her in a very bad way, on the side of a road clutching a baby in her arms. He took her on to his coach, and Nance told him that the man she had left him for had turned out to be a highwayman who was married to someone else. Nance and her baby both died later that night from malnutrition.

Several years later Nance's ex-boyfriend was driving his coach precariously through dense fog, when suddenly the reins were seized from him by invisible hands. Nance then appeared behind him, looking exactly as she had done on the night of her death. She took over the driving of the horses and successfully drove the coach safely into the yard of the *Black Swan*. It is said that her ghost can still be seen on foggy nights, moving in the glare of car headlights. Any driver fortunate enough to see her will be directed safely through the fog, while the cat's eyes on the road will be clearly seen through her translucent form.

A143
Between Geldeston and Bungay, Norfolk

THE ROAD to Bungay is haunted by a phantom coach-and-four.

ABBEY CHURCH
Waltham Abbey, Essex

THE CHURCH was built in 1060 in honour of a cross that had been carried here. From then on it has been visited by many pilgrims, and is a possible burial-place of King Harold, killed at the Battle of Hastings in 1066. During the 1970s there were sightings of a ghostly monk in the churchyard.

ABBEY HOUSE
Barnwell, Cambridge, Cambridgeshire

ABBEY HOUSE was built around 1580 from remnants of Barnwell Priory, itself established in 1112. In its time the house has played host to some intriguing hauntings, which may have mysteriously contributed to the sudden departure of two former tenants from the house at 2:00 in the morning. No reason for their flight was ever given however. During the 1920s the wife of the owner, Mrs Ascham, saw a woman's disembodied head at the foot of her bed on three separate occasions, once in the middle of the afternoon. News of the haunting reached the ears of Professor F J M Stratton, President of the Society for Psychical Research (1953-1954) who rented the house for a month. The Professor reported hearing muttering and singing from an empty room.

1968 was a vintage year for the haunting of Abbey House. The daughter of the house repeatedly heard strange noises night after night, and her dog would rush barking to one corner of a panelled room. A phantom Grey Lady (almost an essential requisite of a haunted house) was seen loitering around the iron gates set in a wall and on the path at the back of the house. This ghost was seen twice in 1969 and is believed to have been one of the nuns of St

Radegund, who was said to have had a lover at the Priory. The story goes that she was walled-up alive when her indiscretions were made public, a common punishment for wayward nuns in the "good old days". There is some confusion as to whether she and the White Lady – who haunted the bedrooms – were one and the same or two entirely different phantoms.

There are spectral animals at the house as well. A red squirrel runs along a wall and disappears when anyone approaches, and a phantom hare is said to appear in the garden, usually when snow is on the ground. Other psychic phenomena includes sheets being pulled off sleeping guests, groans, raps, rustling and the sound of furniture being moved about.

In recent times three clergymen performed exorcisms at the house, which seem to have vanquished the supernatural forces for the time being … but some say that disquieting shadows can still be seen around the house from time to time, especially on Autumn afternoons.

ACONBURY (CHURCH)
Hereford & Worcester

ACONBURY CHURCH is bogged down in myth and legend, chiefly concerning the exorcism of one Roger de Clifford. He was a monk whose tomb is in the church.

The clergy trapped his restless spirit in a bottle and buried it underneath his tomb, but in the church wall so that he was neither inside or outside the building. The exorcism didn't work though as a tall, shadowy, hooded figure in flowing garments has been seen since then.

ADELPHI HOTEL
Lime Street, Liverpool, Merseyside

A GIRL STAYING HERE woke-up at 5:00 in the morning to find a man standing by her bed. But she needn't have worried because this was only the resident ghost, affectionately nicknamed "George" by the staff, and he is thought to be a fairly harmless old fella.

ADELPHI THEATRE
The Strand, London

ON 16 DECEMBER 1897 an actor called William Terris, aged 49, was starring here in a thriller called *Secret Service*. His career was cut short when he was stabbed to death as he left the stage door at the end of the performance by a bit-player, jealous of Terriss's success. Since then Terriss has haunted the building in the form of tapping and footsteps, as well as the lifts appearing to operate themselves and electric lights switching on and off. In 1928 an actress felt the couch in her dressing-room lurch violently whilst she was sitting on it, and her arm was seized by an invisible force, leaving a bruise. It was discovered that she was using the dressing-room of Terriss's leading lady, and this room was also afflicted with a green light which hovered in front of the mirror, and mysterious knocks on the door.

Sometime during the 1950s a man walking down Maiden Lane, outside the stage door of the theatre, saw the ghost of Terriss in full evening dress, coming towards him. In 1965 a nightwatchman reported that he often felt as though he was being watched by unseen eyes. Other nightwatchmen have had this spooky and unnerving feeling over the years.

ALCESTER (CHURCH)
Warwickshire

IN THE EARLY YEARS of this century a woman cleaning in the church saw a figure standing in the shadows by the tomb of Sir Fulke Greville. She assumed it was a visitor, but as he stepped forward she noticed that he was dressed in 16th century costume and with the same style of beard as the one on Sir Fulke's effigy. As she watched he started to dissolve, starting slowly at the head. The poor woman fainted from shock.

ALDGATE UNDERGROUND STATION
London

THE SUPERNATURAL PHENOMENA on this Circle Line tube station was frequently recorded in the station's logbook. Strange footsteps were heard regularly on the line, and an engineer once watched as a colleague, working on the line, had his head stroked by a little old lady. The same man later accidentally touched a rail that sent a 22,000 volt shock through him. He was lucky not to have been killed. He remembered nothing of the old lady or her affectionate caressing. An unnerving whistling sound has also been heard in this area.

ALSCOT PARK
Preston-on-Stour, Warwickshire

A MAN HAUNTS the main road by the entrance here. He usually appears at midnight, walks across the road and then disappears into a wall. Ursula Bloom, the novelist, once saw him as she was cycling home from Stratford with her mother. She narrowly avoided running over him, but didn't realise until later that she had actually seen a ghost.

The theory is that he was a farmer, who died in 1882 after being swept from his horse by a low branch as he was riding past Alscot Park.

ALTHORP PARK
Northampton, Northamptonshire

BUILT IN 1508 by Sir John Spencer and famous nowadays for being the childhood home of the Princess of Wales, it is also haunted by a former servant. The ghost was given credence when he was seen by Archdeacon Drury in 1867, when he stayed there as a guest of Lord Lyttleton.

The guests were escorted to their rooms late at night by a servant, who diligently reminded them to snuff out their candles before going to sleep. The Archdeacon was suddenly woken in the night by a light shining directly on him. A man with a lantern was standing at the bottom of his bed. The Archdeacon abruptly asked him his business, but the stranger didn't reply, instead he disappeared into the dressing-room, which had no other entrance to it.

The following morning, the Archdeacon mentioned his mysterious nocturnal visitor to Lady Lyttleton. She informed him that what he had seen was the ghost of a footman who had died a few weeks before. One of his duties had been to make sure that all the bedroom candles were extinguished. The ghost has also been seen by a tourist, who was walking through the grounds one day when he saw a man leaning against a tree. He spoke to him but received no reply. He walked on and met an estate-worker. He mentioned the unsociable man and demanded to know if he was a member of staff. The reply was that, apart from himself, there were no other staff members

working in the grounds that day and that probably the
tourist had seen the resident ghost.

ALTON TOWERS
Uttoxeter, Staffordshire

NOW FAMOUS practically everywhere in the known world
as an adventure park, Alton Towers was once the estate of
the Earls of Shrewsbury, and before that the site of an Iron
Age encampment.

Earlier this century, when the railway line used to run
along the south side of the estate and the Talbot family
were still in residence, an estate worker had taken his girl
friend to catch a train and as he was walking back to the
house via the Step Walk, he saw a figure in the distance.
The young lad thought nothing of it and assumed it was
only a guest. The figure then started to descend the steps.
It was a man elegantly dressed in a top hat and cape,
carrying a cane. The estate-worker respectfully greeted
him, and the man vanished. The young lad ran back to the
house and blurted it all out to the old foreman, who calmly
asked him if the ghost had had a black dog with him, as he
himself had always seen him accompanied by one.

The story goes that in the 19th century there was a party
nearby at Farley Hall. A guest, who was staying at Alton
Towers, was returning from the party via the Step Walk
when he had a sudden heart-attack and died on the spot.
His ghost has been seen several times since then.

AMERSBURY BANKS
Theydon Bois, Essex

THIS IRON AGE hillfort is reputedly haunted by Queen Boadicea and her daughters.

ANGLER'S ARMS
Goodramgate, York, North Yorkshire

THE TOP FLOOR spectre on these licensed premises is noticeable mainly by its aroma of lavender, while the first floor stairs are haunted by a Victorian child who likes to frolic with the pub cat. The child has been seen by a regular customer at the pub.

The gas taps that pump beer from the cellar to the bar have been known to be turned off with considerable force, and this is usually accredited to the pub's resident 'Nasty Ghost'. This ghost lurks in the cellar and is widely reckoned to be of an evil disposition. The cat and dog refuse to go down there, and the landlady won't venture into its depths at night.

ANTONY HOUSE
Torpoint, Cornwall

THIS QUEEN ANNE house was built from 1711-1721, intentionally as a home for Sir William Carew. In October 1880 Lady Helen Waldegrave paid a visit. Whilst there her maid, Miss Helen Alexander, somehow acquired typhoid, and a woman called Frances Reddel was brought in to nurse her. Early one morning at 4 o'clock Frances heard a bell ringing in the passage outside the sick-room. This was followed by a stout woman wearing a red flannel nightdress entering the room. She crossed over to the bed and vanished. Miss Alexander died two hours later.

At the funeral Frances was somewhat startled when she recognised the maid's Scottish mother as none other than the red-flannelled spectre! Another equally bewildering experience was had by a gentleman called John Butler many years later, who was visiting Cornwall with a friend. One day they came across Antony House and decided to explore it. Everything was going well until they reached the top of the stairs, where Butler felt a disturbing and inexplicable compulsion not to go any further. A female acquaintance of Butler's later looked into the history of the building for him. She discovered that the inhabitants of the house at the turn of the century were also called Butler. Whether they were related to John in any way and what happened to them at the house is a mystery worthy of investigation. At the moment though, the last page to this particular whodunnit is still missing.

ARTHUR'S QUOIT
Reynoldston, West Glamorgan, Wales

THIS PARTICULAR haunting seems to have more than a touch of whimsy about it. The legend goes that when the moon is full, King Arthur's ghost is said to walk down to the sea, dressed in glowing armour.

ARUNDEL CASTLE
West Sussex

BUILT AT THE END of the 11th century by Roger De Montgomery, Earl of Arundel, it has been home to various Dukes of Norfolk ever since. The castle was extensively damaged by fire in 1643 and it took three successive dukes several years to restore it. British castles tend to be a goldmine where ghosts are concerned and Arundel is no exception. There are a motley collection of four spirits wafting around this place, a girl, a boy, a 17th century dandy and a white bird. The boy was employed in the kitchen about 200 years ago and was severely ill-treated by the head cellarer and as a consequence the boy died young. His ghost has been seen since, industriously cleaning pots and pans in the kitchen late at night, which means the poor little lad knows no rest in the After Life either! A young girl in white roams the vicinity of Hiorne's Tower on moonlit nights. The story attached to her is as tragic as one would expect where ghostly White Ladies are concerned. She is said to have killed herself by jumping off the tower due to unrequited love. It is depressing how often this tragic little scenario explains the presence of female phantoms.

A spectral white bird flutters against the castle windows when a death is imminent, and the ghostly dandy is said to emanate from the era of King Charles II. He has been seen at night browsing through books in the library. The sound of Cromwell's cannon has been heard occasionally as well. In 1958 a young footman was walking down a passage late at night when he saw a man in a light grey tunic slightly ahead of him. The man vanished whilst the footman watched.

ASH RECTORY
Aldershot, Hampshire

IN 1938 REV. BLAKEY livened up the parish magazine by recounting a rather strange little experience he had had at the rectory one night. He said that he had been woken by the sound of galloping horses and went on to report that a phantom coach-and-horses had then driven right through his bedroom! The rectory which is Queen Anne, was built on an old coach road, and previous rectors had also witnessed the same extraordinary phenomenon.

ASSEMBLY ROOMS
Bath, Avon

REFERENCES TO this area's ghostly Man in Black were recorded in private documents as far back as the 18th century. He achieved public recognition on 16 March 1950, when the *Bath and Wiltshire Evening Chronicle* quoted a report by Mrs Cynthia Montefiore that she had encountered the ghost at the end of Savile Row.

Mrs Montefiore described him as wearing a large black hat, not dissimilar to that of a Quaker. He crossed the road noiselessly and when she glanced back he had vanished completely. She also obligingly made a sketch of him, in which he came across as being small and thin, and walking with a stoop. In 1972 Mrs Harrison and Mrs Jill Dixon also made a sketch of the spectre, and in May 1974 Mrs Eileen Parrish saw him as she was parking her car in Savile Row. She watched him as he walked towards the Assembly Rooms and remarked that he was dressed like Guy Fawkes.

ASTON PARK
Aston, Birmingham

IN 1974 A WITNESS saw a woman on sitting on the grass next to the tennis court. She was described as wearing an old-fashioned maroon dress and had her hair in a bun. She vanished when the witness and two companions were about 25 yards away from her.

ATHELHAMPTON HALL
Athelhampton, Dorset

THIS MEDIEVAL family house was built in 1485 on the site of King Athelston's palace. The house was later to have such a strong effect on Thomas Hardy that he wrote several poems and a rather macabre short story around it. The house has an intriguing secret stairway which is haunted by none other than a monkey! This animal was once the pet of a young lady of the Martyn family, who had lived at the house for nearly 300 years.

The girl had had a rough time of it in love and naturally decided that the only option left was to kill herself. She went through the secret door and up the stairway to a room where she knew she would be left alone to top herself in peace. Unbeknown to her, her pet monkey had followed her onto the stairs, and she was too distressed to notice that by slamming both doors on him she was sentencing him to death as well. The monkey starved and he has since been heard scratching the panelling in an effort to break out of his prison.

Other phantoms at the house include a Grey Lady who has been seen in the Tudor Room by a housemaid who mistook her for a visitor. The Grey Lady has also been seen by a previous owner, Sir Robert Cooke. Other ghosts at the house are a pair of spectral duellists, a priest wearing a hooded robe who was sighted in the Great Chamber, and the ghostly hammering of a long-dead cooper who seems hard at work in the wine cellars.

AVEBURY
Wiltshire

AVEBURY is known primarily for its huge and mysterious ancient stones dotted around the village in a circle. During World War I lights and music were seen and heard amongst the stones at night. One theory put forward was that it was a possible re-enactment of the annual fair which was discontinued there in the 19th century. In more recent times a witness noticed strange, small figures amongst the stones on a moonlit night.

The Manor House is also credited with being haunted. A monk has been seen in the library and a Cavalier in the garden. A ghostly Lady in White has also been seen around the village by several witnesses. The village pub doesn't escape spectral interference either. The landlord at the *Red Lion* in the High Street once put all the clocks in the inn forward one hour to mark the start of British Summer Time. The next morning he found they had all been put back again. On another occasion a customer was eating lunch in the bar when a girl approached and asked him courteously if he had enjoyed his meal. When the waitress asked him the same question a few minutes later, he said that he was already being attended to, thank you very much. No doubt he was disconcerted to learn that there was only one waitress on duty that day, and she was that waitress.

BADDESLEY CLINTON
Solihull, West Midlands

BADDESLEY CLINTON is a 14th century manor house complete with moat, and a haunting that seems to have evolved from a domestic crime of passion that occurred here in 1485. One day the owner, Nicholas Brome, returned home unexpectedly to find his wife and his domestic chaplain having a good time together. Nicholas killed the wayward clergyman, and immediately did penance for his crime by pressing donations on the two local churches! Nicholas died in 1517, presumably unscathed by any judicial punishment.

The haunting was so prolific in the 19th century that the resident Ferrars family were prompted to keep a diary of supernatural phenomena. In 1884 a lady visitor was sleeping in the Tapestry Room, when she suddenly awoke to see a Woman in Black gliding across the room and through a closed door. The visitor returned to the house three years later and was accommodated in the State Room, but if she thought this would keep the Woman in Black away from her she was mistaken. She had the same experience as before. At the turn of the century Miss Henrietta Knight arrived for a short visit. She reported footsteps on the landing outside her room, along with a strange rapping on the walls and floor of her room. The poor woman was also plagued with the sound of cloth being torn and heavy breathing nearby. A service of exorcism was held, but the haunting of Baddesley Clinton resumed again forty years later, when a ghostly priest was observed conducting mass in the chapel.

Over the years the haunting has been very versatile. Sounds of a muttered argument between several men were heard from an empty room. Shadowy, silent forms have been sighted in the passages, footsteps heard in deserted parts of the house, and objects appearing to move by themselves. A lady visitor once felt an overwhelmingly oppressive feeling in the library, which is also known as the Ghost Room. A clergyman was once a guest at the haunted house and one evening, on going up to his room, he found a phantom lady sitting on a chair. She vanished. Seventy years after the death of Major Thomas Ferrars, his ghost was seen in the Blue Room. An exorcism helped to lay him to rest. In the chapel a phantom was seen moving vestments from a box. The solar is suspected to be the room where Nicholas Brome murdered his amorous chaplain, and it is here that a visitor was held back from entering the room by an unseen force. The ghost of a Waterloo soldier is said to appear in the Red Room, and lastly, Mr G Howard Heaton was at the house many years ago for a Red Cross party. He found vestments mysteriously scattered over the floor of the chapel closet. Whether the murdered chaplain was responsible is not known.

BALMORAL
Grampian, Scotland

THE QUEEN is among the select few who have claimed to have seen the ghost of John Brown, close friend and 'confidant' of the widowed Queen Victoria. He is said to stalk the corridors and entrance hall.

BANK OF ENGLAND
Threadneedle Street, London

THE GHOST at this worthy institute has been nicknamed the Black Nun because of her excessive mourning apparel. The spectral lady is Sarah Whitehead, and she eternally roams the building searching for her brother Philip. In 1811 Philip worked as a clerk here but was arrested on a charge of forgery. The brutal judiciary system of the time demanded that he be hanged. Sarah went to the bank looking for him. On hearing of his death she went insane.

Shortly after she returned to the bank, now completely clad in classic mourning garb complete with thick, heavy veil.

Sarah kept this routine up for the next 25 years until her own death. But shortly after her burial she was seen performing her little ritual again, and her appearances became something of a local legend. One man claimed to have also seen her in a churchyard pounding at a stone slab and sobbing.

BARDSEY ISLAND
Gwynedd, Wales

BARDSEY was known at one time as 'The Island of 20,000 Saints' and was an important pilgrimage site during the 5th and 6th centuries. The 'saints' were all monks and some of these holy men are buried in the churchyard here, and their ghosts are reputed to haunt the shore.

BARNOLDBY-LE-BECK (CHURCHYARD)
Humberside

A BEAST known locally as the 'Shag Foal' haunts this spot. It is a cross between a dog and a horse. It is said to sit on its haunches and howl, and has also been seen in lanes and fields around the village.

BARROCK
Carlisle-Penrith Road, Cumbria

HIGHWAYMAN John Whitfield shot a man on this road in 1768. A small boy hiding nearby witnessed the whole incident and informed the appropriate authorities. Whitfield was apprehended, gibbeted alive and then hung in agony for several days, until a passing coachman put him out of his misery by shooting him. His agonised screams still haunt the road.

BASING HOUSE
Basing, Hampshire

IN 1645 this house was blown up by the Roundheads, and for reasons best known to himself, the ghost of Oliver Cromwell now walks in the ruins.

BATEMAN'S
Burwash, East Sussex

THIS 17TH CENTURY house is famous for being the home of Rudyard Kipling from 1902-1936 and Kipling's ghost is now said to haunt the house and garden, along with his wife. In 1975 John Harvey, a member of the prestigious Ghost Club, saw Kipling in his old study. The form was looking out of the window and vanished when another person approached the room. Invisible presences have been felt here by both visitors and guides alike, and an intriguing atmosphere of energy and enthusiasm has been sensed in Kipling's study at dusk.

Mrs Lees, who occupied the house during the 1940s, claimed she often felt uneasy in Kipling's bedroom. A local person told of seeing Mrs Kipling in the garden one evening carrying a basket.

Kipling himself was a believer in the supernatural, and firmly believed that the nearby Glydwich Wood (now unfortunately gone) held an evil presence. He claimed to have been held back by an invisible force when walking there one evening. A man with the grand name of Thurston Hopkins organised a ghost-hunt in the woods. One member of the party saw a man scramble out of the undergrowth and run towards him clawing at his throat and making choking sounds. The witness noticed that the man's face was unpleasantly decayed. Hopkins researched the story behind the haunting and found that in 1928, a person called David Leany was charged with committing a murder there and was consequently hanged for it. Unfortunately for Leany, it was later discovered that his 'victim' had really died of a heart-attack. Leany had protested his innocence right to the very end and swore that he would return and haunt the people who had hounded him to such an awful death.

BATTLE ABBEY
Battle, East Sussex

KING WILLIAM the Conqueror founded the Abbey on the site of the Battle of Hastings in 1066 as a thanksgiving for his victory. The High Altar of his church was sited, almost gloatingly it would seem, on the spot where King Harold had fell. The main battlefield site lies on a hillside to the south, and the ground is said by some to run red with blood when it rains! Numerous ghosts have been seen in the area in recent years, including a Norman knight in the Abbot's House, a Lady in Red on the stairs of the Abbot's House and in the ruins, a Grey Lady near the Great Hall, and a monk in the Abbey gateway. On the anniversary of the battle, the ghost of a man killed in combat rides across the battlefield.

BEAUCHIEF ABBEY
Sheffield, South Yorkshire

THE WEST TOWER is all that remains of this 18th century Abbey. It is supposedly haunted by a Lady in White and a monk.

BEACHY HEAD
Eastbourne, East Sussex

THE CLIFFTOP has a morbid fascination for those wishing to take their own lives, so it is perhaps inevitable that it is rumoured to be haunted. One of the ghosts is a suicide victim eternally stepping over the edge. A Grey Lady has been seen on the cliffpath, and even more disturbing is a sinister black monk who beckons people to their deaths.

BEACON EDGE ROAD
Edenhall, Cumbria

IN AUGUST 1767 Thomas Nicolson was hanged here for murdering his godfather. His skeleton is reputed to still swing on rotting gallows on stormy nights.

BEAR INN
Woodstock, Oxfordshire

DATING BACK to the 12th century this market town inn has a haunted bedroom. Occupants of Room 16 have reported their possessions being mysteriously moved and hearing strange footsteps. In 1967 an actress staying there heard footsteps inside the room, and found her dressing table lamp switched on. Many people have asked to be moved out after only one night.

BEAULIEU ABBEY
Beaulieu, Hampshire

A POSSE OF MONKS visited King John in 1201 to petition him for their exemption from taxes. The King, not having gone down in history for his kind and generous disposition, had them imprisoned for their audacity and ordered that they were to be trampled to death by horses the next day. That night the King slept uneasily and dreamt that he was being flogged. When he awoke the next day to find whiplash marks all over his body, he took it as a painful omen. He released the monks and gave them permission to build Beaulieu Abbey. The Abbey was in the possession of the monks until 1538 when it was handed over to King Henry VIII at the Dissolution.

Supernatural phenomena reported at the Abbey includes the smell of incense, and footsteps heard at night on the staircase. One of the hauntings is the stuff that legend would be made of, if it hadn't occurred as recently as 1928. A monk appeared to a lady visitor, and told her to dig in a certain spot. She did as she was bid and found some bones, which she then insisted on giving a Christian burial. Since then a ghostly devotional chanting has been heard.

In 1965 another visitor saw a monk sitting reading a scroll of parchment, and in 1977 yet another woman saw two monks walking along a path until they disappeared. But the most curious haunting of all occurred in 1960, when the Curator of Montagu's Motor Museum, whose cottage overlooked the old burial-ground of the monks, heard footsteps, the sound of grave-digging and chanting late at night.

BEDRUTHAN
Cornwall

THESE 60 ACRES of National Trust cliff-top overlooking Bedruthan beach are haunted by the sound of miner's boots and the 'Knocker's' picks. The 'Knockers' were withered, dried-up creatures of small height with large eyes in ugly heads. They are still fervently believed in in the West Country and as recently as 1981 a local man told how he had fled from one.

BELL INN
Stilton, Cambridgeshire

THIS OLD COACHING INN was in a state of near-dereliction until it was restored to former glory in recent years. Notorious highwayman, Dick Turpin, stayed here just before his capture, and as in a lot of other places in England, his spirit is said to roam here. When a new landlord moved in during 1962, he decided to leave Turpin's old room empty.

In 1963 the pub dog made a habit of howling at midnight, and always on a Wednesday. Eventually the poor animal had to be given tranquillisers to calm him down. Whether this had anything to do with the landlord (who seems to have had an uncanny obsession with the highwayman) naming the dog 'Dick Turpin' remains a mystery as well.

BELLISTER CASTLE
Haltwhistle, Northumberland

JUST FOR A CHANGE this castle is haunted by a Grey Man. In 1542 the de Blencansopp family were in residence here. The story goes that an old traveller visited them on a regular basis, and would offer an evening's entertainment in return for bed and board for the night. All went well until one night when the old man was astounded to find himself being unceremoniously turfed out. The reason being that the Lord of Bellister had got an indelible fixation in his head that the old fella was a spy for a Scottish raiding party. Trouble is, not satisfied with merely showing him the door, his Lordship sent his servants and dogs after the traveller as well

The dogs tore the old man to pieces on the banks of the River Tyne. His horrific bloodstained form now haunts the woods and grounds of the castle. Another story is that he was hanged on a tree in front of the castle, now known, incredibly enough, as the 'Hanging Tree'. The legend of the Grey Man is known fairly well throughout the North East of England. He is seen rarely nowadays, which is perhaps just as well, as he is generally regarded as a harbinger of doom.

BELMONT ROAD
Nr Bolton, Lancashire

THIS WAS the stamping-ground of a highwayman called Horrocks (for some reason he doesn't appear to have been credited with a first name). In 1780 Horrocks was interrupted during the course of a robbery. In panic he threw his booty into the bushes. A man called Grimshaw found it and decided that the phrase 'finder's keepers' applied primarily to him. When the stolen goods were later found in his possession he was hanged on suspicion of being Horrocks the Highwayman. The unfortunate Grimshaw now haunts the road with the noose still around his neck.

BEN MACDHUI
The Cairngorms, Grampian, Scotland

BEN MACDHUI is the haunt of a very famous and fascinating spectre known as the 'Big Grey Man'. Documented sightings of the phantom now cover a 100 years. In 1891 Norman Collie heard mysterious footsteps behind him in the mist. Norman became so unnerved by this that he started running and didn't stop until he reached Rothifmurchus Forest. During the summer of 1904 Hugh Welsh and his brother spent a week camping near the summit. On the first night they heard the footsteps following them. They also heard them during daylight hours but failed to see anything.

George Duncan was driving along Denny Road one twilight in 1914, when he saw a figure in a black robe ambling along. It appeared to be waving its arms wildly as it walked. During the 1920s Tom Crowley heard the footsteps on the mountain, on looking behind him he saw a huge, grey figure in leisurely pursuit. In 1941 Wendy Wood fled in panic from Lairig Ghru Pass. She said she had heard a low voice beside her, as well as those incessant footsteps. She swore that they couldn't possibly be an echo. A year later a gentleman with the delightful name of Syd Scroggie was standing innocently at the shelter stone at twilight, when he saw a tall human figure appear out of the gloom on one side of Loch Etchachan and then disappear into the shadow on the other side. He found no footprints to account for the presence of the creature, and when he shouted he received no reply.

In October 1943 Alexander Tewnion was near the summit one afternoon when a dense mist suddenly fell. He decided to retreat down Coine Etchachan path. On hearing loud footsteps in the nearby vicinity he instinctively felt for his revolver, which for reasons unexplained he always carried on his person. He recalled how a huge shape loomed up and he nervously fired at it three times before running away.

In more recent times Joan Grant was walking with her husband in Rothifmurchus Forest in 1982, when she suddenly felt an inexplicable sense of terror. It was so unbearable that she fled the scene. She recalled later that she had also heard the pounding of hooves. Other stories from the mystery mountain include the experience of Dr A M Kellas, who was resting near the summit one June day with his brother. Dr Kellas watched as a strange figure appeared out of the Lairig Ghru Pass. The form walked around for a little, as though stretching his legs, and then sauntered back into the Pass. Dr Kellas said that the form had been about 10 feet tall. On another occasion a reporter from *The Times* said that he had been pursued on the mountain by "something sinister".

Mountain hauntings are always difficult to give credence to, simply because everybody usually has a sound and rational explanation to cover it. The weather is the most common excuse, and the fact that some mountains possess such an inordinate amount of atmosphere that people can easily see what they want (or don't want) to see. The Brocken Spectre, which for many years terrified the living daylights out of people on the Brocken mountain in the Hartz range in Germany, has been scientifically disproved as the combined effects of sun and mist. Ben Macdhui is harder to explain away. The mist on mountains can make people see things, but the Big Grey Man has been sighted on many clear days. For every aspect of the haunting of Ben Macdhui that can be explained away, there is another that can't.

BERKELEY CASTLE
Berkeley, Gloucestershire

BUILT IN 1153 Berkeley is now the oldest inhabited castle in England and has its fair share of black history. At one time any 'commoner' who dared to offend the noble Lord Berkeley in any way was drowned in a well. Then again, any nobility daft enough to do the same were imprisoned in a cell above the dungeons, where they could inhale the aromatic odour of the rotting corpses below. The castle's most famous captive, King Edward II, was imprisoned here on the orders of his wife, Queen Isabella, who went down in history nicknamed the 'She-Wolf'.

On 21 September 1327 the King's captors decided that His Royal Highness was too much of a threat to their power while he was alive The trouble was, a King's corpse had to be displayed in public to prove that he hadn't died from any foul play. They realised he would have to be murdered in such a way that would not leave any marks on the outside of his body. The King's homosexuality, which was common knowledge the length and breadth of the land and had led mainly to his downfall, gave them an ingenious and horrifyingly sadistic idea for the murder. They shoved a funnel containing a red hot poker up his rectum. The agony of the King's last minutes on earth do not require much imagination. His agonised screams now haunt the castle.

50 BERKELEY SQUARE
London

MAGGS BROTHERS, the Booksellers, have owned this property since 1939 and claim that in all that time they have not been troubled by any unnatural presences. It seems that at last the evil ghoul is resting in peace. It is not before time. The house was built in the 18th century and was once the home of Prime Minister George Canning. It is not clear, however, when the disturbances first started, or how much of the haunting was due to the restless spirit of a former owner. Mr Myers was widely regarded as an eccentric, due no doubt to spending the major part of his life trying to come to terms with the fact that a former fiancee had jilted him for another man. In 1873 Mr Myers appeared in the local newspapers on a charge of not paying his taxes but other than that he seems to have kept an abnormally low profile. Rumours were that he lived in one room at the top of the house and would only let his manservant in to see him, and he would emerge at night when he was said to roam the house in a state of unrelieved misery. The poor chap died in 1878. Then the 'fun' started in earnest .

Neighbours reported cries and moans from the empty building at night. There was also the sound of furniture being moved, bells ringing and books thrown out onto the street. In 1880 the Bentley family moved in. Apart from a strange odour and occasionally a whimpering noise nothing untoward was noticed about their home. Then the eldest daughter's fiancé was invited to stay. The housemaid was sent upstairs to prepare the guest room for his arrival the next day. Her screams were later heard ringing throughout the house. The family discovered her in the room suffering from a convulsive fit. She died in hospital the following day. The fiancé arrived and was determined not to let such an insignificant occurrence spoil his stay. He insisted on sleeping in the Guest Room. Needless to say, exactly the same thing happened to him. The family decided that enough was definitely enough and moved out.

The spectral killer had now claimed two victims but had no intention of stopping there. On Christmas Eve 1887 two sailors, Edward Blund and Robert Martin, docked with their ship and went looking for cheap digs. They didn't come much cheaper than 50 Berkeley Square, which now stood empty and in a state of considerable neglect. They broke into the house and inspected it for somewhere to 'crash down'. Inevitably they found themselves in the sinister Guest Room on the second floor. Being blissfully unaware of its reputation they settled down for the night. Blunden woke to hear footsteps outside the room. He woke Martin and they both waited anxiously for their fellow intruder to approach. Suddenly something large, dark and shapeless rushed into the room and made a dive for Blunden. Martin took the opportunity to flee for his life. He found a policeman in the nearby vicinity and took him to the house where they discovered Blunden dead near the basement steps. He had fallen out of the window and been impaled on the railings.

The house in Berkeley Square had now become something of a tourist attraction for the Victorians and tales of the murderous ghoul were all over London. It wasn't long before the ghoul was facing fresh challenges. Sir Robert Warboys accepted a challenge at his club that he would spend a night in the haunted house. At the time the house was owned by a man called Benson, who was understandably rather nervous of the idea, but Warboys agreed to take a gun with him and he didn't object to having his friends on guard in the room below the Guest Room. Warboys was to ring a bell if he sensed danger. Warboys retired upstairs at 11:15 PM. At midnight the bell was heard ringing furiously. On reaching the room though, the men found Warboys already dead. The look on his face spoke volumes. He had died of sheer fright.

Another curious 'silly-arse', Lord Lyttleton, decided that he wanted to confront the ghoul as well. To be extra safe he took two guns with him, one of which was filled with silver sixpenny pieces: charms to ward off evil. These seemed to work because his Lordship lived to tell the tale and he recounted how he had fired them at a huge shape that had charged into the room.

Early tales from the house include the suitably tragic Victorian melodrama of a young woman who lived there with her lecherous uncle. In desperation to escape his clutches she threw herself from a window. Witnesses later reported seeing her ghost hanging from the window-ledge and screaming. The ghost of a child was seen sobbing in the upstairs nursery and there is a peculiar tale of a man who went mad in the Guest Room waiting for a message to appear on the wall. The Berkeley Square haunting is unique and crammed with true horror in the best Victorian gothic tradition. But perhaps it is just as well that the ghoul, (whoever or whatever it was) seems to have finally exhausted himself.

BERRINGTON HALL
Leominster, Hereford & Worcester

HENRY HOLLAND built Berrington Hall from 1778-1781, and the park was designed by Capability Brown, but it is the staircase which is reputedly the haunted part of the house. In May 1981 a dark figure was seen walking in the South East Wing. The phantom emerged from the Upper Ward, (so-called because it was used as a hospital in both the World Wars) and then turned as if intending to go downstairs. Was the ghost perhaps, one of the wounded who was treated here during the wars?

BERRY POMEROY CASTLE
Totnes, Devon

THE DE LA POMERAI family used Berry Pomeroy Castle as their home from 1066-1548 and in 1550 Edward Seymour, Duke of Somerset and brother of Jane Seymour, built a large mansion within the castle walls. The Seymours lived there until late in the 17th century, when they were forced to evacuate the place due to the structural damage incurred during the Civil War. The building suffered further when a disastrous fire broke out in 1708.

One day, towards the end of the 19th century, Sir Walter Farquhar called at the castle to attend to the wife of the steward, who was seriously ill. While waiting to see his patient he was shown into a room which had a flight of stairs going to the floor above. While he was alone the door opened and a richly-dressed lady entered. She was wringing her hands in distress and totally ignored Sir Walter as she hurried across the room and charged up the stairs. At the top she paused, then looked directly at Sir Walter before disappearing. On his next visit Sir Walter casually mentioned his sighting of the beautiful lady to the steward who responded by getting very upset. When he had calmed down he explained to Sir Walter that he had seen a ghost and even worse, she was generally acknowledged to be a messenger of death! The steward's wife died a few hours later.

This banshee woman is one of a pair of ghostly sisters who used to live at the castle. They were called Eleanor and Margaret de Pomeroy. At the risk of making the whole legend sound like a Grimm's Fairy Tale, one was beautiful and the other was plain. They both loved the same man, and Eleanor, the plain one, was insanely jealous of her beautiful sister's relationship with him. Unable to control her bitterness any longer, Eleanor had the fair Margaret chained up in the dungeons to keep her out of the way. Eleanor now had the lothario all to herself. He responded equally eagerly and didn't seem too fussed by Margaret's rather rapid disappearance. Eleanor would leave while he was still recovering from her attentions and dash down to the dungeon to relate the entire experience to her poor sister. Margaret eventually starved to death. Legend has it that she now rises from her old prison and wanders the ramparts in flowing garments beckoning to anyone unfortunate enough to see her. She has also been seen close to the arches near the gatehouse, clad in a long blue hooded cloak, and her profile was captured in a photograph in 1968. A mysterious gentleman in a tri-cornered hat, who has yet to be named, has also been pictured.

A phantom baby has also been reported crying in the castle several times during the past 50 years. It was rumoured to have been murdered by his mother soon after birth, but whether this was the work of the dreadful Eleanor is not known.

An atmosphere of loneliness, dread and even downright evil has been noted at the castle ruins by extra-perceptive visitors. Some claim to have been lured by a peculiar urge to an unsafe spot in or near the ruins.

BETTISCOMBE MANOR
Lyme Regis, Dorset

THE MANOR is the home of one of several Screaming Skull legends that are dotted around the British Isles with fair regularity. The story is typical of its kind; if the skull is taken out of the house it will let out an earsplitting scream, crops will fail and the cattle perish etc. etc. But this one is unique in that it is also said to sweat blood when the outbreak of war is imminent, and any person silly enough to remove it will be dead within a year.

A former tenant once threw the skull into the duckpond opposite the house. Consequently he became so disturbed by some unpleasant noises that he raked the pond until he found it again. On another occasion the skull was buried underneath 9 feet of earth, but it worked its way to the surface accompanied by dramatic screams and thunderclaps. At one time the squire stowed it away in a haystack and the skull protested so loudly that farmers working in the fields for miles around could hear it.

One theory behind the legend is that it is the head of a 17th century negro slave. On his deathbed he warned that his spirit would haunt the Manor unless he was taken back to his homeland for burial. The warning was dutifully ignored and on his death he was quietly interned in the local churchyard. Immediately wild screams were heard from the tomb. The Manor was rocked by bumps, crashes, cries and moans. The body was hastily disinterred and kept in the loft from then on. Unfortunately this story was given the kiss of death when Professor Gilbert Causey examined the skull for he said that it was in fact that of a Prehistoric woman, and she was probably a foundation sacrifice. A hill called Pilsdon Pen, behind the house, was a Celtic sacred place of worship.

Incidentally on one occasion a psychic investigator spent the night in the house. He reported hearing a slithering noise as if someone in carpet slippers was creeping along the passage. At 2: 00 AM the door creaked open. The investigator closed it but half-an-hour later it opened again, and a yellow light floated in through the doorway. It swelled into the size of a human head and then

67

shaped itself into a skull.

The skull is now kept in a cardboard box and treated with the due respect that any sensible person with more than half-a-brain gives to it.

BINGO HALL
Clapham High Street, London

THE STORY GOES that at the turn of the century a budding music hall singer was brutally told that she had no talent. She was so distressed by this that she climbed up onto the roof, where, legend says, she sang to the stars before throwing herself to her death. The more cynical and realistic theory is that she was blind drunk when she accidentally fell off. Her ghost then haunted the roof and the stairs leading up to it.

In 1972, the year that the haunting got public recognition in the press, people claimed to be spooked by doors opening, and hearing mysterious bangs and footsteps. A security man got curious and left a tape-recorder on the steps to the roof and on the tape being played back, the sounds were of a woman singing. A year later there were sightings of a headless woman in the stage area. Whoever she was will probably never be known, and certainly not while the management still suffers from embarrassment over the haunting, and refuses to talk about it.

BINHAM PRIORY
Norfolk

NOW LIKE SO MANY other ruins, Binham Priory is rumoured to have an underground tunnel that runs for no less than three-and-a-half miles. There is a legend that a fiddler and his dog decided, against their better judgement it would seem, to go for a walk along the tunnel. The fiddler disappeared without trace and the dog returned alone, scared out of its wits. This story would be quite fascinating, if it wasn't for the fact that it crops up all over the country whenever there are rumours of an underground tunnel in the vicinity.

BIRCHAM NEWTON
Norfolk

THE BIRCHAM NEWTON aerodrome, built in 1914, has been largely disused since World War II. Students were once staying there on a construction course when they reported having their bedclothes pulled off and their curtains torn down. An engineer working in the attic of the mess was tapped on the shoulder by an invisible presence and one witness saw a man in RAF uniform walk through a wall.

A film crew went there to make a training film in the officer's mess and during the course of the filming a studio lamp fell near a man named Peter Clark. Nothing more would have been made of this incident if it wasn't for the events that followed.

One of the crew members went to the disused squash court to get some practice but whilst there he heard footsteps in the gallery, which rather unnerved him as he remembered locking himself into the building. On glancing up he saw a man in RAF uniform watching him but the figure suddenly vanished. He joined forces with Peter Clark and they returned later that night to see if they could record the sound of the ghostly footsteps on tape. They had noticed a distinct drop in temperature in the building when setting up the tape recorder to operate by itself, and when they left the building. On playing the tape back later they were astonished to hear what appeared to be the sounds of a busy wartime aerodrome accompanied by a mysterious groaning noise. They had the tape technically examined by a BBC engineer who reported that he could find no possible fault with the tape.

A medium was then taken to Bircham Newton. Once in a trance the ghost came through easily and informed them that his name was 'Wiley', and he had killed himself there during World War II.

When the tape was broadcast by the BBC on television they were inundated with complaints from viewers, who said that their pets had reacted violently to the noises. The BBC became sufficiently intrigued to visit the site themselves, armed with two Spiritualists. The psychics reported feeling a "presence" in the squash court, and a medium called John Sutton, said that one of the ghosts was a man named Dusty Miller who had been killed with two colleagues during the war. The three men had all been keen squash players who had made a pact to meet together on the court if they were all killed in action. They were shot down and killed together when their 'plane crashed in the village. The mediums exorcised the place and that would appear to be the end of the airmen's rather contradictory story.

BIRCHEN BOWER
Hollinwood, Nr Manchester

HANNAH BESWICK was a spinster who hid all her treasure away in 1745 when she feared an invasion by the Scots. She died in 1758, leaving various firm instructions of things that had to be done after her death. She was plagued by the thought of being interred too soon, and with just cause, it would seem! Her brother had nearly been buried alive and had been rescued at the funeral in the nick of time. Because of this Hannah ordered that her body had to be kept above ground, and that every 21 years she was to be lain in the granary for 7 days. During this unofficial lying-in-state her body would be mummified and her face left uncovered. For a while Hannah's eccentric wishes were obeyed, then her body was moved to the Manchester Natural History Museum for convenience. It was finally decided to bury the old girl on 22 July 1868 in Harpurhey Cemetery. Hannah didn't like this at all.

Hannah's ghost began to wander the house and the surrounding grounds dressed in her habitual black. She was also sighted near the barn and the pond. Even more disturbing were reports of a strange glowing light occasionally seen coming from the barn.

In time Birchen Bower was transformed into labourer's cottages, but the tenants confirmed that Hannah's ghost still walked. One tenant, a weaver, often saw her hovering in the corner of his parlour. He naturally became curious and pulled up a corner flagstone. He was astonished to find that he had discovered Hannah's crock of gold! Hannah's ghost became even more troubled after this, a strange blue light was seen darting from her eyes and spine-chilling noises were heard from the barn, which is beginning to sound like Aunt Ada Doom's infamous woodshed in *Cold Comfort Farm!*

Eventually the cottages were destroyed and Ferranti's built a factory over the site of Hannah's old home. But that was not the end of Hannah Beswick's restless and troubled spirit. A factory worker was reported to have seen a strange little old lady in black on the shop-floor.

BISHAM ABBEY
Marlow, Buckinghamshire

THE TUDORS AND ELIZABETHANS were harsh and expected a lot from their children. Education was rigorous and sometimes downright miracles were expected of very small children as regards the absorbing of knowledge. Dame Elizabeth Hoby, a member of the Court of Queen Elizabeth I, was no exception, and it was a thorn in her side that her youngest son William was a slow learner. Out of sheer exasperation she locked him in a cupboard so that he could do his schoolwork with no distractions.

Dame Elizabeth was unexpectedly summoned to Court by the Queen, which was an order that didn't pay you to ignore. She charged off, and in her hurry forgot all about her poor son locked in his small prison. When she returned in the evening she was devastated to learn that William had died. Dame Elizabeth passed away in 1609, aged 91, constantly blaming herself for William's death right to the bitter end. In 1840, workmen were carrying out repairs to the house when they found a tear-stained school-book lodged between the Tudor floor joists.

The ghost of Dame Elizabeth Hoby now wanders the grounds, and she presents a pitiful figure as she constantly washes her hands in a bowl that moves in front of her. Her spectre is unusual in that she is said to appear like a negative, with black hands and face and white clothes. This opens the door to all sorts of theories about ghosts. A ghost appearing like an undeveloped photograph, or like a bad video recording, would add fuel to the theory that a ghost is an image from a past age that has managed to transpose itself onto our present time, like a double exposure on a camera film. Unfortunately this is far from adequate in explaining *all* supernatural phenomena.

BLACK DOG INN
Haye Lane, Uplyme, Devon

THIS PUB is named after its ghost. The black dog is a phantom hound that is rumoured to haunt the lane outside. Apparently the lane used to be called Dog Lane but its name was changed to appease the neighbourhood. The sinister inn sign has been replaced as well, with a nice picture of a smiling retriever! Well one has the customers to think about ...

BLENKINSOPP CASTLE
Nr Carlisle, Cumbria

BUILT 600 years ago, Blenkinsopp Castle was once the home of a certain mercenary-minded gentleman called Sir Bryan de Blenkinsopp. Sir Bryan once vowed that he would only marry if his bride brought along a chest full of gold with her as a dowry. To the astonishment of his friends Sir Bryan returned home one day with a bride who satisfied his greedy obsession.

Everything in the garden was lovely until the couple quarrelled, and to spite him, his wife hid her dowry in a secret place within the castle. Sir Bryan stormed out, and meant it when he said he wasn't going to return. A year later his wife grew rather lonely and decided to follow her husband. One of the great mysteries of the castle is that neither ever seemed to return!

By the time the 18th century rolled round, the castle had been neglected for a very long time. A labourer and his family arrived and squatted in two of the rooms. Things took a disturbing turn when one of the children woke up screaming hysterically one night about having a visit from a mysterious White Lady. This happened on three consecutive occasions.

Within a few years several poor families had taken up residence at the castle, but eventually even they grew sick of the place, and a farmer decided that it might just about be fit to store his cattle in. He decided to make a start by clearing out the vaults, which was when he came across a dark and dank passage which a colleague volunteered to explore. He walked along gingerly until he came to a flight of steps leading down into the bowels of the earth. At the bottom, the candle went out and he quickly returned. When on a second attempt exactly the same thing happened, the bold explorer abandoned any further thoughts of exploration.

In 1875 the castle was purchased by Edward Joicey, and he set about the unenviable task of restoring it. Amazingly, he accomplished this within five years and although he estimated the underground passage to be about one-and-a-half miles long, no-one seemed to be very keen to confirm this. The castle was reduced to a shell by a bad fire in 1954. The West Wing was eventually rebuilt to become a poultry farm, which seems to be the last great event in this building's rather joyless history, and even the White Lady hasn't been seen for over 10 years now. The haunting at Blenkinsopp Castle has been acquired merely because of some ancient legend regarding the original owner, which is all par for the course with hauntings, but this one seems even more depressing and vague than most.

BLETCHINGLEY (CHURCH)
Surrey

VERY LITTLE detail is forthcoming concerning this haunting, but even so several people have seen the ghost of a woman in "old-fashioned" costume, standing close to the memorial of Sir Robert Clayton. Who she was, what era she dates from, and why she has an after-life affinity with Sir Robert is not known.

BLICKLING HALL
Aylsham, Norfolk

THE PRESENT house was built on the foundations of an earlier one between 1616 and 1624, and the site itself has a right royal history. Its inhabitants over the years have included King Harold, and King Charles II. It is even rumoured that King Henry VIII courted Anne Boleyn here. Legend has it that a former owner, Sir Henry Hobart, was killed in a duel here on 21 August 1698. A duelling stone now marks the spot where he fell, and sounds of ghostly sword-play have been heard here. The ghost of Sir Henry also visits the South-West Turret Bedroom on the anniversary of his death.

The house is acclaimed in some circles, as being the place where Anne Boleyn was born, although no-one seems to want to say categorically where this fascinating lady actually did start life. But if her birth wasn't considered important enough for recording, her death was a different matter. It has been written about trillions of times. She was beheaded by the sword at the Tower of London on 19 May 1536. Her ghost also seems to be even more active in death than she was in life, for her spectre is one of the most commonly sighted of ghostly historical figures in the British Isles.

Like Sir Henry, Anne returns to the house on the anniversary of her death. At midnight she makes a dramatic entrance, being driven up the main drive in a carriage pulled by headless horses and cradling her head in her lap. Anne's brother George was executed just before her, on what was almost certainly a trumped-up charge by the King, of committing incest with his sister. His wretched ghost is to be seen being dragged by horses with his head still tucked neatly under his arm.

Anne's ghost has also been seen in the passages of the house and in the garden by the lake. A butler called Sydney Hancock once claimed to have spoken to her.

Another less awesome haunting is by a cat. Once upon a time the cook's old cat was lost in the attic and it's pitiful wailing has been heard frequently since. As well as the lost cat the attic once played host to a dramatic scene when two menservants fought to the death over their joint passion for a serving-girl. Apparently their fight can still be heard at the full moon.

In more recent times the son of the house decided that he would dress up in a suit of armour, in the early hours of his 21st birthday, to frighten his parents. Sadly he was killed soon after but his ghost has been clanking down the passages since then, as though he is on an eternal practical joke. There is also, for good measure, a phantom black dog at the house.

BODIAM CASTLE
Nr. Robertsbridge, East Sussex

BODIAM CASTLE is a moated fortress that was built in 1386 and is still largely preserved in spite of being attacked during the English Civil War. The haunting of Bodiam is elusive and has been largely non-existent for the last 50 years. But during the 1920s the controversial king of psychic investigation, Harry Price, gave a lecture on *Hauntings in Sussex* which included Bodiam. He claimed that sounds of a party had been heard at the castle by passers-by on winter nights.

Faint refrains of "foreign" music have been heard there as well, usually for some inexplicable reason on Easter Sunday. Peter Underwood current President of the Ghost Club, has concocted a very credible theory that certain psychic phenomena runs down steadily over several years, like a battery. Perhaps the sounds of merrymaking and music at Bodiam were fairly strong at one time, but in recent years they seem to have dissipated.

BODMIN MOOR
Cornwall

THIS HAUNTING has a touch of 'Faust' about it, in that the culprit tried to save his damned soul by buying salvation. During the 17th century Jan Tregeagle was a magistrate who was as vindictive and corrupt as Judge Jeffries. He was well aware that he was a complete bastard, and had enough conscience to fear for his own soul after death. As such, he bribed the local clergy to ensure that he would be buried in consecrated ground, St Breock's Churchyard.

After his death all his wicked misdeeds were made public, and the local clergy decided they had better try and save Tregeagle's soul. They thought that if Tregeagle was kept busy in the afterlife he might not look so bad on Judgement Day. They set his spirit the task of emptying Dozmary Pool (rumoured to be bottomless), with a cracked limpet shell. He was supervised in his task by a pack of headless hounds.

One night Tregeagle's ghost became terrified by the storm that was raging all around him and he ran for shelter into the Hermit's Chapel on Roche Rock. The death hounds mistook his sudden flight for an escape bid, and chased him. When they caught up with him at the chapel they tore him to pieces. A priest, tormented by Tregeagle's agonised screams, exorcised the place and banished him to the moors.

It is said that Tregeagle's ghost can still be seen in the eerie moorland mists, wandering the lonely moors and wailing in despair at his eternal fate.

BOLLING HALL
Bradford, West Yorkshire

BOLLING HALL is haunted by an anonymous Grey Lady, who is credited with having once saved the entire population of Bradford from extinction during the English Civil War. The story is as follows. In 1643 Bolling Hall was owned by a Royalist supporter called Richard Tempest. The Earl of Newcastle stopped there as a guest on the same night that he had given orders for the massacre of the Bradford people. His excuse for this barbaric command was that the Earl of Newport had been killed during the laying of the siege.

The Earl of Newcastle didn't get much rest that night, and it wasn't entirely due to his conscience pricking him. Three times he had his bedclothes pulled off him by a mysterious woman, who implored him passionately to spare the people of Bradford. The Earl was considerably shaken by all this, and then had to put up with being called a drunk by sceptics who heard his story. Others claimed that the ghostly Grey Lady was really a wench who lived nearby. Whatever the truth may be, the incident had a considerable effect on the Earl, and he accordingly spared the lives of the people.

BOLTON PRIORY
Nr Skipton, North Yorkshire

BOLTON PRIORY was built around 1160 and monks were empoyed here for the next 300 years, successfully fending off a raid by the Scots in 1330, but finally being defeated by King Henry VIII who ordered them away at the Dissolution. The present Rectory now stands on the site of the old priory gatehouse.

The Marquis of Hartington stayed here as a boy in 1912 and during his visit he claimed to have seen an old monk with a wrinkled face standing at his bedroom door. The boy stood watching the mysterious figure from the top of the stairs, and noted that the old man was ponderously looking into his room, before he vanished. A year later the Rev. MacNabb caught the ghost watching him from a doorway, and he was sighted again by Lord Cavendish in 1920. In 1965 a man entering the gatehouse saw the ghostly old monk coming towards him. In addition to this familiar spectre, is the muffled sound of sandalled feet walking about, which has been heard in the Rectory.

The ghostly monk can be more commonly sighted during daylight hours in July and August.

BORLEY
Essex

BORLEY RECTORY has become something of an old chestnut in the world of the supernatural. At one time it was described as the World's Most Haunted House, when in fact it would be nearer the truth to say that it was the World's Most Written About Haunted House. But even now, several years after the Rectory burnt down in 1939, the village of Borley still holds a magnetic fascination for anyone interested in ghosts.

For many centuries the villagers were plagued by the ghost of a strange woman wafting around the churchyard, but it was when the infamous Rectory was built that things became seriously dramatic. The Rev. Henry Dawson Ellis Bull built the Rectory in 1863. Soon after he and his family had moved into the 14-roomed house they were besieged with supernatural phenomena, such as footsteps and tapping, bells ringing, disembodied voices and ghostly chanting from the church nearby. One of the children was rudely woken by a slap in the face. Another saw a man in old-fashioned clothes standing by her bed. There were sightings in the grounds, of a nun, a phantom coach-and-horses, a headless man, the obligatory Woman in White, and just about every other form of ghostly phenomena ever noted.

The Bull family seemed to bear up remarkably well under all this psychic pressure, for there were no sudden flights from the haunted house in the middle of the night. In fact the Rev. Bull became so fascinated by the ghost of the Grey Nun that he had a summerhouse built near the path where she walked, (nicknamed 'the Nun's Walk'), so that he could watch her take her daily constitutional. On 28 July 1900 the four daughters of the house were returning from a tea-party when they all saw the nun on the lawn.

In 1929 Harry Price, the author and psychic investigator, went to the house and recorded various poltergeist phenomena such as pebbles and keys flying through the air. Then the Rev. Lionel Foyster and his wife Marianne moved into the Rectory in 1930 and soon after messages started appearing on the walls and scraps of paper, urging Marianne to get help. She also heard a female voice calling her, and then when she was viciously attacked by an invisible assailant, the couple moved out.

Harry Price seized his opportunity. He advertised in the

Times for a trusty band of supporters and rented the house for research purposes. His work on Borley was to make him a household name, but due to allegations of fraud, he became a controversial figure and his opinions are loath to be accepted seriously nowadays by psychic investigators. Harry's team recorded sharp drops of up to 10 degrees in temperature, smells of incense, and stones and cakes of soap being hurled across the room, and a monk who attempted an exorcism was pelted with pebbles. Due to Harry, the Rectory became the most famous haunted house in the world, but it also became a topic of much heated controversy. Whether Harry bent the facts about Borley or not (and this I find hard to believe for he may have been an innate showman, but he also had a tremendous respect and regard for the field of the supernatural) is irrelevant, because after he and his team left the phenomena continued.

Captain H Gregson acquired the Rectory in 1938, and he wasn't to escape the antics of the ghosts either. His two dogs mysteriously disappeared and were never seen again. On 27 February 1939 an oil lamp fell over of its own accord, and started the inferno that completely gutted the building. Onlookers gathered to watch the destruction of the Rectory and noticed the figure of a nun at an upstairs window.

During the war, chauffeur Herbert Mayes claimed he heard invisible hooves as he drove past the shell of the building, and ARP Wardens were constantly called to the ruins by reports of mysterious lights at the windows. In 1949 a young girl saw a lady in a nun's veil in Borley churchyard. The Grey Nun was seen on her path by a male visitor in 1951 whilst other phenomena in Borley since the demise of the Rectory includes car headlights, cameras and torches all failing to work on the site of the house and footsteps being heard approaching the church and going in. Ghostly organ music has also been heard and, it has been claimed, the communion wine has been turned into ink.

So what caused the haunting of Borley? In 1937 a London medium called Helen Glanville said that the haunting was caused by a nun called Marie Lairre. Marie had been forced to abandon her vows and marry into the Waldegrave family at Borley Manor and she was strangled on the site of the Rectory in May 1667. In 1943 excavations carried out on the site revealed a woman's jaw bone buried in a well with some religious pendants. This would all seem to tie up the haunting nicely, but then so much about Borley is controversial and uncertain that it would be unwise to reach any conclusion.

The Rectory may be long gone and new houses now surround the site, but the eerie reputation of Borley refuses to lie down. Any study on British ghosts would never be complete without a mention of dear old Borley!

BOSWORTH HALL
Husbands Boswell, Leicestershire

THIS HOUSE plays host to a ghost that creaks and moans, and a bloodstain on a floor that has stubbornly remained indelible for 300 years. In less tolerant times the house was a Roman Catholic stronghold, and Masses were held there in secret during the Civil War. The resident priest would be hastily bundled under the attic floor if any Roundheads approached. On one such occasion he cut his hand in his hurry to be hidden and the bloodstain still marks the chapel floor.

In spite of all that the ghost is not, as one would imagine, the priest. In 1881 Lady Lisgar, a Protestant, married Sir Francis Fortescue-Turville. The lady must have had a heart of steel because she refused to let a Roman Catholic priest give final comfort to a dying servant. She seems to be paying for her coldness after death, because her ghost restlessly roams the house. A doctor saw her climbing the stairs but when he spoke to her she didn't reply. She has also been seen in her old bedroom, and in the passages. Eerie groans and creaks have been heard at night. One guest even claimed to have been hurled out of bed by an invisible force. Whether Lady Lisgar was responsible is not known.

BOTTLEBUSH DOWN
Sixpenny Handley, Dorset

THE PHANTOM HORSEMAN that haunts this area dates back 2,500 years to the Bronze Age, and as such could be credited with being the oldest ghost in Europe. He usually appears close to the A3081 road. Farmworkers and shepherds have reported seeing him galloping across the fields, and in the late 1920s two young girls were terrified out of their wits as they cycled home one night. They told the police that the horseman had suddenly appeared from nowhere and ridden alongside them for some distance before vanishing.

In 1924 archaeologist R C Clay came face to face with the horseman, and for about 100 yards, the ghost kept pace with his car. Mr Clay reported that the horse was small with no bridle or stirrups, and the rider had bare legs, a long flowing cloak and was holding a weapon over his head. He then simply vanished. The following day Mr Clay returned to the scene of the haunting and found a low burial mound where the horseman had vanished. He dated the ghost between 700 and 600 BC.

BOULEY BAY
Jersey, Channel Islands

I HAD GIVEN UP all hope of finding anything of the supernatural kind in the Channel Islands, until I was given an old map of Jersey which asserts that Bouley Bay, on the idyllic north coast, is haunted by a phantom hound with saucer eyes. One of the bars, The Black Dog, in a local pub is named after the beast.

BRADGATE PARK
Newtown Linford, Leicestershire

IN 1554 ONE OF the most pitiful characters in British history was executed. Lady Jane Grey was the victim of a shameless power struggle by her relatives. She was made Queen for nine days in a futile attempt to keep the Catholic Princess, Mary Tudor, off the throne. The plan backfired and Lady Jane was beheaded for treason. She is said to return to her old home on Christmas Eve, driving up to the house in a coach drawn by four headless black horses. (If the story sounds familiar it is because Anne Boleyn, who suffered the same death, returns home in an almost identical manner to Blickling Hall in Norfolk). Lady Jane's coach then disappears into the ruins. There are also rumours that she sometimes appears as a White Lady.

BRAMBER CASTLE
Steyning, West Sussex

A FORMER OWNER of Bramber Castle, William de Braose, was a nasty piece of work who murdered several people and then gave large endowments to the church out of guilt. He had five children, four of which lived with him at the castle. King John, an even nastier piece of work, heard of de Braose's wealth and became extremely jealous. He sent his equerry, Sir Peter Maulne, to the castle to demand the children as hostages until their father surrendered all his money. De Braose refused which was not a wise move. An enraged King John ordered his army to march on the castle. The family tried desperately to flee to Ireland, but King John had them seized and taken to Windsor Castle.

At this point in the story things become rather muddled. There are two theories as to what happened next. One is that King John had the entire family starved to death at Windsor, another is that de Braose fled to France and the rest of the family starved alone.

Three ghostly children in an emaciated state are now said to appear to witnesses, holding out their hands pathetically for food, usually in the month of December.

In 1954 the residents of Bramber claimed to have heard a woman wailing in the castle ruins. This particular haunting dates back to the 15th century, when Lady Maud de Hurst watched helplessly as her husband Hubert walled her lover up alive in the castle. The cries of despair are said to be hers. Lady Maud died the following day, from what is not clear, but I assume her husband killed her. When the castle was attacked in later years by Parliamentarian troops they found the skeleton of the unfortunate lover, William de Lingfield, within the castle walls.

BRAMFIELD ROAD
Nr Knebworth, Hertfordshire

A CERTAIN hardworking gentleman called Clibbon worked as a pie-man at fairs, and moonlighted on the side as a highwayman. One day his luck ran out when some local farmers caught him redhanded, attempting to commit a robbery on Bramfield Road. They punished him by tying him to a horse which dragged him around until he was dead. The phantom horse can now be seen dragging a writhing body along the road, calling out for mercy. Sometimes only the galloping hooves can be heard, along with a scattering of gravel and agonised moans.

BRAMSHILL HOUSE
Hartley Wintney, Hampshire

THIS OLD HOUSE, which in parts dates back to the 14th century, is now used as a police training college. It also houses a large and motley collection of spooks which earns it the well-deserved title of Most Haunted House in Hampshire.

One of the hauntings can be fitted neatly in the section in paranormal legend, known as the Bride in the Chest. Several areas in the British Isles seems to have such a tale. A bride playing hide-and-seek with her wedding guests on her wedding night hides in a chest, which the silly girl then realises she can't get out of, and so she eventually starves and/or suffocates to death. Her ghost can inevitably be seen at Christmas, dressed in white and clutching a sprig of mistletoe. The Bramshill Mistletoe Bride tends to favour the Fleur de Lys Room as her favourite haunt. Shortly after World War II the Romanian Royal Family stayed at Bramshill, and complained about a mysterious Lady in White who had a disturbing habit of rampaging through their children's room at night.

Bramshill also has a Grey Lady, a fetching creature in a grey robe with golden hair, always accompanied by an aroma of lilies-of-the-valley. In 1962 she was seen by a man from the Ministry of Works in the Long Gallery, and in

1980 her pungent aroma was noticed by a college engineer. The girls in the accounts office claimed to have been puzzled by her scent in the Long Gallery. Another employee also encountered her unexpectedly in the Long Gallery when he noticed a sharp drop in temperature, and his dog gave a howl of terror before running off.

In relatively recent years ghostly sightings at Bramshill include a man in a grey suit, walking through a wall in the entrance hall, witnessed by a security officer. Another official was patrolling the house one night in 1976, when he saw a young man clutching a tennis racquet disappear into a fireplace.

Other ghosts at this psychically overcrowded site are an eccentric character dressed in green, who drowned himself in 1806. His ghost has been sighted on the bridge near the gatehouse and the footpath around the lake has been known to have a strange effect on dogs, for they will try to avoid it at all costs. The hallway of the house is frequented by a ghostly old man with a long beard and the chapel drawing-room has a phantom woman in 17th century costume. An upstairs bedroom houses an invisible child who touches visitors gently, and a first-floor room has phantoms which float around above the floor!

Finally, mysterious footsteps have been heard in the chapel and drawing-room, and another Lady in White was once sighted on the terrace by a former owner, Sir William Cope and his family. She vanished as they watched.

BREAMORE HOUSE
Fordinbridge, Hampshire

THIS BUILDING dates back to 1583 and is haunted by a woman in a poke bonnet. She is said to be the wife of a former owner who died at the murderous hands of her own son. She has a disturbing habit of appearing when whoever is in residence is soon to die.

BRECKLES HALL
Attleborough, Norfolk

SINCE THE TURN of the century another ghost has been added to what was already an infamous place. It comes in the form of the pained voice of poacher Jim Mace. He and a friend decided to go partridge shooting in the deserted grounds of the Hall one night after the pubs had closed. There they were somewhat startled by the screams for mercy, banging doors and footsteps which were echoing through the empty house. On peering through one of the windows they saw a host of spectral dancers careering around the ballroom. Suddenly a phantom coach-and-horses galloped into the grounds and a beautiful, bejewelled woman stepped out. She stared straight into Mace's eyes, and instantly he fell to the ground screaming. His distraught companion ran hell-for-leather to the village to get help but no-one would venture near the Hall after dark. The next morning the local vicar felt brave enough to lead a posse of villagers to the house. They found Mace where his friend had hurriedly left him. He was dead, with a look of absolute terror on his face.

BRIDGE Nr SHATTON
Bamford, Derbyshire

A GHOSTLY FARMER carrying a lantern was seen walking over the bridge by several people early this century.

BRIGHTON ROYAL PAVILION
East Sussex

THIS 18TH CENTURY pavilion, which boasts of being "the most fantastic palace in Europe", has the ghost of King George IV in the underground passages. He has been sighted in an underground passage that leads to what was once the stables, and is now the Dome, and also in a tunnel which once linked the Royal Pavilion cellars with those of the *Druid's Head Inn*. Sometime between the two world wars, a caterer was checking his work on the night before a special banquet, when he saw a ghostly woman in a white dress complete with bonnet and shawl, walking through the room where the tables were laid out.

BRISTOL CATHEDRAL
Avon

THE CATHEDRAL is haunted by a monk in grey robes.

B.B.C.
Langham House, London

THE GHOST at this unlikely spot opposite Broadcasting House, seems to have finally laid himself to rest, he was last sighted in 1973. He has been described as a butler carrying a tray along an upstairs passage, and he walked with a limp. He was seen by half-a-dozen people in that particular year, including an engineer who came across him in a control room on the 8th floor. The phantom butler vanished into thin air. Witnesses, including two BBC producers, noticed that the ghost always seemed to vanish at a certain door. Curiously no-one ever saw his face, no-one knows who he was, and it seems fairly likely that no one ever shall.

BROCKLEY
Avon

A GHOSTLY LITTLE LADY dressed in brown rushes down the aisle of Brockley Church and up to the altar, or into the vestry, whichever takes her fancy. She simply vanishes when spoken to.

A valley in Brockley Wood, known as the Combe, is credited with having no less than three phantoms. One is a coach that drives through the area at high speed causing road accidents, another is the ghost of a clergyman, and there is also a perfect menace of an old woman who causes death or madness to anyone who has the misfortune to see her.

BRODICK CASTLE
Isle of Arran, Strathclyde, Scotland

ONCE THE HOME of the Dukes of Hamilton and now under the care of the National Trust, this 13th century castle is haunted by another of those incorrigible Grey Ladies, and like all the wonderful female phantoms of her breed, a question-mark hangs over her identity.

Legend has it that in 1700 three ladies riddled with a fatal dose of plague were confined to the castle, and the Grey lady is reckoned to be one of them. She has aimlessly roamed the corridors ever since.

At one time a housekeeper, Mrs Munsey, credited herself with psychic powers and announced that she had seen the ghost, looking like a dairy maid, on several occasions on the back stairs. A butler once came across her apparently speaking to an odd-job man in a passage but the man said he hadn't heard or noticed her at all. Mrs Munsey decided to find out about the female phantom, by using the controversial means of 'Automatic Writing'. The ghost responded and described how she had worked as a serving-girl at the castle during the Civil War, when Cromwellian troops were stationed there. The girl had an amorous liaison with a general and as a consequence found herself pregnant by him. The girl was considerably distraught by this and committed suicide by jumping off the quay below the castle. Whether she and the plague victim are one and the same, or two different Grey Ladies is hard to say.

Another resident ghost is a bewigged man dressed in green, who has been sighted sitting in a chair in the library. Less affable is a ghostly white dove which usually appears just before the death of the head of the household.

BRODIE CASTLE
Nairn Moray, Grampian, Scotland

FOR REASONS best known to himself, Lord Lewis Gordon set fire to this property in 1645 and the castle was largely rebuilt during the 17th-19th centuries.

In September 1889 Hugo, the 23rd Chief, died in exile in Switzerland. Whilst abroad he had let the castle, with instructions to the tenants that his ground-floor study had to stay locked and undisturbed during his absence. On the evening of 20 September 1889 the butler told the tenants, who were sitting together in the drawing-room, that he could hear someone in the Master's study, which was rather puzzling as the door was still locked. As they all listened outside the door they could hear papers being shuffled and a low moaning noise. Then there was complete silence. The next day they were informed of the death of Lord

Brodie the previous evening. The tenants could find no rational explanation for the curious noises in the locked study, and the obvious answer is that it was the newly-deceased Lord Brodie searching in desperation for something. As such the haunting of Brodie Castle appears to have been a one-off wonder.

BROUGHAM HALL
Penrith, Cumbria

A TYPICAL Screaming Skull Legend is attached to this place. The skull screamed brattishly whenever it was moved from the house. It was eventually bricked up inside a wall, and the screaming stopped.

BROUGHTON HALL
Eccleshall, Staffordshire

THE GHOSTLY LEGEND around this Elizabethan house dates back to the Civil War when it was attacked by Roundheads. The young heir to the property saw the army approaching, and rebelliously shouted down to them his undying allegiance to his king. He was shot for his pains but he managed to drag himself into a nearby room where he could die in privacy. His bloodstains still remain in the Long Gallery and are said to be totally irremovable whilst his ghost continues to haunt the room, usually seen standing at a window.

During the late 19th century a young girl playing hide-and-seek hid in the Long Gallery. She noticed a strange man standing at the window, looking thoughtfully outside. She crept past him thinking he was a guest she hadn't met yet, but when she got downstairs she found that this wasn't the case. On another occasion a woman scrubbing the stairs to the Long Gallery looked up to see a young man watching her, but when she moved her bucket so that he could pass, he walked straight through her.

BROUGHTON MOOR
Nr Flimby, Cumbria

THANKFULLY the gruesome apparition that haunts this area has not been seen since 1972. 'Bele Sheephead' appears as some kind of freakish half-human half-sheep apparition. The story goes that when a young girl she had a pet lamb which was killed by a fox and far from being upset, Bele suddenly felt a bestial impulse to drink the lamb's blood. It wasn't long before she acquired a craving for its taste.

Many unfortunate motorists have come to grief in this area. One of the more horrific instances occurred when a man and wife ran out of petrol late at night on the moor. The husband walked off with a petrol can, whilst his wife fell asleep in the car. Sometime later she was woken by the siren of a police car and the arrival of a policeman who asked her to get out of the car, but told her not to look round. Naturally she did so, and saw her husband's corpse lying on the road, with his severed head placed on one of the fence-posts. The unfortunate gentleman was buried in Flimby churchyard and the horrific murder remained officially unsolved, but the locals believed he had been a victim of the spectral killer, 'Bele Sheephead'.

Even more curious is the legend that the moor is haunted by an equally strange character called 'Bible John', so-called because he carries a Bible in which is secreted a pistol. Is there a tenuous link with the Glasgow killer, nicknamed 'Bible John', who was never caught?

BROWSHOLME HALL
Clitheroe, Lancashire

IN 1536 A PERSON was killed here following a Pilgrimage of Grace, and this started yet another Screaming Skull Legend. In 1703 the skull was taken from the top of the house into the family chapel, where it remained until the 1850s when schoolboy Edward Parker removed it for a "joke". He buried it in the garden, and then all hell broke out. Fires started and there were deaths in the family. Eventually the boy remorsefully dug it up and returned it to the house. Normality resumed once more.

BUCKINGHAM PALACE
London

PROBABLY THE most famous building in England, but it can only boast one ghost. It is haunted by Major John Gwynne, who was a secretary in the household of King Edward VII. He shot himself in his first floor office, and the dim shape of him has been seen in that area several times.

BUCKLAND ABBEY
Yelverton, Devon

REPUTEDLY COMPLETED in three days by preternatural means, this 13th century Cistercian monastery was the home of Sir Francis Drake from 1581, when he returned home after circumnavigating the world. Drake himself makes the odd dramatic appearance driving a hearse pulled by headless horses.

One of Drake's relics now preserved at the house is a drum, which was beaten as he lay dying in Nombre de Dios

Bay. He vowed that it would beat whenever England was in danger. It was heard, beating by itself, just before the First World War in 1914, and again in 1939. There are also some rather unusual headless hounds on the site, whose baying is said to foretell the death of any dog that hears them.

BULL INN
Henley on Thames, Oxfordshire

AN AROMA of burnt candles lingers in the bar here, and one guest staying at the inn reported seeing a cowled figure bending over him as he lay in bed.

BURFORD NUNNERY
Burford, Oxfordshire

THIS AREA is haunted by a monk and a gamekeeper. Mysterious footsteps, the ringing of a bell and ghostly singing have been heard in the garden of the nunnery.

BURITON
Hampshire

A PHANTOM FRIAR has been seen around the village in recent years. During the 1960s a boy working at the manor saw the ghost in the stable-yard. A woman and her daughter encountered him in a narrow lane, where he vanished. From 1936-1952 the Vicar often saw the friar in his garden, and his wife reported hearing strange foot-steps outside, but nobody was ever there.

BURNMOOR TARN
Eskdale, Cumbria

AT ONE TIME a fell pony used to pull coffins across the moor. Nowadays it appears out of the mist and then vanishes again. It is usually noiseless.

BURTON AGNES HALL
Bridlington, Humberside

ONE OF THE MOST famous Screaming Skull Legends in England is to be found here. 'Awd Nance' has been a source of trouble for various inhabitants of the Hall for many years. For more than 300 years the skull has resolutely insisted on staying within the confines of the house.

Burton Agnes Hall was built by three spinster sisters during the years 1598-1610. Anne, the youngest, so loved her home that she insisted that her head should be kept in the walls after her death, but her sisters were so horrified by this ghoulish idea that on her death Anne was interned intact. Barely seven days after the funeral there was a loud crash from an upstairs room which woke the entire household. A week later the family were woken again by doors slamming in every part of the house. Yet another week after that came the most disturbing aspect of the haunting so far. The family lay in bed all night as the whole house shook with the sound of invisible people thundering along the corridors and up and down the stairs, and agonised groans echoed throughout the rooms. The family had Anne's body exhumed and were disconcerted to find that the skin on her head had shrivelled away, leaving the skull bare, whereas the rest of her corpse was relatively the same as when it had been laid to rest. The skull was severed from the body, and the sisters carried their unenviable souvenir back to the Hall. The haunting immediately ceased, and the women lived with their gruesome family heirloom for the rest of their lives.

Several owners have since tried foolishly to rid themselves of 'Awd Nance' and all have lived to regret it. Subsequent hauntings have included mysterious scratching sounds, slamming doors and loud groans, resulting in Anne's skull being respectfully taken back into the fold. One incident of the skull's power occurred one day when a servant-girl threw the skull out of a window where it landed on a passing cart. The horse stopped in its tracks and refused to move until the skull was retrieved.

'Awd Nance' was kept on a table in the Great Hall for many years, until she was eventually bricked up into a wall where she remains to this day. But her ghost is still restless, although less violent now her wishes are being adhered to. In 1915 the owner saw the ghost of a lady in a fawn dress. The family were having tea in the garden when the phantom walked along the path, up the steps and into the house through the front door. The ghost has also been seen by visitors in an upstairs corridor, and it is also known to haunt the Queen's State Bedroom. There is no cause for alarm though, 'Awd Nance' is just checking that everything is to her satisfaction.

BURY ST EDMUNDS ABBEY
Suffolk

THE ABBEY was named after a saint who was murdered by Danes in 870 AD. By 1327 the people of the town felt considerable resentment over the wealth of the abbots and rioted, destroying the gateway in the process. The abbots ordered them to rebuild it and the task was finally completed in 1347. But several monks were killed in the course of the riot, and one now haunts the cellars of two buildings in Abbeygate Street. In 1967 a local workman saw the phantom in the vaults of a wine merchant's building whilst another monk haunts the Abbey Gates. A local vicar once claimed to have received spirit messages from monks telling him where St Edmund was buried. As a consequence the church authorities ordered that the ground was to remain unsullied.

BUSBY STOOP INN
Northallerton, North Yorkshire

TOM BUSBY married the daughter of Daniel Auty, his counterfeiting partner-in-crime in the 18th century. During an argument Busby killed Auty with a hammer, and in 1702 he was hanged for the murder directly opposite the inn. His favourite chair used to stand next to the pub's piano, and was superstitiously reserved for Busby's ghost. There was a belief that anyone who sat in it would soon die. Naturally this happened rather often in the course of 200 years, but the brewery finally decided to remove the infamous chair out of "harm's way". Its 20th century victims are said to include an RAF fighter pilot, a motorist, a motor-cyclist, a hitch-hiker and a local man. All died within a mere few days of sitting on Busby's chair. Like all superstitions this one would be very hard to prove, but then some things are definitely not in the realm of rational calculation. There are a lot of aspects of supernatural phenomena that are worthy of serious investigation. I'm afraid that this isn't one of them.

CADEBY HALL
near Conisbrough, South Yorkshire

A PHANTOM coach-and-horses, a prowling hooded monk and the sound of clanking chains all haunt this abandoned 18th century house deep in the heart of the Lincolnshire countryside. Cadeby Hall is an aristocrat amongst haunted houses, it is said to have been cursed by a grief-stricken mother whose young son disappeared in the grounds and was later found lying dead in the hollow of a tree. It is now considered to have such an unlucky atmosphere that the present owners choose to live elsewhere.

The phantom coach-and-horses are said to career along the drive whenever anyone living at the hall is about to die. The ghostly monk, who is a relic from the days when a monastery stood on the site, creeps stealthily along a path in the garden known as the 'Monk's Walk' (shades of Borley Rectory here), and the clanking chains were frequently heard in some underground passages which have been sealed up in recent years.

The old Roman road, Barton Street, which runs past the house is also haunted, but not by any Roman Centurions as you might think. George Nelson was riding past Cadeby Hall during a thunderstorm one night in 1885, when he was suddenly struck by lightning and killed. Mr Nelson and his horse are now said to terrorise unsuspecting motorists by hurtling out in front of them. His horse usually rears up and tosses him headfirst into a ditch before they both disappear.

CAERPHILLY CASTLE
Mid Glamorgan, Wales

THE CASTLE RAMPARTS here are allegedly haunted by a lady described as having big eyes in a large head, and wearing a long green veil. This "charming" apparition is sometimes accompanied by soldiers in chain mail.

CAESAR'S CAMP
Easthampstead, Berkshire

THE CAMP is an Iron Age hillfort situated half-a-mile north of the Devil's Highway. During World War II two ladies living nearby heard strange footsteps at the camp. They also claimed to hear voices and the sound of soldiers marching and one local woman even awoke to find a red-haired man standing by her bed. Unfortunately he was a ghost!

CALGARTH HALL
Windermere, Cumbria

NOWADAYS there is considerable scepticism as to the authenticity of this legend, especially as to whether the characters really existed. Even so, it's a good yarn in the best ghostly tradition. "A tale of power and revenge" is probably how it would be described in present-day format.

During the 16th century a certain dastardly scoundrel called Myles Phillipson was said to own much of the countryside around here, and he had ambitious plans to build a glorious mansion for himself. Unfortunately the particular bit of land he had in mind belonged to a couple named Kraster and Dorothy Cook, who had a farm there. Not to be thwarted, Phillipson invited the couple to his house for Christmas dinner. Whilst they were there he astonished them by presenting them with a golden bowl as a Christmas present. The following day soldiers turned up at the Cook's farm accusing them of stealing the golden bowl. The case was against the couple from the start as Phillipson was also the local magistrate! Theft in those days was a capital offence and the couple were sentenced to hang, but whilst in court Dorothy soundly cursed Phillipson no less than seven times. Undaunted, Phillipson built his house on the site of the farmer's home, overlooking the lake.

The following Christmas Phillipson invited some friends to his new house for dinner, but the festivities were cut short when when two grinning skulls suddenly appeared on the bannisters. Phillipson threw the skulls into the courtyard in a terrible rage, but if he thought that would be the end of his troubles he was mistaken. In the small hours his guests were woken by horrific screams to find the skulls had reappeared on the stairs. The skulls continued to persist haunt Phillipson, and eventually he died, a broken man. On the night of his death the house rang with the demonic laughter of the skulls, but they still found it hard to rest, even after the death of their sworn foe. The heads continued to haunt the house on Christmas Day and on the anniversary of their execution for many years after, and the hauntings only ceased when the Phillipson family finally had enough and sold the Hall. The revenge of Kraster and Dorothy Cook was finally complete.

CAMMERINGHAM
Lincolnshire

IN 62 AD Queen Boadicea faced defeat here by the Romans, and unable to stand such a humiliation, she poisoned herself. At the turn of the 20th century she was seen in her chariot being pulled by two phantom horses in the village near the old Roman road.

CANTERBURY CATHEDRAL
Kent

THIS 12TH CENTURY cathedral is haunted by a monk who appears to be deep in thought, walking into the cloisters, where he vanishes.

CAPESTHORNE HALL
Monk's Heath, Nr Macclesfield, Cheshire

THE MOST commonly-sighted ghost in this 18th century house is a Grey Lady, but one of the residing Bromley-Davenports also claims to have seen a line of figures going down the steps into the family vault in the Georgian chapel. His son also saw a ghostly arm in his bedroom when it was reaching towards the window just before it disappeared.

CARACTACUS STONE
Exmoor, Somerset

A WAGON DRIVER tried to move this stone to get at the treasure which is rumoured to be buried beneath it. The stone fell and killed him. He now haunts the area complete with phantom wagon and horses.

CARDIFF CASTLE
South Glamorgan, Wales

A GHOSTLY MAN in a red cloak has been seen by both visitors and staff here. He has been sighted on the stairs, in the chapel doorway and in the hall. The 2nd Marquess of Bute died in the chapel and many say that the ghost looks like that of the figure in his portrait.

CAREW CASTLE
Dyfed, Wales

VISITORS HERE have reported seeing a Woman in White amongst the ruins. The theory is that she is probably Nest, daughter of the last king of South Wales, much famed at the time for her ravishing good looks. She was kidnapped from here in the 11th century.

CARLETON CASTLE
Lendalfoot, Strathclyde, Scotland

THE RUINS of this castle, standing atop a rocky ridge, are said to be haunted by ghostly screams. According to legend, the one-time Baron of Lendalfoot was rumoured to have been a regular Bluebeard. He pushed seven of his wives to their deaths over the ridge but the eighth pushed him over. Poetic justice.

CARSHALTON HOUSE
Sutton, Surrey

NOW OWNED by the Daughters of the Cross and used as a convent and school, it has just a murky past as many other British houses. In 1713 a messenger arrived to beg the services of Dr John Radcliffe. Although the request had been sent by Queen Anne, who was suffering from a bad attack of gout, the doctor refused point-blank to be rushed to the Queen's side. The messenger became so insistent that the good doctor lost his temper and ended the argument by pushing the man down the stairs, resulting in a broken neck. However, Dr Radcliffe thwarted justice by dying before he could be brought to trial. The next owner of the building, Sir John Fellowes, had a similar debate with a taxman on the landing. The argument became so heated that Sir John knocked the official over the bannisters, where he fell to his death. Both the messenger and the taxman now haunt the staircase.

CASTLE HALL
Winchester, Hampshire

BUILT IN THE 13TH CENTURY, Castle Hall is now used as an Assizes Court. In 1973 a prisoner cleaning the cell-block in the basement saw a man wearing a frock coat and a tri-cornered hat walking into a wall.

CASTLE HOTEL
Conwy, Clwyd, Wales

GHOSTS CAN either be a curse or a blessing to a business. In the case of hotels and pubs nine times out of ten they are a blessing. One of the more recent places to jump on the supernatural bandwagon is the 15th century *Castle Hotel*. It was reported in a local newspaper on 29 January 1991 that the hotel had suddenly acquired a ghost called 'George' (a popular nickname for ghosts it would seem). 'George' doesn't appear to do very much, filling ashtrays with water being his most strenuous activity. Even so, the hotel is planning a whole cavalcade of activities to encourage him to appear more often, including a guided tour of local haunted hot-spots and a fancy dress Spook's Ball.

CASTLE RUSHEN
Castletown, Isle of Man

THE UNDERGROUND PASSAGE here links Castle Rushen to Rushen Abbey. At 2:00 AM it is frequented by a Grey Lady. She has been seen by visitors and caretakers alike.

CATOR COMMON
Postbridge, Devon

DURING THE LAST 50 years or so there has been sightings of what some say is the ghost of a large white dog in this area. Once when a woman spoke to it, the animal promptly vanished. Yet others believe the creature to be the ghost of a deer.

CHAMBERCOMBE MANOR
Ilfracombe, Devon

A SMILING LADY in grey wanders amongst the visitors to this house. Her name is Kate Wallace and she was shipwrecked near here over 400 years ago. Her corpse was robbed of her possessions by the occupants of the Manor and then walled-up inside the house. Her skeleton was discovered in 1885 when a farmer, engaged in re-thatching the roof, looked down and saw her bones in a room that he didn't know existed. The bones were taken out and buried in Ilfracombe but Kate was seen as recently as 1976 and again in 1981.

CHARFORD MANOR
Devon

DURING THE EARLY 1980s there were reports of the hotel cellars here being haunted by the ghost of an elderly man. Strange footsteps were heard and bottles were moved around by invisible hands. His ghost has been sighted floating around in the dining-room.

CHARLECOTE PARK
Stratford-upon-Avon, Warwickshire

THE CONSTRUCTION of Charlecote Park was started in 1551 by Sir Thomas Lucy. He was a man of some considerable importance, who even entertained Queen Elizabeth I to breakfast here in 1576. The ghost of a young girl has been seen at the Gatehouse, where she usually runs down to the water and then disappears. Once while a daughter of the house was sleeping in the Green Room, she awoke to find a crowd of strange people milling all around her. Raised voices have also been heard from this room. A footman who committed suicide is sometimes seen near the waterfall.

CHARTWELL
Westerham, Kent

CHARTWELL was the home of Sir Winston Churchill for 40 years. His son, Randolph Churchill, claimed to have once had a long discussion with Sir Winston's ghost in the studio here.

CHATWALL
Shropshire

EASTER 1965 – a couple driving near Chatwall village saw a phantom rider on a horse. The ghostly image was quite colourless, and no sound could be heard at all, even though the windows of the witnesses' car were open.

CHECKLEY (CHURCH)
Staffordshire

IT WAS AT ONE TIME very difficult to get gravediggers to work here, purely because they claimed that they felt that they were always being watched. This disturbing but inexplicable sensation has often been noticed by sensitive people aware of psychic atmosphere. In the late 1930s the village schoolmistress, Miss Stonehouse, tried to take a shortcut across the graveyard one evening after dusk. She suddenly felt herself being held back by an invisible force, and had to hastily retrace her steps. Miss Stonehouse also practised the organ in the church, and on a couple of occasions she saw a hooded figure by the altar. The Vicar also claimed that he had seen the ghost and said he thought it was the Abbot of Croxden, who had been buried in the chancel.

CHEQUERS INN
Burry End, Amersham, Buckinghamshire

THE REPORTED HAUNTINGS here in this 15th century inn include moaning sounds and a white hooded figure which floats through a bedroom. In 1971 the barman calmly told the landlord that he had seen a cloaked man trying to climb up the bar-room chimney! One of the customers informed the landlord that he thought it was only the ghost of 'Old Osman'. Other phenomena at the pub includes shrieking screams heard in the passages at night, doors opening and closing by themselves, and the daughter of a former landlord once saw a hooded figure walk round her dressing-table and then through a locked door. It wasn't long before the girl's father, a former private detective, decided that he could take no more of the weird screams that wrecked his family's sleep and their nerves every night, and moved out.

The story behind the haunting is that 400 years ago some religious martyrs spent their last night on earth chained to a beam at the inn, under the guard of a man called Osman. The following morning the prisoners were all burnt at the stake in the Rectory Woods. Osman died in his early thirties, legend says out of pure misery. The phantom screamer is reckoned to be the daughter of one of the martyrs, William Tylsworth. The poor girl was forced to light the fire that burnt the martyrs, so I'm not surprised that the unfortunate creature is still screaming.

CHESTER
Cheshire

A PHANTOM MONK was seen by several people near St John's Church during the 1970s. He spoke to two witnesses and was most put out when they made it clear that they didn't understand him. In December 1973, a man was walking home late one night along a cobbled footpath when he met the monk. The phantom spoke to him in some strange language, and again got upset when the man said that he didn't understand him. Other rather peculiar hauntings from this town include, in November 1984, a witness seeing the ghost of a man hanging in a tree, in 1985 a woman leaving a shop heard a disembodied voice bidding her goodbye, whilst in January 1986 a girl claimed to have conversed with a dead man.

CHIDEOCK (GRAVEYARD)
Dorset

BEFORE WORLD WAR I a man and a friend were walking home late one winter night when they saw a phantom black dog walk towards a gravestone and vanish.

CHINGLE HALL
Goosnargh, Nr Preston, Lancashire

IT USUALLY induces a sense of "oh-no" when somebody boasts that a certain building is the "most haunted in ..." but I think Chingle Hall deserves its claim of being the

'Most Haunted House in England'. It is certainly the house with the most active supernatural phenomena at the present time, and one of those elusive buildings where the keen ghost-hunter is rarely disappointed in his quest. Chingle Hall is now so confident of its ghostly fame that it allows sponsored charity sit-ins and midnight visits by psychical researchers wanting to investigate the hauntings in St John Wall's Room otherwise known as the Priest's Room.

Adam de Singleton built the house in the form of a cross in 1260, making it the oldest brick house in Britain. The house was the birthplace of a priest called John Wall, who became a Roman Catholic martyr. He was executed in 1679 and his head was secretly interred in the cellar. Varied phenomena at the house has been so extensive that it would be easier just to note some examples of it during the last 30 years.

In January 1977 a visitor came across two monks praying in a downstairs room. They melted into the wall as he approached. In May 1979 a couple of Ghost Club investigators were holding a vigil in the Priest Room when they heard loud bangs and thuds from the Priest's-Hole. A chair shook with vibration, and the owner, Fred Knowles, demonstrated how he communicated with the spirit, using knocks. Two months later on 28 July, another party of ghosthunters heard bangs and felt a drop in temperature. In September 1979 a psychic investigator felt something invisible brush against her leg, and heard a mysterious knocking sound. On 15 August 1980 some more psychic investigators heard strange taps and Knowles again demonstrated his knocking technique. In 1985 a psychic investigator heard footsteps along a passage, and felt icy fingers grab his hand. Banging was also heard in the Priest's Room.

A former owner, Mrs Margaret Howarth, heard footsteps in the rooms and passages. They also seemed to make a spectral journey over the bridge across the moat, through the front door and across the hall. Mrs Howarth also reported door latches moving and doors opening, dogs getting agitated and objects being moved. Water was known to appear from nowhere, and monkish figures were seen in the house and garden.

A monkish face has been known to appear at a window and then vanish again. From a window in the Priest's Room, 12 feet from the ground, a man with long hair was seen to glide past. A visitor watched as a greenish figure walked from the porch to the dining-room and then vanished. A Mrs Walmsley was pushed violently whilst she was standing alone in the centre of the lounge and a Mrs Moorby felt a sharp drop in temperature and experienced that strange feeling of being watched by unseen eyes. A Mrs Robinson heard footsteps climbing the stairs followed by three raps from the Priest's Room, whilst a Mrs McKay felt a waft of cold air in the same room and watched as some flowers were lifted out of a vase. Later a table-lamp and a picture rattled. One evening two ladies, Mrs Rigby and the owner, Mrs Howarth, were having tea in the lounge when a wooden plaque shot off the wall and landed in the middle of the room.

But again and again we keep coming back to the Priest's Room. A man called Michael Bingham heard bricks being moved in there. He said he saw a hand moving them which then vanished and he also made a video recording of a shadowy figure in the passage. On another occasion ghostly monks were photographed on the South Lawn.

Chingle Hall rightly deserves its eminent standing in the world of the supernatural.

CHURCH OF ST LAWRENCE
Bradford-on-Avon, Wiltshire

THIS 10TH CENTURY church was 'lost' until 1856, because it had been used as a private home. A priest taking communion once saw a group of strange people dressed in medieval costume standing by the altar rail. In 1932 the well-known American medium Eileen Garrett, went into a trance inside the church, and claimed to have seen a group of people taking communion. She said afterwards that she felt that they could have been lepers.

CITY PALACE OF VARIETIES
Leeds, West Yorkshire

REGARDED AS the most famous music-hall still standing, it was opened in its present form on 7 June 1865. It conjures up images of bygone glamour. For instance, in 1898 King Edward VII, then Prince of Wales, came to watch Lillie Langtry perform here, watching her from Box D. Mysterious sounds of a piano being played have been heard, but whether this is of the ghostly lady is not known.

A TV producer, Len Marten, took his production assistant to the theatre whilst on a visit to Leeds. Afterwards they were invited to the Circle Bar for a drink, but when he visited the cloakroom in the bar area, all the lights inexplicably went out. He groped his way back to the bar only to find that room was in darkness as well and the door was locked. When no-one heard him shouting he realised he was locked in for the night and eventually dropped off to sleep in front of the coal-fire. When he suddenly woke up feeling cold, he saw the ghost of a crinolined lady standing by the fire, looking directly at him. She then vanished. Once she had gone, the room became warm again but Len Marten's ordeal only ended when the nightwatchman came to let him out in the early hours of the morning.

CLANDON PARK
West Clandon, Guildford, Surrey

IN 1896 Ada Goodrich-Freer wrote an article for *Borderland* magazine about the ghosts of Clandon Park. Her interest had been caught by rumours that a former tenant had even terminated his lease because of the haunting. It was reported that, in the early hours of the morning, the servants had seen a woman rushing across the lawns brandishing a hunting-knife. Shots were fired at her by the keepers but she thwarted them by vanishing into a wall. More than 20 people were a witness to this phantom. The owner of the estate, Lord Onslow, claimed to have also seen the ghost of a girl in black and a man with a long beard. Miss Freer made it known that she was very sceptical about the stories, but in 1897 she produced another article on Clandon Park in which it appeared that she had considerably changed her tune.

In the interim period Miss Freer had been invited to stay at the house, and on 29 January 1897 she gave a talk about her experiences at Westminster Town Hall. She related how, on going upstairs to dress for dinner, she had seen a bejewelled and begowned woman in the upstairs passage. The beautiful phantom vanished as they drew close to each other.

It is believed that the history of the house goes back to about 1735 when it was built by Giacomo Leoni on the site of an earlier house. The grounds were, it is thought, once in possession of the Knights Templar. The mysterious lady phantom is said to be one Elizabeth Knight, the deeply unhappy wife of a former baron, who ended her days by drowning herself in the lake. What she intends to do with the hunting-knife is not clear.

CLASSIC CINEMA
Lenton Abbey, Nottingham

THE RESIDENT GHOST here haunts the projection room and the circle. Mysterious footsteps have also been heard walking down the aisle and doors open by themselves in the foyer. In 1973 usherette Maureeen Longford saw the ghost of a man in a suit standing in the circle and projectionist Henry Chamberlain saw the same figure in the projection room, where it vanished in front of him. The reports insist that the ghost seems to be of a friendly disposition.

CLAYDON HOUSE
Middle Claydon, Nr Winslow, Buckinghamshire

LEGEND HAS IT that Sir Edmund Verney haunts the little chapel in this 18th century house, searching for his hand which was cut off at the Battle of Edgehill in 1642. In 1923 Mrs Walker, a forester's wife, was staying at the house when she heard footsteps in the corridors at night, but they stopped at the trapdoor entrance to the Priest's Hole. Her sisters had exactly the same experience several years later.

The noiseless ghost of a certain eccentric Mr Lightfoot has also been seen in shadowy parts of the house. Lightfoot appeared to a carpenter who was working on the demolition of the ballroom, and then vanished. In 1892 Ruth Verney, aged 13, saw a man near the Cedar Room on the first floor. She described him as wearing a plumed hat and he carried a sword. Andrew Lang, who was sleeping in the Rose Room, woke to see a beautiful lady in grey vanish into the wall of what had once been a secret room. There is some speculation as to whether this ghost is Florence Nightingale. She did stay here but the theory is much disputed. The house, and an earlier one on the same site, has been the home of the Verney family since 1620, and there is more reason to suppose that she is a female member of the family instead.

CLODACK (CHURCH)
Hereford & Worcester

A PHANTOM BLACK DOG was said to haunt the lane near the church. It would run alongside horses and vehicles before disappearing.

CLOUDS HILL
Wool, Dorset

T E LAWRENCE BOUGHT this cottage in 1925 and was so fond of it that he spent much of his time here until he was killed in a motorcycle accident in May 1935. There were many reported sightings of his ghost, dressed in his favourite Arab garb, usually seen entering the house at dusk. The roar of his powerful motorcycle has also been heard in the area of his fatal accident at night. A Mrs Little heard the motorcycle in 1973. A woman, as she was leaving the house in the evening, passed his ghost dressed in Arab costume. She was with a friend when she heard the roar of the motorcycle in the road.

COCK AND BOTTLE
Skeldergate, York, North Yorkshire

THE SUPERNATURAL phenomena recorded here includes the usual mixture of doors opening and closing, bangs, footsteps, sharp drops in temperature, and small objects disappearing and returning again. Landlady Brenda Stanley saw the ghost of a very ugly man with one eye bigger than the other. The ghost of a man in a cavalier hat has been sighted, and any unsuspecting customer wearing a crucifix has it suddenly and rudely snatched from them by an unseen force.

A man once related an occasion when he was walking along an upstairs passage and suddenly found himself being held against the wall by an invisible attacker. The same man also reported seeing the ghost of a milkmaid.

COGGESHALL
Essex

THIS PART of England seems rich in supernatural phenomena, and the entire village of Coggeshall appears to spawn ghostly beings. Cradle House has an occasional visit from a procession of ghostly monks, a house in Church Street which used to be a pub has experienced poltergeist phenomena, strange lights have been seen in the attic at Guild House, and there have been sightings of a little old man suddenly appearing at the foot of a bed here.

COLISEUM THEATRE
St Martin's Lane, London

A YOUNG SOLDIER visited here on the night before he was called to the front during World War I. It was to be his last bit of pleasure on this earth, for he was killed on 3 October 1918, one of the last casualties of the bloodbath that destroyed so many young men. On the night he died his ghost was seen at the theatre; a uniformed figure seen moving to the front row just before the show started. He has been seen less frequently since World War II.

CONYGAR HILL
Dunster, Somerset

IN JULY 1951 two ladies holidaying in Dunster, decided to walk up Conygar Hill. As they walked back down again they noticed a drop in temperature and a cold wind, then they heard the sound of marching feet. The women were panic stricken and ran the rest of the way down.

COOKHAM DEAN (CHURCH)
Berkshire

THE VICAR'S WIFE saw a man-sized shadow in this church in 1979, and also noticed a drop in temperature whilst her husband admitted that he often felt as though he was being watched. There's a possible theory that this haunting is caused by the ghost of a previous vicar, who has been seen a few times in the church. Nearby is the northern edge of Windsor Forest, where the ghost of the enigmatic character Herne the Hunter, was seen disappearing into an oak tree one summer's evening in the 1920s.

CORFE CASTLE
Purbeck, Dorset

LIKE ALL ROYAL buildings Corfe Castle has a long and bloody history. In 978 AD King Edward the Martyr was murdered in the grounds on the orders of his mother, Elfrida. The infamous King John used the castle as his treasure house but he also used it for other purposes – he had 22 French nobles starved to death in the dungeons. During the Civil War, Parliamentary troops gained possession and the castle was blown up in 1646, reducing it to ruins.

In the evenings a vague shape resembling a headless woman, has been sighted here. The shape was seen in 1967 by a local resident, who said it might be connected with the nearby manor house, and a secret underground tunnel which is said to lead the the Castle. He described the phantom as a white headless figure that drifted across the road and he felt a distinct sharp coldness at the same time. In 1971 it was seen in the same place by a visitor, and then again in 1976 by no less than three visitors.

CORTACHY CASTLE
Tayside, Scotland

SUPERNATURAL messengers of death come in all guises and in various places. This castle's prophet of doom appears in the shape of a ghostly drummer, who is said to haunt the area when a demise is imminent in the resident Airlie clan. During the 1840s the drummer sounded the death-knell of the Countess. By 1848 the Earl had remarried and threw a dinner-party in honour of his new bride. Unfortunately one of the guests, Margaret Dalrymple, innocently mentioned over dinner that she had heard a drummer in the courtyard. Understandably the happy couple went considerably pale at the news.

Dalrymple's maid, Ann Day, got upset herself when she heard the drummer the following morning, yet on looking out of the window she saw that the courtyard was empty but on hearing it again a day later Miss Dalrymple decided to cut short her stay. A few weeks later she learnt that the new Lady Airlie had died in Brighton. In 1853 some estate workers heard the drummer just before the death of the Earl. In 1881 two relatives visiting the castle heard the drummer, and a week later the 10th Earl, David Ogilvy, died in America.

COTEHELE
Calstock, Cornwall

COTEHELE was built between 1485 and 1520 on the site of an older house, and was once the home of the Earls of Mount Edgecumbe. A permanent bloodstain indicated where a man was killed in the entrance archway. Unfortunately for those wishing to see the gory reminder of the death, the bloodstained stone was moved to the bridge by Cotehele Quay and painted over. One of the tales surrounding Cotehele concerns Caroline, Countess of Mount Edgecumbe, who died in 1881. Whilst the sexton was busy removing jewellery from her corpse, she sat bolt upright and the sexton fled. A strong herbal smell has been noticed around the house from time to time, with no apparent source. Ghostly music has also been heard in the building.

A nurse, who was attending the 5th Earl during his fatal illness, watched as a spectral young lady in white passed through his room, and the girl in white was also seen at Christmas 1980. Friends of Mrs Julyan, who lived at the house, once saw the ghost walking down the main staircase.

COTGRAVE COLLIERY
Nottinghamshire

IN OCTOBER 1987 miner Gary Pine saw a ghost in a black helmet and dark overalls. He couldn't recall seeing a face to the apparition, and watched as the figure vanished into a wall. The witness had hysterics and had to be carried away from the mine on a stretcher.

COUGHTON COURT
Alcester, Warwickshire

LEGEND HAS IT that the ghost of a pink lady makes a regular journey from the Tapestry Bedroom, across the dining-room and onto the front stairs. At the turn of the 20th century, Sir William Throckmorton's agent arranged for a Catholic priest to carry out an exorcism, which might explain why things have been a bit quiet on the supernatural front here in recent years.

CRAB AND LOBSTER INN
Sidlesham, West Sussex

DURING THE CIVIL WAR the *Crab and Lobster Inn* became the centre for Royalist underground activities. One story goes that Sir Robert Earnley and friends were waiting at the Inn to cross to France and safety but they were thwarted in their plan by the sudden arrival of a party of Roundheads. Fighting broke out and six cavaliers were killed in the lane outside the Inn. The pub is now haunted, both inside and out, by a tall figure wearing the Civil War costume of a Royalist.

In 1965/66 the haunting attracted tourists from all over the world (although in recent issues of the *Good Pub Guide* it is stated that the inn is relatively untroubled by such characters nowadays). Anyway, the pub cat has been known to act strangely, always trying to avoid certain parts of the saloon bar floor, and one of the bedrooms has been reported to have an unpleasant atmosphere. Heavy footsteps were once heard downstairs late at night on a regular basis, but whenever the landlord went to investigate there was never anyone there. During the summer of 1969 a couple called in for a meal. On going past the saloon bar on their way to the dining-room the woman gave a cry of alarm for she had just seen a man in Civil War clothing lying on the floor trying to plug a gunshot wound with "a hankie". There were people sitting all around him drinking, totally oblivious to the wounded 400 year-old Royalist lying in their midst.

CRAIGIEVAR CASTLE
Lumphanan, Grampian, Scotland

THE BLUE ROOM at this tower house is haunted by a member of the Gordon family, who was shoved out of the window by the 3rd Laird, 'Red' Sir John. The Forbes-Sempill family as such would not let any guest of theirs pass a night in the haunted bedroom.

Footsteps have been heard going up and down the stairs, and Lady Cecilia once related an extraordinary story of how she had seen a crowd of people in old-fashioned costume in the entrance hall late one night. She had been talking with her solicitor in the drawing-room, discussing some financial trouble being experienced by the family, and left the room to see where her husband was.

The hall was lit by only four candles, and in the dim light she saw a man getting something out of the chest near the door. Mistakenly thinking that it was her husband she spoke to him, upon which he hurried out of sight. It then dawned on Lady Cecilia that the hall was full of strange people; in her understandably anxious state she had brushed through the throng, intent on only finding her husband. She found him contentedly fast asleep in the notorious Blue Room. On relating the strange incident to two elderly ladies at a later date, she was astonished when one of them said that "they" would always return whenever the family was in trouble.

CRANHAM
Hornchurch, Essex

IT WAS AT Christmas-time in 1977 when Richard Sage was driving with some friends that he saw a monk appear out of nowhere. He said the figure crossed the road in front of them and then vanished. The same incident was reported again in December 1979. Similar reports place other sightings of the ghostly monk at Christmas-time in 1976 and 1978.

CRASTER TOWER
Alnwick, Northumberland

ONE MORNING an anxious maid appeared to the owner of the premises, urgently asking him to accompany her to the dining-room. The room was in a peculiar shambles; two Chinese vases on the mantlepiece had been broken, a pile of soot lay behind the firescreen, and there was the outline of a naked, sooty, human foot on the windowseat. It was roundly assumed that this was the work of something unearthly. Bangs and thumps had also been reported from the wall between the two libraries, along with sightings of a ghostly Grey Lady. In August 1955 a young girl saw the Grey Lady walk upstairs to the drawing-room and it is this female phantom who may also be responsible for the occasional sound of rustling skirts.

A phantom coach-and-horses has also been known to stop at the front door, but discernable by sound only as nothing has ever been seen. The phantom coach usually then heads for the stables. Naturally.

CRATHES CASTLE
Banchory, Grampian, Scotland

THE LAND HERE was granted to the Burnett family by Robert the Bruce in 1323. The castle was built later during the 16th century. A ghostly Green Lady has been known to appear just before a death in the household. She was once sighted by Queen Victoria when she was a guest at the castle and it is claimed that the Queen watched as the phantom glided across a room to the fireplace where it stopped, picked up a child and then vanished. It is extremely likely that the ghost has a connection with the skeletons of a woman and child found beneath the fireplace. The most intriguing part of this story is, how did their bodies get there?

CROFT CASTLE
Leominster, Hereford & Worcester

CROFT CASTLE, mentioned in the Domesday Book, has an exterior which is 14th and 15th century, but the hall and gallery belong to the 18th century.

Hauntings reported over the years seem to indicate that the castle houses two ghosts, one usually seen in the Oak Room, and the other more frequently in the hall. During the 1920s a friend of the late Sir James Croft (the 11th Baronet) was playing billiards in the Oak Room, when he turned and encountered a huge man clad in leather! This ghost is one of the more commonly-sighted ones, and many people reckon that it is the ghost of Owen Glendower, hero of many a Welsh terrorist.

In 1926 some of the Oxford Boat Race crew were staying at the castle for the weekend. An oarsman coming downstairs for dinner saw a tall man in a leather jerkin loitering in the portrait gallery but the ghost faded away after a few seconds. A short while later another of the guests almost collided with the same figure near the Oak Room, but again the apparition faded. Also during the 1920s some guests were foolishly playing the oujii board in the saloon, when they were startled by a prolific tapping at each window in the room. At the same time the dogs started to panic and began to show signs of great distress. The Oak Room phantom was also seen by a cousin of the family in daylight hours and again he vanished in front of her. A different phantom is one in Elizabethan costume sighted in one of the Tower bedrooms. This gentleman, in doublet and hose, was seen early one morning by the Archbishop of Brisbane as he was drinking his early morning tea. The apparition looked in his direction before it disappeared into a wall. He later saw a portrait of Sir James Croft, comptroller of Queen Elizabeth I's household,

124

which provided a good likeness of the ghost.

CROSS KEYS HOTEL
Peebles, Borders, Scotland

IN SEPTEMBER 1975 there were reports of supernatural phenomena occurring in Room 3. A radio interviewer taped a ghostly voice, but unfortunately when the tape was played back, all it revealed was the voice of Donald Duck at high speed!

CROSS ROADS
Edale, Derbyshire

AS A SMALL GROUP of men were walking home one night they heard the sound of galloping horses. Although they could see nothing, the sound continued until it passed right by them. The hooves then turned up the lane towards the village of Hope. In 1930, a few miles away at Upper Booth, a girl out walking one evening, saw a phantom black dog pass through a wire fence.

CROWN HOTEL
Askern, Nr Doncaster, South Yorkshire

MRS BANKS once lived here whilst her parents ran the business. Although her bedroom was on the first floor she hankered after a room on the floor above, yet the particular room she had in mind was never used by the guests and was full of junk and dust. Mrs Banks asked her mother if she could move into this room as it was bigger than her own. Her parents agreed and the room was cleared out and redecorated. Eventually the young Mrs Banks changed rooms, settled down, and was soon asleep. After a short time she awoke with a strange feeling, and said later that she felt as though she was being watched.

Suddenly the curtains flew open and the room was filled with moonlight. When she realised that she was still quite alone in the room she fled, running back down to her old room where her brother found her the next morning. Later, he said that he found it rather odd that the second floor room had bars on the windows, and a lock and two bolts on the *outside* of the door. The mystery remains unsolved, and the answer could lie anywhere in the building's 200 year-old history.

CROWN HOTEL
Market Street, Poole, Dorset

DURING THE 1960s the upper floor of the stable block of the hotel was converted into a nightclub. In 1966 people talking in the courtyard, heard a piano tinkling away to itself in the club, what was disturbing was that they knew that the stables were empty at the time. On another occasion not long after, a hammer and some nails resting on the piano lid suddenly flew into the air.

Other phenomena includes a ball of fluorescent mist resembling a child's head seen floating downstairs and out into the street. The sound of a heavy object, suspiciously resembling a body, has been heard being dragged across an upper floor of the hotel, and was once heard by licensee Mrs Marie Hughes. Some men working in the stable block once watched as the door slowly swung open.

News of the stable block haunting reached the ears of a sceptical guest. He painted five crosses on the door and bolted it. To his amazement the door still persistently swung open. In 1974 the local milkman told the landlord that he had heard children's screams coming from the empty stable block when he made his 5:00 AM delivery. This was verified by the landlady at the time, Mrs Eeles, who had also heard the screams. As with a lot of juicy hauntings there appears to be a suitably gruesome legend behind this one. The story goes that a former landlord in the 19th century had killed and buried two deformed children in the stable block, after imprisoning them for a while in the attic, where during the 1960s a hidden, doorless room was discovered.

CROWN INN
Trellech, Gwent, Wales

FROM 10-24 DECEMBER 1981 there was a short outbreak of poltergeist activity at this pub, which ended on Christmas Eve with a violent shaking of the Christmas tree!

CULLODEN
Nr Inverness, Highland, Scotland

ON 16 APRIL 1746 the last pitched battle of the House of Stewart took place at Culloden. Bonnie Prince Charlie's army was defeated by the Duke of Cumberland's troops, resulting in a huge loss of life, and a green mound still marks the burial-place of the soldiers. A visitor to the area in recent times saw the body of a Highland soldier lying on top of the mound, his clothes were dirty and plastered with mud, and he wore the tartan of the Stewarts. The visitor turned and fled the scene. Wendy Wood told how on looking into the nearby 'Well of the Dead' she not only saw her own reflection but the face of a man with long dark hair and a scar across his forehead, and immediately felt an acute pain in her brow, which took four days to ease.

CULZEAN CASTLE
Maybole, Strathclyde, Scotland

CULZEAN CASTLE was built by Robert Adam between 1777-1792, and is haunted by the sound of a ghostly piper. Gilbert Kennedy, 4th Earl of Cassillis, arranged for Allan Stewart, Commendator of Crossraguel Abbey, to be taken prisoner when he visited the castle. Stewart was dragged into a vault and roasted on a spit. Under such torture he naturally agreed to sign a document releasing the Abbey to the Earl. On completion of this "business agreement" Stewart was obligingly set free. Kennedy was fined for his rather unorthodox methods by the Privy Council and ordered to pay Stewart a life pension. The Earl still managed to keep the land though. Nowadays, on autumn mornings, the sounds of a fire crackling and anguished cries can still be heard.

In 1946 an apartment in the castle was given to General Eisenhower as a gift. This particular suite of rooms is haunted by a beautiful girl. One afternoon at 5:00 Mrs Margaret Penney met the ghost in the corridor and said that she was dressed in a beautiful evening gown. As she pressed herself against the wall to let the ghostly vision pass by she felt a cold chill when she spoke to the phantom. The ghostly lady answered her by replying that she didn't require much room nowadays, and vanished.

In 1972 three servants noticed a strange shape in the passages leading to the dungeons, and in 1976 two visitors saw a misty shape near a staircase. They watched the shape travel up the stairs and vanish and just to add an extra dose of atmosphere to the area, fairies are said to meet in the Coves of Culzean at Halloween.

CWM HELDEG
Cilfynydd, Mid Glamorgan, Wales

THE WOODED SLOPES here are said to be haunted by a White Lady. In 1968 the editor of the local newspaper saw the vision himself. In recent times she has been sighted in front of the trees, and moving amongst them, with a luminous mystery being in a white cloak.

DALLINGTON (CHURCH)
Northamptonshire

IN 1907 two young girls decided to visit Dallington Church as dusk was falling. One entered the building but immediately came back outside again obviously distressed. The second girl went in to see what had upset her friend and she recalled seeing an entire congregation knelt in prayer, but they appeared to be insubstantial as they were composed entirely of bubbles. A very, very curious haunting.

DARLINGTON RAILWAY STATION
County Durham

ONE EVENING a porter was sitting in the porter's cellar when a man walked in, accompanied by a black retriever. Suddenly the stranger struck out at the porter, who struck back in sheer bewilderment, and was then even more disconcerted when his fist hit nothing but air! The dog then set-to and grabbed the porter's leg. The porter was relieved when the man and his dog took themselves off to the coalhouse. When the porter plucked up the courage to look into the coalhouse a short while later, he found there was nobody there.

The porter later learned that the ghost was a man who had killed himself at the station by jumping under a train. His body was laid out in the coal cellar whilst everyone waited for the undertaker to call. He had owned a black retriever – which incidentally left no bite mark on the porter's leg.

DARTMOOR PRISON
Princetown, Devon

NOBODY HAS much chance of mistaking this gloomy old pile for anything but a prison as they drive past Princetown, isolated up on the moors. It was originally built to cage French prisoners-of-war in 1806, and was put into general penal use in 1850. Many ghosts are said to haunt the prison cemetery and have been seen frequently over the years by prisoners and warders alike.

This prison also has its own version of the 'Birdman of Alcatraz' in David Davies, who was sent to Dartmoor in 1879, and was to spend the next 50 years of his life there. He occupied his time looking after a herd of sheep, and after several years he was even allowed to camp out on the moors during the lambing season, totally unsupervised. When the authorities eventually decided to release him, he begged them to let him stay and keep his old shepherding job which he had grown to love. This wasn't quite what they had expected and they released him, whether he liked it or not, only to have Davies get himself re-admitted a few weeks later. He died in prison in 1929. His ghost has become legendary in the area for he continues to haunt the direct vicinity of the prison, still tending his beloved sheep.

DEADMAN'S COVE
Hudder Down, Cornwall

IN 1978 a couple saw a strange man in black standing on the beach, at the edge of the waves. He faded away as they approached.

DEARHAM BRIDGE RAILWAY STATION
Maryport, Cumbria

NOT LONG after the station opened in the 19th century, a man was walking over the bridge with his wife and young child, when he suddenly seized the baby and hurled it under a moving train. The man was hanged for this incredible act of insane cruelty. Since then several people claim to have heard the ghostly, and ghastly screams of the poor baby.

DENTON
Lincolnshire

ON 29 JANUARY 1961 a rally driver competing in a race, encountered a ghostly horseman near Denton.

DEVIL'S DEN
Fyfield, Wiltshire

THIS NEOLITHIC tomb is said to be haunted by a phantom dog with large, fiery eyes.

DITCHLING BEACON
Ditchling, East Sussex

LEGEND GOES that phantom witch-hounds were believed to race overhead here, chasing the Souls of the Damned, whilst the road between Ditchling and Westmerton, on Black Dog Hill, is haunted by a phantom headless, black dog.

DOLPHIN INN
The Quay, Penzance, Cornwall

IN 1588 THE INN was used by Sir John Hawkins as his headquarters, when he was recruiting men to fight against the Spanish Armada. Judge Jeffries was believed to have held one of his infamous courts here, where the prisoners were kept in the cellar. The pub was also used by smugglers, who once thrived along the coastline hereabouts and were responsible for spreading a lot of false yarns about ghosts, to help them carry out their illegal trade unmolested at night. The pub is haunted by an old sea-captain who sports a tri-cornered hat. Footsteps were heard as recently as 1985, usually crossing the room above the bar.

The haunting here seems to have become more substantial in recent years. Tenants Brian and May Clark both heard the distinct sound of footsteps walking along the upstairs passage and down the stairs early one morning. The footsteps sounded as though they were crossing bare boards, even though the corridor and stairs were carpeted. Mrs Clark also saw, twice in one week, the apparition of a young fair-haired man who faded away. The discovery of pipe tobacco ash scattered untidily over the floor of Room 5 by a chambermaid, has been attributed to tobacco-importer Sir Walter Raleigh, who stayed here in 1586. The maid also reported that the bed in the room often appeared to have been slept in, even when the room was unused.

DOVER CASTLE
Kent

DOVER CASTLE was built just after the Norman Conquest, and is said to be haunted by a headless drummer boy who was killed during the Napoleonic Wars.

NO.10 DOWNING STREET
London

NO. 10 IS BELIEVED to be haunted by a Regency politician at times of "national crisis". He was sighted by workmen in the garden in 1960.

DUNBLANE
Perthshire, Scotland

IN 1974 writer A C McKerracher was living on a newly-built housing estate above the town. One September evening he decided to step outside to get some air. The town was covered in mist, and he thought he could hear the movement of a large group of people walking across the fields. At first he thought nothing of it and went back indoors. Twenty minutes later the sound of tramping feet seemed to be even louder and nearer. Next he heard what sounded like a legion of men walking directly past his house but amazingly, this still didn't concern him very much and he went to bed! A week later he paid a visit to an elderly couple who lived nearby. They mentioned the ghostly legion without any prompting from him, and remarked that their dog and cat had reacted to the sound even if Mr McKerracher hadn't. The couple reported that the animals had sat and watched as though something invisible was crossing the lounge. McKerracher told them of his own experience and found that both the incidents had occurred at the same time.

McKerracher later discovered that a Roman road used to run through the area. In 117 AD the IX Hispania Legion had marched through Dunblane to quell a tribal uprising. The 4000 men of the Legion were a rough bunch who are notorious in history for having flogged Queen Boadicea's tribe and raped her daughters. The Queen put a curse on the Legion, and soon after they vanished without trace after passing through Dunblane.

In October 1984 McKerracher gave a lecture on local history. One of the members of the local history club, Cecilia Moore, said that she had heard the ghostly legion as well. She added that they'd seemed to pass right through her front garden. The date that she heard them coincided exactly with the experience of McKerracher and the elderly couple.

DUNSMORE HEATH
Stretton-on-Dunsmore, Warwickshire

A THREE MILE STRETCH of the A45 road crossing Dunsmore Heath, and centering on Knightlow Hill, is said to be haunted by, of all things, a phantom lorry. The vehicle was notorious for causing accidents when cars swerved to avoid it and one of the witnesses to it included an ex-policeman who lived locally. He was helping out at a traffic accident one winter's night sometime in the early 1950s when he saw the lorry. Bonfires had been lit to warn approaching vehicles of the accident, but the lorry drove straight past, and as the police officer turned, he saw with disbelief that the fires were visible through the vehicle. Needless to say, the lorry didn't crash into the accident pile-up.

DUNSTANBURGH CASTLE
Alnwick, Northumberland

BUILDING OF the castle was started in 1313 after the line of the previous lords of the site became extinct in 1244. Now in ruins, Dunstanburgh was once the largest castle in Northumberland. In more recent centuries a knight called Sir Guy (who doesn't appear to have been credited with a surname) got caught in a storm, and sought refuge in the castle ruins. He was waiting with his horse in the archway of the keep gatehouse for the storm to pass, when a figure appeared and ordered Sir Guy to follow him. The figure led him through passages beneath the castle, until they came upon a room in which lay some comatose knights and a beautiful lady. Sir Guy was told to choose between a horn and a sword, and was also informed in no uncertain terms that the fate of the beautiful lady lay upon his decision. Sir Guy innocently chose the horn and blew on it, at which the knights all woke up. Before he knew it Sir Guy found himself outside in the rain again. Sir Guy searched for many years after for the door to the sleeping beauty, but he never found it.

Strangely though, the high-pitched wail of a horn can still be heard amongst the ruins at night, and a stumbling figure in armour has been sighted.

DUNWICH
Suffolk

A VERITABLE RASH of spooky goings-on in this area it would seem. The hauntings include the bells of a sunken church ringing mournfully and the appearance of a Victorian squire on horseback. During World War I the ghost of the squire was sighted by some soldiers. He is said to have been a member of the Barne family who lived nearby. Miles Barne bred Arab horses and exercised them on Dunwich Heath. There is also the ghost of an Elizabethan lady who walks down to the sea and then disappears.

Old Dunwich was once a city which boasted no less than 52 churches. The entire town was destroyed by a storm in 1328, and now the bells of one of the old churches can still be heard just before Christmas.

At Grey Friars the son of the lord of the manor was refused permission to marry his sweetheart. He died of a broken heart and his ghost now desolately roams the sand dunes, but leaves no footprints. Dunwich is also haunted by 'Black Shuck', (the local name for a phantom black hound), and just for good measure the ghosts of the former inhabitants of Old Dunwich can sometimes be seen frequenting the shore. Other spectral phenomena include the chanting of monks in the ruins of Grey Friars Priory, deformed shapes in the graveyard near the leper hospital, and a young man searching for his wayward wife on the pathways near the priory.

DYLIFE
Powys, Wales

IN 1984 a man in the disused mineshafts heard a low
humming noise. He called out but got no reply. Then he
saw a small, white or pale blue glowing shape, but when
the witness switched on his torch it vanished. On telling of
his strange experience to local men he learnt that
mysterious lights had often been seen emerging from the
cave and rising into the air.

Whether this really classified as a haunting, or is some
kind of UFO phenomena, is open to conjecture but then
Wales is UFO country. Dylife is certainly an atmospheric
place, and well worth the long, winding drive over the hills
for anyone who wants to imagine that they are on the edge
of the world.

EAST RIDDLESDEN HALL
Keighley, West Yorkshire

THIS 17TH CENTURY manor house has a multitude of hauntings, first of which is the essential Grey Lady. She has been seen roaming the corridors, as well as drifting aimlessly in and out of the rooms. The story behind her is that she was once a lady of the manor, but her husband returned home unexpectedly one day to find her in the arms of her lover.

The cuckolded husband locked her in her room, and then walled up her lover (quite a few husbands seem to have resorted to this form of rough justice at one time). Both she and her lover eventually starved to death, and her ghost now shuffles up the stairs and along the landing to the master bedroom. A former caretaker, an old lady saw the ghost on many occasions and although taking her appearances with a pinch of salt, used to get very annoyed because the ghost never acknowledged her greetings!

A later resident, Major Morris-Barker, never saw the Grey Lady personally, but his wife and family frequently heard disembodied footsteps on the stairs and landing, and on three occasions a female voice was heard bidding them "goodnight" from the top of the stairs. The Grey Lady's unfortunate lover is said to appear at the window of the bricked-up room where he died. The son of a former caretaker claimed many years ago that the bricked-up room had certainly existed, and when it was broken into a male skeleton was found. There is also a ghostly White Lady, and she is said to be yet another lady of the manor. Her story is that she had been riding around the estate and turned in at the gates to return home. Mysteriously the horse arrived at the house alone, and in spite of extensive searching, the woman was never found. The theory is that the horse shied, threw her into the lake and she drowned, for her ghost has been seen walking around that area.

There is also a phantom coachman. He drowned when his horses mysteriously bolted, and dragged him and his coach into the lake. He has been seen searching for his coach ever since.

EDGE HILL
Radway, Warwickshire

THE FAMOUS Civil War Battle of Edge Hill took place here on 23 October 1642. The result was a calamitous loss of life.

The following Christmas Eve some shepherds tending their flock saw, not a bright star in the East, but a complete ghostly re-enactment of the battle which lasted an entire three hours. The following day news of this festive spectral entertainment spread like wildfire, and the entire village turned out to witness another vivid re-run of the battle. The haunting became big news indeed and King Charles I himself, not unnaturally, became very interested in it. He sent some of his men to witness it for themselves. The clarity of the spectral battle has diminished considerably over the years, which lends more weight to the theory that incredible psychic phenomena like that slowly runs down, like a battery, over a long period of time. But not to despair, phantom horses and some of the soldiers have still been seen here from time to time in recent years.

EGGARDON HILL
Nettlecombe, Dorset

ANOTHER HAUNTING steeped in fascinating Pagan folklore. This Iron Age hillfort is said to be haunted by the Goddess Diana and her hounds, collecting the souls of the dead.

EILEAN DONAN CASTLE
Loch Duich, Highland, Scotland

THIS 13TH CENTURY castle is haunted by the ghost of an 18th century Spanish soldier.

ELLESBOROUGH (CHURCH)
Buckinghamshire

SHORTLY AFTER World War II an organist here saw the ghost of a man dressed in medieval costume. The ghost was seen again a few years later by a lady arranging the altar flowers. He was last sighted by a visitor in 1970.

ELM PARK GARDENS
Chelsea, London

MILD POLTERGEIST activity broke out in one of these houses in 1937. It centered mainly on a young servant girl, and consisted mostly of thumps and knockings on a dividing wall. It is an interesting aspect of poltergeist phenomena that the haunting usually centres on a person of puberty or post-adolescent years, which suggests that poltergeist activity is created by some powerful force emanating from the human body at times of physical and emotional turmoil. This separates it from other supernatural phenomena quite neatly.

ELM VICARAGE
Elm, Nr Wisbech, Cambridgeshire

THIS 17TH CENTURY vicarage is haunted in part by a bell that sounds a death-knell, for shortly after hearing it the vicar would usually learn of a death in the village within 24 hours. Over a period of 2/3 years this depressing incident occurred 30 times. The most interesting haunting of the vicarage occurred when the Rev. and Mrs A R Bradshaw were in residence. First they heard footsteps at night in the vicarage but then Mrs Bradshaw had the strangest experience. She was walking along an upstairs corridor when she brushed against a monk who she really hadn't expected to be there.

Over a period of time she gained the confidence of this spectral holy-man. He informed her that he was Ignatius the Bellringer, and was condemned to wander the earth forever as a penance, because he had accidentally caused the death of his fellow monks. He had fallen asleep on watch duty and thus failed to warn the brothers in time that the monastery was in danger of being flooded. Several monks drowned on the site on which the vicarage now stands.

One September, Mrs Bradshaw was asleep in one of the bedrooms with her dog when the animal suddenly gave a start and fled the room. Then she had a most unpleasant experience of the supernatural kind for she felt as though she was being strangled and was then thrown violently across the bed. She said later that her attacker was a dark shape with gnarled hands, and she was only saved by the intervention of her friend, Ignatius the ghostly monk. The vicar's wife had marks on her neck for several days after this nasty incident. Ignatius told her that by saving her life he had been released from his penance and his ghostly form would no longer have to aimlessly roam the earth.

From then on the room was kept locked-up, and the theory is that her gnarled would-be murderer was himself killed in that room. A neighbour of the late Rev. and Mrs Bradshaw swore that this most unusual and aggressive haunting was definitely true, and that two ghosts did indeed once haunt the vicarage – one good and the other bad.

ENCHMARSH
All Stretton, Shropshire

IN APRIL 1965 two London art lecturers were passing through the village of Enchmarsh, when they came across a horse standing in the middle of the road, bearing a rider in 17th century costume. The horseman seemed oblivious to the approaching car, and the two lecturers watched in fascination as the colourless, noiseless phantoms galloped away across the fields.

EPWORTH PARSONAGE
Humberside

BUILT IN 1709, the parsonage is famous for having been the childhood home of John and Charles Wesley, and is reckoned to be the oldest Methodist shrine in the country.

But the redoubtable Mr John Wesley was himself host to a fascinating and detailed haunting that once took place here. It all started in December 1716 with strange knocks on the front door and a corn-grinding handmill seen turning by itself. Wesley's sister, Molly, was sitting alone in the library one evening, when the door opened and she heard disembodied footsteps walking around her chair, accompanied by the noise of rustling petticoats. Soon after there appeared to be a wealth of psychic phenomena breaking out all over the house. There were rappings on a table, footsteps on the stairs, loud bangs in the hall and kitchen, and the sound of an invisible cradle rocking in the nursery.

At 9:45 precisely each evening footsteps plodded from the northeast corner of the house to the library. Eventually Wesley's father, Samuel, challenged this spectral creature of habit to a confrontation. Before he could do so though, a powerful force pushed the study door back onto him, followed by a loud knocking on each wall in turn. The phenomena lasted precisely two months, which is a not uncommon length of time for an outbreak of poltergeist activity.

ETTINGTON PARK HOTEL
Stratford-upon-Avon, Warwickshire

THE ORIGINAL HOUSE was Saxon, was mentioned in the Domesday Book as Eaton Done, and it was rebuilt during the 18th and 19th centuries. The terrace beside the main entrance seems to be the focal point for the haunting. A woman in white glides along the tiled-floor passage at dusk, which always seems to be a favourite time of day with ghosts. Doors have also been known to open and close by themselves in the old servant's quarters in the Turret Rooms.

EWLOE CASTLE
Clwyd, Wales

A CUSTODIAN of the castle in recent years reported hearing ghostly singing and saw a phantom walk through a hedge. His dog, poor creature, died two days later from shock. Singing has been heard from the tower on three occasions, and always during a thunderstorm. There were no telephone wires or electric cables in the nearby vicinity to cause the sound.

EXETER CATHEDRAL
Devon

A PHANTOM NUN haunts the cloisters here, and she usually appears about 7:00 in the evening, near the south wall of the nave. She walks for a few yards before vanishing.

FARDON BRIDGE
Cheshire

FARDON BRIDGE, spanning the River Dee, links England to Wales and was built in 1345. The story goes that Prince Madoc left his two sons in the care of Roger Mortimer and the Earl of Warren when he died. The loving guardians threw the children over the bridge into the river, and the two pathetic spectres now haunt the area on stormy nights.

FARNHAM (CHURCH)
Surrey

A VISITOR kneeling in prayer in what he thought was an empty church, was rather taken aback to see a high mass taking place at the altar. The scene vanished when the rector and the churchwarden arrived. During World War II somebody reported hearing Latin chanting coming from the church at night. Small pinpoints of light have also been seen moving at the end of the nave.

Most curious of all was when a former vicar was delivering a sermon, for he saw a misty veil come down, and dim figures and strange lights moving behind it. The curate and parson have reported seeing a ghostly old lady as well.

FEATHERSTONE CASTLE
Haltwhistle, Northumberland

THIS TURRETED castle, which in parts dates back to the 12th century, plays host to a very dramatic haunting - that of a ghostly bloodstained wedding procession. The bride was Abigail Featherstonhaugh. Her father, Baron Featherstonhaugh, had refused to let her marry her lover, one of the Ridleys of Hardriding. The reason for his distaste for this arrangement varies either from the boy being his illegitimate son, or that the Ridleys were longstanding enemies of his. Whatever the reason, the Baron thought it would be a much better idea if Abigail married a distant relation of his.

Lady Abigail went tearfully through with the wedding ceremony and then set off with her guests for the traditional wedding day hunt. Unbeknown to her, the spurned lover accompanied by some chums, was hiding in a secluded area called Pinkyne Claugh, with the intention of kidnapping his sweetheart. But in the bloodbath that followed Abigail was accidentally killed, and her new husband and the jilted lover were all slain in direct combat.

The bridal phantoms returned to the castle and calmly seated themselves at the wedding feast, where they then slowly vanished. The bride's anguished father, judging by their bloodstained faces that he was in the company of the dead, sent out a search party for the bodies of his daughter and her friends. Their corpses were found where they had fallen. It is hardly surprising that after this terrible experience the Baron collapsed and completely lost his marbles. He never recovered his sanity. The ghostly party are still said to ride up to the castle gates on the anniversary of their slaughter.

FELBRIGG HALL
Norwich, Norfolk

AMONG THE former owners of this 17th century house are John Ketton, a Quaker who died in 1872, and John Wyndham (1840-1866) who was a keen railway enthusiast. The Ketton ladies were convinced that Wyndham still visited the library after his death. In 1885 the women informed the Victorian ghost-hunter Augustus Hare of their haunting. In December 1969 Felbrigg Hall was given to the National Trust, and one of the Trust's curators was checking books in the library when he saw a man sitting in one of the chairs reading. The figure slowly faded from view. When the curator informed the butler of his experience, he was calmly informed that it was probably the ghost of John Wyndham.

Far less pleasant than the benign spirit of Wyndham is the occasional, inexplicable smell of rotting flesh in a passage.

Another story is that the last squire at the hall was once drinking port in the dining-room with his brother, when his three dogs suddenly started and pointed in extreme anticipation at the door. This was followed by the movements of someone walking the length of the room. A drop in temperature was also noticed at the same time.

FERRY BOAT INN
Holywell, Cambridgeshire

THE FERRY BOAT INN lays claim to being the oldest pub in England, but this is arguable as I can think of a couple of others which also lay claim to that title. The pub has a resident ghost in the form of Juliet Tewsley, (the spelling varies), a dreamy young lady who suffered from acute, terminal romanticitus. She hanged herself after being cruelly rebuffed by a local lout who obviously didn't deserve such adoration.

The *Ferry Boat* makes a great fuss of Juliet's ghost and has even named it's restaurant after her. Her tombstone has pride of place in the bar-room floor, underneath a framed cutting from a newspaper showing Juliet appearing in the bar. The typed promo sheets distributed around the bar describe Juliet's story in pure Victorian melodramatic style.

According to yet another framed press cutting in one of the bedrooms, Juliet was evidently big business back in the 1950s. Legend decrees that Juliet manifests on 17 March, and in one ghost-vigil in 1954 local police had to be drafted in from St Ives to control the crowd.

Not surprisingly Juliet got stage-fright and refused to appear in front of such a vast and unruly audience.

Juliet's storytellers, however, claim that the pub came after her, which makes her about a 1000 years old now. That is a very long time for Juliet's gentle spirit to be seen so vividly. The last witness to see her died back in the 1960s, and since then she has stubbornly refused to appear, for cases of doors opening at will and faint strains of ghostly music are hardly impressive and extremely difficult to investigate.

The ghost is obviously a good peg for successive landlords to hang publicity on and as she is benign, so much the better. It is very hard to sell a disturbing haunting to punters. Anyway I'll close this particular haunting with the Ferry Boat's slogan "Capture the Spirit!" Oh dear.

FLAGG HALL
Tunstead Milton, Derbyshire

THERE IS NOT really much need to go into this haunting in

too much detail, simply because the particulars can be found in many other Screaming Skull Legends. Various methods for disposing of the resident skull here have had little success. Once a funeral was arranged for it, but the horses pulling the hearse bolted at Chilmorton Church, and the owners had to return it to the house.

FLEUR DE LYS
Norton St Philip, Somerset

REBELS SUPPORTING the Duke of Monmouth's uprising were put on trial in a makeshift court at the *George Inn*, across the road from here. Those sentenced to death were led to their execution in an orchard behind the *Fleur de Lys*, via a passage beside the bar. A traveller held open a gate for the prisoners, and had the sheer rotten luck to be bundled along with the convicted men by mistake. The guards hanged the innocent man in error. In 1974 William Harris became landlord of the haunted pub. He reported hearing jangling chains in the passage whilst his wife saw a shadowy figure walk along the corridor of the empty pub. An earlier landlord locked his dog in his office for an hour whilst he went out. On his return he found the animal had gone mad. The poor thing bolted out into the road and was run over.

FORDE ABBEY
Chard, Somerset

FORDE ABBEY was once a Cistercian monastery, founded in 1140, and it has been a private house since the 17th century. A ghostly monk has been seen in the cloisters and in the Great Hall.

FORMBY COAST
Merseyside

PHANTOM HOUNDS pop up all over the British Isles, and are known by different names in each area. The Lancashire/Merseyside phantom hound is called 'Old Trash' supposedly from the sound that his feet make on the beach. On Hallowe'en Night 1962 he was seen by two reporters and a photographer who had set up a vigil for him. One of those rare occurrences in the supernatural world when a ghost appears on demand! But the phantom hound left no footprints in the sand.

FOTHERINGHAY (CHURCH)
Northamptonshire

THIS 15TH CENTURY church is haunted by ghostly drums and trumpets, which some say may date back to the Battle of Agincourt. The reasoning behind this theory is that Edward, Duke of York, was killed in the battle in 1415, and is now buried here.

GARGOYLE CLUB
Soho, London

THIS PROVES once and for all that ghosts can appear practically anywhere. *The Gargoyle* is now a strip-club, but it also has the distinction of being the oldest nightclub in Europe, and was one of the 'in' places around the time of the second World War. There are fond rumours that the ghost here is none other than dear old Nell Gwynne, who worked as a barmaid in this area and lived in Dean Street. The ghost is usually seen in the early hours of the morning wearing a large hat and accompanied by the alluring scent of gardenias. She glides across the floor and disappears into the liftshaft.

A male witness who saw her said that she was old, which disproves the Nell Gwynne story, because "poor Nellie" died at the age of 37. The more substantial theory is that she is Fanny Kemble, an indomitable lady who built the Royalty Theatre, which stood next door to the Gargoyle until it was destroyed in World War II. Fanny, an actress herself, opened the theatre in 1840, and supplemented her income by teaching acting to young ladies.

The theatre had a fairly distinguished career, (Charles Dickens played here in September 1845), but unfortunately it's success was short-lived and it eventually closed down, until it reopened in 1905. Whilst the theatre still stood, Fanny's ghost could be seen sitting in the stage-box, usually at 1:00 AM, or walking down the stairs where she would vanish in the vestibule. Fanny was believed to have killed herself, and like a lot of suicides, her spirit has been restless ever since. When the Royalty Theatre was destroyed, Fanny moved into the club next door and now makes her home amongst the strippers of Soho.

GATCOMBE PARK
Gloucestershire

THE HOME of the Princess Royal is believed to be haunted by a phantom black hound, curiously nicknamed the 'Hound of Odin'.

GAWSWORTH HALL
Macclesfield, Cheshire

GAWSWORTH HALL is a rather quaint-looking 15th century Tudor manor house situated close to the medieval church. In February 1971 Monica Richards was sleeping in a bedroom directly below the Priest's Room. She complained about a curious smell of incense, which was also noticed by four people in March 1977. Whether this has anything to do with a human skeleton found next to the Priest's Room after a cupboard was removed in 1921, is not known.

Among the hall's former inhabitants was one Mary Fitton, who was lady-in-waiting to Queen Elizabeth I and also something of a good-time girl at her court. She is thought to be the 'Dark Lady' of Shakespeare's sonnets. Her ghost now walks, usually on autumn evenings, down an avenue of lime trees to the *Harrington Arms*, which was merely a farmhouse in Mary's day. She has also been seen in the vicinity of the church, where she sometimes pops out from behind the altar. A man returning home late from the Hall saw her cloaked figure crossing the road at 2:00 AM. The old rectory nearby is also haunted; smashing glass and a woman's voice has been heard, accompanied by inexplicable raps and bangs. Monica Richards saw a man with dark eyes and a pointed beard standing in an alcove at the bottom of the stairs and a student priest, who was staying as a guest, complained that he couldn't sleep at the rectory until 2 o'clock in the morning.

On a more lighter note we come to Samuel Johnson, who was the last professional jester in England. He was buried in Maggoty's Wood near the Hall. One winter's day a visitor saw a colourful figure prancing about in the woods but the figure vanished, without leaving any footprints in the snow. A servant who was employed at the Hall, was walking in the woods one bright summer's day, and remarked that in spite of the fine weather, the spot near Johnson's grave had felt icy-cold.

GEORGE AND DRAGON
Liverpool Street, Chester, Cheshire

ALTHOUGH THE PUB is relatively modern, it was built on the site of a Roman cemetery, and as such appears to be haunted by a Roman soldier on permanent sentry duty. Steady footsteps have been heard pacing around the upstairs floor of the pub and in the early hours of the morning, footsteps have even been heard passing through several brick walls.

GLAMIS CASTLE
Tayside, Scotland

THIS STRIKING castle, setting of Shakespeare's atmospheric tragedy *Macbeth*, has a bloody and fascinating history, and houses a positive legion of spooks.

Among the many mysteries of Glamis are the strange ringed stones set in the floors of some of the bedrooms, and a permanent bloodstain where Duncan was allegedly killed by Macbeth. The ghost of Lord Crawford appears in an uninhabited tower, where legend says that he gambled with the Devil. Stamping and swearing have been heard coming from here, and many guests claim to have actually seen the sinister Lord Crawford. Furniture in this part of the building has a disconcerting habit of changing to that of a different era when a ghost is present, so it is understandable that this part of the house is no longer used.

Other sinister rooms at Glamis include the Hangman's Chamber, which is reputedly haunted by a butler who hanged himself there. There is also the economically-named Haunted Chamber, which is now kept sealed, and is where the Ogilvie clan imprisoned the Lindsay clan and starved them all to death. Lord Strathmore was considerably disturbed by the unearthly noises coming from this chamber, and decided to investigate them for himself. On entering the room he collapsed. A tall, dark figure has a tendency towards entering a locked door halfway up a staircase. A figure in armour passes through a bedroom into a dressing-room and a ghostly little black boy sits on a stone seat beside the door of the Queen Mother's sitting-room.

A Grey Lady haunts the chapel. She was witnessed by Lady Glanville who sighted her kneeling in a pew and Lord Strathmore saw her several times. There is also (of course!)

155

the White Lady, and a strange apparition called Jack the Runner, who sprints across the park on moonlit nights. A more gruesome spectre is the Tongueless Woman, whose tongue was cut out to stop her revealing one of the castle's many sinister secrets.

Another of the castle's grisly inhabitants was the servant who was caught taking blood from a victim and was thus bricked-up in a secret room. Another Grey Lady haunts the Clock Tower, and has been seen there by the Queen Mother. This particular phantom is believed to be Janet Douglas, wife of the 6th Lord. She was burned alive in Edinburgh in 1527 on a charge of witchcraft, and of trying to poison King James V of Scotland.

Possibly the most fascinating legend of all about Glamis though is the 'Legend of the Deformed Earl'. Gossip was rife in Victorian upper-class society that a mis-shapen freak had been born into the Strathmore clan. As he was the first-born son he would, under normal circumstances, have inherited the Earldom. This was unthinkable to his parents, so they locked him away in one of the castle's numerous secret rooms. There is much dissention as to how long the poor creature actually lived, but the hairy freak was only seen by a handful of people during his entire lifetime.

Guests staying at the castle added extra fuel to the rumours. Many claimed to have been woken by strange snarls and grunts. One woman saw a mournful pale face with huge eyes staring at her from across the courtyard. The figure vanished, and then the lady heard screams and saw a woman charging across the courtyard with a large bundle in her arms. In 1869 a Mrs Munro woke in the night to feel what she described as a beard brushing her face. Then she saw a strange form stumble into the next room where her young son was sleeping. The boy woke screaming and told his distraught parents that he had seen a giant. A loud crash was heard by other guests in the castle that night.

In 1865 a workman accidentally stumbled into the secret lair of the freak. He was paid a substantial sum of money to emigrate to Australia. In 1877 ghost-hunter Augustus Hare overheard Lord Strathmore talking to the Bishop of Brechin about his "burden", and how he assured the Bishop that he should thank God it wasn't his! Exactly when the creature died is anybody's guess, as no record of death exists. He is believed to be in a coffin bricked-up within the thick castle walls. A rooftop lead path where the creature took his daily exercise is now known as the 'Mad Earl's Walk'.

GLEN SHIEL
Highland, Scotland

PHANTOM WARRIORS are said to re-enact the 1719 Battle of Glen Shiel between the Jacobites and Hanoverians here.

GODLEY LANE
Burnley, Lancashire

OLD TRASH, or 'Striker' as he is also known in these parts haunts this area.

GOLDEN FLEECE
London Road, Brentwood, Essex

THE GOLDEN FLEECE stands on the site of a 12th century priory. Lord Nelson was said to have stayed here, during the days when the Inn was on the London to Harwich coach route. A lady guest staying in an upstairs room once saw a ghostly monk watching her. He vanished. Pots, pans and glasses have also been known to move around the bar and the kitchen from time to time.

GOLDEN LION
Market Place, St Ives, Cambridgeshire

IN 1970 the Cambridge University Society for Psychical Research was invited by the landlord to arrange a ghost-watching vigil on his premises. This was after a man staying at the pub had reported that at 2:00 AM he had woken to find his door unbolted and all his bedclothes pulled off. To his considerable exasperation this happened three times. A member of staff once reported seeing a female ghost standing in this room, Room No.12.

The story goes that this room was used by Cromwell and his men. It is also said to be haunted by a cavalier, whom I wouldn't have thought would have been too popular in Cromwell's company! The cavalier was sighted by a chambermaid in 1970, also gliding into Room 12. Other phenomena centering on this room included two pictures falling mysteriously to the floor.

Needless to say that in spite of all this, the psychic research group experienced absolutely nothing. Just to prove that ghosts have an excessively awkward streak in them, the ghostly phenomena resumed again immediately after the investigators had left. Bells rang, doors opened,

and the bedclothes were once more pulled away from
hapless sleepers. Room 14 has also been credited with
harbouring supernatural phenomena.

GOLD HILL
Shaftesbury, Dorset

IN 979 Edward the Martyr's body was taken to Shaftesbury
Abbey for burial. He is now to be seen being carried up the
cobbled hill by two ghostly men leading phantom
packhorses.

GOODRICH CASTLE
Hereford & Worcester

DURING THE 17TH CENTURY Colonel Birch's niece Alice
eloped and took refuge here at the castle. Her loving uncle
besieged it while she attempted to escape with her love,
Charles Clifford. Unfortunately they both drowned in the
nearby River Wye. Rumour goes that their screams can be
heard from the river on stormy nights but their ghosts also
haunt the castle.

GOODWIN SANDS
Deal, Kent

THE COASTLINE here is haunted by the schooner 'Lady
Lovibond' which ran aground on 13 February 1748, sinking
and killing all on-board. Fifty years later the ship was seen
once more heading for the sands, and witnesses heard the
sound of a celebration coming from the doomed vessel.
The phantom ship was seen again by several people on 13

February 1898. With the sound belief that the boat appeared regularly every 50 years, a group of watchers set up vigil on 13 February 1948, but the weather conditions were too poor to allow any clear visibility to the disappointed watchers.

GOP CAIRN
Trelawnyd, Clwyd, Wales

THIS PREHISTORIC 40-ft cairn possibly has a Roman Centurion buried underneath it, which would account for the haunting associated with the area. A local man was walking past the cairn one moonlit night when he saw Roman soldiers in the field, being led by a centurion on a white horse. The intriguing scene was lost to view when the moon clouded over, and when it was clear again the ghostly soldiers had disappeared.

GRACE DIEU PRIORY
Thringstone, Leicestershire

A LADY IN WHITE is said to haunt the A512 road, close to the ruins of the priory. In 1961 she was seen by the village policeman who was walking in the fields but the phantom vanished into a hawthorn hedge. The policeman's dog growled and he also noticed a sharp drop in temperature.

GRAND THEATRE
Lancaster, Lancashire

THE GREAT tragic actress Sarah Siddons is one of the elite group of ghosts, like Dick Turpin and Anne Boleyn, who seems to get around a fair bit in the 'After Life'. One of her favoured sites includes this theatre. She has been sighted by a watchman, and the late actress Patricia Phoenix once saw her cross into an aisle and vanish.

GRAVEL WALK
Victoria Park, Bath, Avon

IN 1976 a schoolboy walking along Gravel Walk, a route designated as one of the walks listed in Bath's Ghost Tour, saw a tall man with white hair. No-one else at the time saw the phantom, but several sightings of him had been reported during the 1970s.

GRAYINGHAM
Blyborough, Lincolnshire

THE ROAD leading into Grayingham is haunted by a phantom black dog who has a tendency to lurk near the pond. One woman who saw it hit it with her umbrella, which went straight through the spectral animal.

THE GRENADIER
Wilton Row, Nr Marble Arch, London

RATED AS the most famous haunted pub in the world, no less, it is haunted by a ghostly soldier, which is not really surprising as it was once an officer's mess. The lane outside is called Old Barracks Road, and the main bar was once the officer's dining-room. The story goes that one September day a soldier was caught cheating at cards and as a result he was brutally flogged for his misdeed, and died in the cellar.

As a consequence the hauntings here are rumoured to reach a peak of fevered activity in the month of September, something that has become increasingly hard to substantiate. A young boy lying in bed upstairs saw a mysterious shadowy figure on the landing. A lady customer saw a man go upstairs and vanish when he reached the top. A guest sleeping in the pub felt someone trying to touch him at the bottom of his bed.

Other strange occurrences include knocks, raps, lights switching themselves on and off, and eerie shadows sighted on the landing and stairs. The pub dog once entered the cellar and started to scratch vigorously at the floor for no visible reason. A brewery inspector (who was also a former CID officer) saw a mysterious wisp of smoke and felt something burn his wrist like an invisible cigarette.

GRETA HALL
Keswick, Cumbria

THE HALL was built in 1800 by William Jackson, initially as a peaceful abode in which to live out his retirement.

Jackson rented a portion of it to the poet Samuel Coleridge, who moved in with his wife in 1803; Coleridge in turn invited his brother-in-law Robert Southey and his spouse Edith to live with them. The following year Coleridge fled the happy little nest. This part of the building was later to become a section of Keswick Junior Girls' School. During the 1914-1918 war, a maid at the school, Sarah Bowe, was sleeping at the top of the house. It was holiday-time and therefore very quiet. She reported that she had fallen asleep in her room with the gas lamp on. She said that she was woken by the sound of pages being turned in a book, and she saw a man with his back to her reading by the light of the gas lamp. Not long after a

French teacher at the school was enjoying a soak in the bathroom when she was horrified to see a man, standing with his back to her, staring out of the window. Many reckon that the quiet phantom bears a resemblance to Coleridge's brother-in-law, Robert Southey.

GUNBY HALL
Burgh-le-Marsh, Lincolnshire

THE DAUGHTER of Sir William Massingberd, who built the house in 1700, fell in love with a servant. This romantic liaison was to prove unlucky for the young man; he was mysteriously killed and his body dumped in the pond. His ghost now walks along the path beside the pond.

Another equally unpleasant tale is that *both* young lovers were killed, which might account for the ghostly couple being seen moving along the path. An eerie coldness has been experienced by witnesses as they watch the lovers fade away.

HADSTOCK (CHURCH)
Essex

THE GHOST of a pleasant old gentleman has been sighted here several times during the last 50 years.

HALL-I-TH WOOD
Bolton, Lancashire

THIS 15TH CENTURY manor house is now a museum. A ghost carrying a sack over his shoulder has been sighted here, usually disappearing into a wall. A phantom man in black has been seen upstairs, and an old lady loiters around the kitchen.

HAM HOUSE
Richmond, Surrey

HAM HOUSE was primarily built for King James I's eldest son, who died in 1612. The house is not haunted by him though, but by the Duchess of Lauderdale, who was rumoured to have been the mistress of Cromwell. In 1672 she married John Maitland, who was a favourite of King Charles II. From her portraits she looks as though butter wouldn't have melted in her mouth, but the Duchess had some highly dubious pastimes, one of which included a delight in putting innocent people on that infamous instrument of torture, the rack. After her death her room was left untouched, and mysterious tappings heard around the house since have been attributed to her walking-stick. These noises have frequently been heard at night. In more recent times a butler employed at the house had his six-year-old daughter to stay with him. The child had a terrifying experience which would probably have left less hardy little souls mentally maimed for life. The little girl woke at dawn to find an old woman clawing at the fireplace in her room. The child jerked upright in bed in surprise, causing the old lady to turn and face her. The woman grasped the bedrail and stared intently at the child, who screamed back at her. Servants immediately ran to her aid.

Papers were later found hidden behind the fireplace which implied in no uncertain terms that the Duchess of Lauderdale had murdered her first husband, and doubtless it was these that the old crow was searching for. A more pleasant spectre is a phantom spaniel, who has often been seen on the terrace in broad daylight. It usually runs along the west passages and then vanishes into a wall. A lady visitor said that it had growled at her before disappearing.

A mystery woman in white has been seen looking out of a terrace window. Other aspects of the Ham House haunting include banging and whispering from locked empty rooms, and a ghostly cavalier who walks the towpath nearby. This ghost was seen by a woman on a July afternoon, and also by that most amazing of ghost-hunters, Elliot O'Donnell, who had a considerable wealth of supernatural experiences to his credit. In 1978 a lady visitor watched as the cavalier slowly vanished. In 1980 two residents from the nearby town of Kingston-upon-Thames met the ghost on the towpath. He disappeared.

HAMMERSMITH (CHURCHYARD)
London

THE HAMMERSMITH AREA was cursed in 1804 by a phantom that cost two people their lives, as well as scaring others out of their wits. It first appeared to a woman as she was crossing the churchyard, seizing her arms as she tried to run away from it. The poor woman fainted and died at home a few days later. After 16 people travelling in a cart were pursued by the phantom, a vigilante group was set up to watch for the ghost. On the fourth night Francis Smith spotted what he thought was the ghost coming down a lane. Smith fired at the figure, and it fell to the ground instantly.

To Smith's dismay the victim was not the phantom, but a bricklayer called Thomas Millward, who was setting off for work early in the morning wearing his white overalls. The courts were surprisingly lenient on Smith (for that era where a child could be hung for scrumping apples) and he spent a year in prison.

HAMPTON COURT PALACE
Kingston-upon-Thames, London

THERE ARE approximately a dozen ghosts connected with Cardinal Wolsey's old house. The palace was home to five of King Henry VIII's six wives, namely Anne Boleyn, Jane Seymour, Anne of Cleves, Catherine Howard and Catherine Parr, so it is not surprising that the spirit of the King himself is said to roam here as well. But the more substantial ghost is his fifth wife, the young and vivacious Catherine Howard.

Residents at the palace have often heard Catherine's plaintive screams as she runs along the Gallery. In 1541 Catherine was accused of adultery, which as she was Queen was classed as high treason, and thus the charge carried the death penalty. On 4 November 1541 she ran through the palace, desperately searching for her ageing husband so that she could beg him to spare her life. Catherine never reached the monarch because she was seized by the guards and dragged away.

Catherine was beheaded at the Tower of London on 13 February 1542. Her screams have been heard echoing along the Gallery ever since. At the end of the 19th century the Gallery was kept mainly locked, as it was then used for storing pictures in, yet residents at the palace still complained of the unearthly screams from the Gallery, which seemed especially prolific during late autumn. When the Gallery was opened to the public an artist was sketching there when he saw a be-ringed hand touch his pad. He later discovered, after looking at a portrait, that the ring was very similar to one Catherine had owned. The numerous witnesses who have all heard and seen her over the years all agree that she has long, flowing hair. One resident saw her on such a regular basis that she took Catherine's agonised wails as part of daily life at the palace. Wife No. three, Jane Seymour, has been seen in the Clock Court. She is usually sighted at night on the staircase wearing white and carrying a candle.

Jane is more commonly seen on the anniversary of her son's (King Edward VI) birth on 12 October. She died a week after giving birth to him. Many servants at the palace have quit after seeing gentle Jane's ghost. Another spectral wife of King Hal is Anne Boleyn, who seems to spread herself around a lot in the 'After Life'. She has been seen, dressed in blue, gliding along the passages. Servants at the palace at the end of the 19th century reported that she looked sad, which is hardly surprising considering her unenviable fate.

Another Tudor ghost is Mistress Sybil Penn, who was foster-mother to King Edward VI, and was much loved by him. Sybil died of smallpox and has been seen by a number of people since, including Queen Elizabeth I. In 1829 Sybil's grave was desecrated when St Mary's Church, where she was buried, was pulled down, which can hardly have soothed her restless spirit. The Ponsonby family heard her voice and the workings of her spinning-wheel in their room. The Board of Works later found a sealed room containing a spinning-wheel. Her ghost is usually wearing a grey dress with a hood. She has been seen by two sentries, one of whom deserted his post on seeing her. Rooms where her presence has been felt are noted to be bathed in an eerie light. She was sighted by Princess Frederica of Hanover, who recognised her from her stone effigy and The Grey Lady, as she is known, was also seen by a resident called Lady Maude, entering a room. Lady Maude mistook her for a housekeeper until the phantom walked through a closed door.

Other ghosts at the haunted palace include a White Lady seen by a party of anglers one Midsummer's Eve, and two cavaliers in the Fountain Court, although the soldiers have not been seen since their remains were discovered by workmen in the courtyard. They were later buried elsewhere and now seem to be resting in peace. In February 1907 a policeman filed a report in which he stated that he had seen a party of men and women on Ditton Walk. He noticed them walking towards Flower Pot Gate where they then vanished. The report is still preserved in the station log.

Actor Leslie Finch saw a grey figure in Tudor costume,

and when he moved to let her pass he felt a cold chill. Lady Grant who was with him at the time saw nothing, but she did note the drop in temperature. In 1966 a visitor swore to seeing Cardinal Wolsey walking through the gates and a ghost in clerical robes has also been sighted in the cloisters, whilst two of Anne Boleyn's alleged lovers walk the narrow passageways. Another old Grey Lady (there seems to be a surplus of them at the palace) haunts the Birdwood apartments, and a distraught woman runs out of the main entrance; perhaps the lack of spectral privacy is getting her down!

HANDSWORTH (CHURCH)
Sheffield, West Yorkshire

THIS 12TH CENTURY church is haunted by a Grey Lady, who has usually been sighted by the font. "Strange presences" have also been felt here.

HANHAM ABBOTS (CHURCH)
Avon

A MAN cycling past the church and Hanham Court at midnight claimed that he felt a "cold, clammy atmosphere". He then saw a Woman in White, who surprised him so much that he fell off his bicycle. When he had recovered the ghostly figure had vanished. A phantom nun has also been seen in the area.

HARDWICK HALL
Chesterfield, Derbyshire

HARDWICK HALL was built in the 16th century (1591-1597) by the then Countess of Shrewsbury, the legendary Bess of Hardwick. In 1976 Mark Gresswell and Carol Rawlings reported seeing a ghostly monk in Hardwick Park. The figure had walked into the lights of the car and disappeared. The couple noticed that he had no hands or feet, but a luminous white face. The landlady of the *Hardwick Inn* (which was once the lodge to the Hall) said that the ghostly monk had been seen twice previously that week. The monk was also sighted by two policemen. In 1983 Fraser Martin, co-founder of Chesterfield Psychic Study Group, watched as a shadowy figure crossed the Blue Room and disappeared through a window.

Several years earlier in 1934 two girls were playing in the ruins when they both saw a man floating in mid-air. They noticed that he was carrying a tray of tankards.

HARVEY'S WINE BAR
Kidderminster, Hereford & Worcester

IN 1963 the landlord reported hearing mysterious footsteps in his otherwise empty building. Other inexplicable noises included banging and the sound of doors opening and closing. A customer who was sitting alone in a room at the back saw an interior door open and close, followed by the street door doing exactly the same. A barmaid, clearing up after a lunchtime session, heard strange footsteps. She then saw the figure of a tall, young woman wearing a brown Tudor-style dress walking towards her across the bar. The lady smiled and walked past through a side door. Another barmaid saw the same ghost a few weeks later.

News of the haunting reached the *Kidderminster Times*, who decided to look into the history of the building. They found that *Harvey's Wine Bar* was built on the site of the *Clarence Inn*. In 1851 the stable floor, which was in the process of being repaired, gave way, revealing a vault filled with human and animal remains. Also among the grisly contents of the vault was a black bottle, a glass, a pickaxe and tobacco pipes. Local historians believe it was once the crypt of the chapel of the nearby manor-house.

HARVINGTON HALL
Kidderminster, Hereford & Worcester

THE GHOST of a local witch is said to haunt the grounds of this moated Elizabethan house, the neighbouring fields and highways. The witch was Mistress Hicks, who was hanged in 1710 for allegedly causing women and children in the area to vomit pins and needles. She was also credited with the power to raise storms. As was the custom of the time she was probably buried at the cross-roads of the present A448 and A450. A cross-roads burial (usually with a stake through the heart) was the customary end of suicides and executed people, because of the belief that it had the power to stop the spirit walking after death. In Mistress Hicks's case it doesn't seem to have worked. Her ghost is more frequently seen near her supposed grave.

HASTINGS CASTLE
East Sussex

HASTINGS CASTLE stopped being a fortress in the 12th century and was then used as a religious house, which would account for the frequent reports of ghostly organ music heard in the area. The ghost of Sir Thomas á Becket can be seen on autumn evenings. There are also stories of the sounds of rattling chains, and the groans of starving prisoners. A mirage of the castle is also said to be seen out at sea on sunny, misty mornings, when once again pennants can be seen flying from turrets of the castle. More recent phenomena at the castle includes a ghostly woman, possibly a nun, dressed in brown who seems to be digging near the entrance to a dungeon. This sounds a rather bizarre occupation for a spectral nun, but doubtless there is some suitably grisly story behind it to help explain things.

HATHERTON HALL
Cannock, Staffordshire

THE ISOLATED POSITION of the house makes it a marvellous setting for a spooky story, and it does oblige in that respect. One Christmas Eve, late in the 19th century, Lord Hatherton was entertaining some local gentlemen to drinks in his study. To make the festivities even more complete he insisted on showing them a human skull, which he said was all that remained of an ancestor of his. He seemed proud to be able to say that he now used the skull as a drinking vessel!

The skull had been separated from the rest of the body when the old chapel was dug up, and all the guests took turns to drink from Sir Hugh de Hatherton's skull. The present lord, who was probably well in his cups by this time, then rashly demanded the presence of Sir Hugh himself and at the stroke of midnight the drinking buddies were startled to hear footsteps in the hall. The skull rolled across the desk, the door flung open, and a headless apparition dressed in armour appeared in the doorway. The figure then abruptly bowed and left. Not surprisingly after that little episode all the men spent a sleepless night and the next day Lord Hatherton discovered that the skull had vanished. It hasn't been seen since.

HAWORTH MOOR
West Yorkshire

As PROBABLY ANYONE who has ever read Victorian literature knows, the talented Bronte sisters resided in Haworth Parsonage, and are buried in the churchyard here. Emily drew her inspiration for *Wuthering Heights* from the moors which she deeply loved, so it is not surprising that her ghost now haunts Top Withens and the path leading to the Bronte waterfall.

HAYMARKET THEATRE
London

THE HAYMARKET was built in 1720, and in 1853 the manager, John Baldwin Buckstone, lived in the building at the back, which is now used as dressing-rooms and offices for the theatre. Frequently his ghost was seen and his voice heard rehearsing lines in the dressing-rooms during the period from 1900 to the Great War. Dressing-room and wardrobe doors would open mysteriously and footsteps were heard in backstage corridors. A theatre fireman followed Buckstone's ghost around a corridor and watched him vanish, and with a cleaner on a separate occasion, saw him crossing the dress circle. Another cleaner watched as the ghost walked through a locked door. A manager and a clerk were sitting in the office at 1:00 AM when they saw the door open and shut but they both knew there was no one else in the theatre at the time.

An actor saw Buckstone sitting in an armchair in his dressing-room and in 1927 an actress who was talking to someone backstage, saw him walk between them. In 1946 the manager, Stuart Wilson, was working in the accounts office when all the lights went out and he noticed a drop in temperature.

The ghost made his most spectacular appearance when he appeared during a performance behind an actor's wheelchair. The stage manager watched as he vanished.

HEATHROW AIRPORT
London

HEATHROW AIRPORT boasts three ghosts, including a rather strange individual who pants. The airline girls have frequently felt him breathe on their necks and four people in the staff car-park have had the same experience. The second ghost is a man in a grey suit. He was sighted by a diplomat, who was so shaken by the experience that he fled from one of the VIP lounges. The ghostly gentleman usually appears in Terminal 1. The ghost has also been seen by a supervisor and an airport policewoman. On 2 March 1948 a DC3 burst into flames on a runway killing all on board. A bowler-hatted man, (who also happens to be the third ghost), kept pestering the rescue-workers to find his briefcase.

In 1970 this spook popped up again when a police patrol-car was instructed to go out on a runway to pick up a bowler-hatted gentleman who was getting in the way. The ghost wasn't there, but there were several more sightings of him all afternoon. Although the invisible figure registered as a human being on the radar screen in the airport control tower, a team of squad cars succeeded in running over him!

HERMITAGE CASTLE
Liddlesdale, Borders, Scotland

HERMITAGE CASTLE, which appears to be partly sunk into the ground, has a fascinating history of black magic associations. An early owner called Lord de Soulis had a bit of a reputation for being the Gilles de Rais of Scotland. He was said to murder little children and use their blood in his black magic activities and to be ably assisted in these unorthodox practices, by a creature with fangs called 'Redcap'. When Lord de Soulis's practices were discovered he was taken to Nine Stane Rig stone circle, rolled in a sheet of lead and tipped into a cauldron. He now haunts the castle. Another spectral inhabitant is the Lady in White, whom many wistfully believe is Mary, Queen of Scots. Her association with the castle is that she nearly died of a fever there, after riding 50 miles in a day to comfort her wounded lover, the Earl of Bothwell, who lay within the walls of the castle.

HERSTMONCEUX CASTLE
Hailsham, East Sussex

THIS BEAUTIFUL fairy-tale castle was built in 1440 by Sir Roger de Fiennes, and up until recent times housed the Royal Greenwich Observatory. Not unnaturally it has several ghosts.

First is a White Lady who swims in the moat. Her story is that several centuries ago she was enticed into the castle by Sir Roger, who harboured dastardly intentions where she was concerned. The girl, who lived locally, tried to escape from his lecherous clutches by swimming the moat. Sir Roger caught her, had his wicked way and then (as all good melodramas should have it) brutally killed her. At the turn of this century the castle was owned by a Colonel Lowther. One night he met a strange girl in the courtyard, who appeared to be in some considerable emotional distress, but when he approached her she vanished.

In 1708 the castle was bought by the Naylor family, and the daughter, Grace, haunts it as well. For some obscure reason she starved to death in the East Wing. Sounds of her sobbing have been heard and her ghost has a habit of flitting around the corridors. At the end of the 18th century another member of the Naylor family, Georgina, dabbled in the occult. She liked to don a white cloak and stalk around accompanied by her favourite pet, a white doe. The doe was torn to pieces by some hounds and the heartbroken Georgina left the castle soon after to live in Switzerland. She died in Lausanne in 1806. Her ghost now sits aside a white ass, and rides in and out of the rooms. Another story of the castle is that in the late 15th century Lord Dacre, the owner, found Lord Pelham's keepers poaching on his land. In the fracas that followed Lord Dacre stabbed one of the keepers. The ghostly keeper now haunts the field, whilst Lord Dacre himself haunts the castle grounds. If anyone dares to approach him he rides his horse into the moat.

The Drummer's Hall is said to be haunted by a giant drummer. He has been seen, with his drum, striding along the battlements above the great hall. One of the stories behind him is that a supposedly dead member of the Dacre family lived in secret at the castle with his wife. Whenever he was annoyed by the suitors who came to the castle to console his 'widow' he would pose as the ghostly drummer to scare them away.

HESKIN HALL
Eccleston, Lancashire

HESKIN HALL was a Catholic household during the Civil War. The resident priest, when confronted by Cromwell's men, tried to prove to them that he had no allegiance to the Catholic Royalist family he was living with, by hanging the youngest daughter of the house. The site of this cowardly murder is now the top of the fire escape, and the girl's pitiful ghost haunts the Scarlet Bedroom. Her appearance is usually marked by a drop in temperature. She is sometimes seen being chased by the priest across the room. The girl has also been seen in the kitchen, where one visitor mistook her for a real person.

HETHFELTON HOUSE
Wool, Dorset

AT MIDNIGHT a phantom coach and horses drives down the lane here towards the River Frome.

HICKLING BROAD
Hickling, Norfolk

THE GHOSTLY SKATER that exercises here was said to be a drummer in the Napoleonic Wars, who drowned as he was crossing the water to meet his lover.

A couple holidaying on the Broads saw a Woman in White punting towards them but she ignored their shouts of warning and they learned later that they had seen a ghost. The White Lady usually punts across from one mill to another.

HICKLING PRIORY
Hickling, Norfolk

THE PRIORY ruins are haunted by a ghostly monk, but I'm afraid that this also seems to be yet another Underground Tunnel Legend.

HIGHER CHILTERN FARM
Chilton Cantelo, Somerset

A FORMER OWNER, who went by the wonderful name of Theophilus Brome, died here in 1670. Like a lot of people in the past who seem to have had a strange fixation about their own heads, he decreed that his should be preserved at the farm, and thus (yes, no prizes for guessing this one) another Screaming Skull Legend was born!

Various attempts to bury Brome's skull have usually resulted in horrid screams resounding throughout the house. During the 1860s a sexton began to dig a hole to bury the skull. He gave up after his spade broke into two pieces. The skull is now respectfully preserved in a cabinet over the door in the hallway of the farmhouse.

HIGHGATE CEMETERY
London

THE 1990 EDITION of 'Historic Houses, Castles and Gardens Guide' describes the cemetery as "a place of tranquillity", which no doubt it is now, but in the past, weird vampire legends grew up about it. Unfortunately the whole case seems to be clouded in mystery, although I understand that the vampire tales are no longer relevant.

HIGHWORTH (CHURCH)
Wiltshire

THE RESIDENT ghost here has been seen many times over the years, but it is arguable as to whether it is the same one each time. In 1907 a Master of Balliol and three companions saw a man whose face appeared to be featureless, with sunken dark shadows instead of eyes. They saw the sinister form near the organ, but a woman standing by the font hadn't seen anything at all. In 1936 the verger saw a figure in a long white robe gliding up the centre aisle.

HINCKLEY (CHURCH)
Leicestershire

IN 1727 Richard Smith upset his recruiting sergeant, who retaliated by running him through with a pike. Smith is now buried in the churchyard here. On 12 April, the anniversary of his murder, his tombstone is said to sweat blood. Mysterious footsteps have also been heard, pacing up and down the aisle inside the church.

HOLY ISLAND
Northumberland

LINDISFARNE CASTLE was built here in 1550 and was converted into a home in 1903 by Sir Edwin Lutyens. The history of Holy Island itself goes back to 635 AD when St Aidan arrived here. In 664 AD St Cuthbert arrived as well, and his ghost is said to haunt the rocks rather delightfully known as 'St Cuthbert's Beads'. Legend goes that in 793 AD whirlwinds blew up and dragons were seen in the sky. All this had a strange effect on the men, who destroyed the church. This legend is explained later. In 1644 the Royalist garrison here were driven out by Parliamentarians, and the ghost of a Cromwellian soldier has been seen since at the castle. A choirboy told Rev A W Jackson that he very often saw a monk sitting reading a parchment, who would then vanish into a wall. In 1968 a story was published called 'Celtic Church Speaks Today?', published by the World Fellowship Press, in which the choirboy claimed to receive communications from Bishop Cuthbert himself.

Irish ghost-hunter Elliott O'Donnell wrote about the haunting of Holy Island in which he said that the ghost of Bishop Cuthbert sits on the rocks. Ghostly hammering in the area has also been accredited to this phantom, who has since been recorded for posterity in a poem by Sir Walter Scott. Holy Island is also frequented by a large phantom white hound, and phantom monks have been seen moving along the causeway.

Regarding the legend these monks were on Holy Island in 793 AD when the invading Danes destroyed the monastery here, but I doubt they needed whirlwinds or dragons for guidance! The monks were killed, and one of them now watches the sands, as if on permanent lookout for any more dastardly Danes. In 1962 two holiday visitors watched as he faded into the sands. The ghost of Cuthbert has also been sighted amongst the ruins of the Norman Priory. Alfred the Great was said to have seen Cuthbert's ghost, and had been assured by him that he would one day be king, a tale that seems straight out of Arthurian legend. Cuthbert's body was kept in a coffin by the altar in Lindisfarne Castle for a while, and was said to be still incorrupt when it was opened 11 years after his death. He is now kept in Durham Cathedral.

HOLY TRINITY CHURCH
Micklegate, York, North Yorkshire

HOLY TRINITY CHURCH is haunted by a former abbess, a woman and a child. At the Dissolution the Abbess stoutly refused admittance to soldiers sent by King Henry VIII. The soldiers killed her but before she died she vowed that she would return to haunt the site. She has often been seen on Trinity Sunday. One August Sunday in the late 19th century a worshipper saw two women and a child cross to the East Window and noticed that one of the women seemed to be trying to soothe the child. One of the women is thought to be the Abbess, whilst the other two figures are of victims of the plague buried near the organ window.

In 1876 another worshipper saw the shape of a woman gliding past the windows. The figure returned with the child, and then made a third trip on her own.

HORNING
Norfolk

IN 410 AD the Romans finally withdrew from East Anglia, and Ella was crowned as the region's new king. Every five years on 21 July his coronation is re-enacted by the River Bure, by groups of ghosts.

HORSEY MERE
Norfolk

HORSEY MERE is haunted by the ghostly voices of children buried here. This ritual water burial was the common internment for children when the Romans dominated the area. On 13 June every year, Children's Night, the spectral infants are said to return to life for a brief hour.

On 13 June 1930 Charles Sampson and friend were fishing on the Mere when they were rather startled to find the water draining away. They were even more amazed when naked children suddenly started appearing on the scene, dancing and clapping. The Mere's ghostly legend was written down for posterity in 1709, when archaelogical transactions referred to the Children's Mere, and the strange happenings that could occur there.

HORTON COURT
Chipping Sodbury, Avon

HORTON COURT is a Cotswold manor house which dates back to Norman times. Anything on the supernatural front has been rather quiet of late, but around 1937 the cook's little boy innocently asked who the little old lady was who tucked him up at night. The boy's bedroom was next to the Norman Hall.

HOUGHTON TOWER
Preston, Lancashire

THE PENDLE AREA around here was referred to by the gypsies as "witch country", and Pendle Hill was a favourite meeting-place of the Lancashire witches, many of whom were brutally executed in the witch trials of the 17th century. Houghton Tower has its own mystery, in the guise of a ghostly lady who wears green velvet.

Her hearty, loud laughter and the rustle of her silk skirts has been heard. Animals, always good barometers when it comes to indicating a paranormal presence, have often reacted dramatically when she is in the locality. The story behind her is that she was Ann, a Protestant lady who tried to commit the heinous sin of eloping with her Catholic lover. The couple were shot dead as they tried to run away, but Ann's presence has been felt ever since. She has often been seen in the Minstrel's Gallery. A former owner was once sitting in the Ladies Withdrawing Room when he heard laughter, the rustling of skirts, and felt someone looking over his shoulder.

HOUSE OF THE BINNS
Linlithgow, Lothian, Scotland

HOUSE OF THE BINNS is the historical home of the Dalyell clan. A ghostly old man in a brown habit has been seen gathering sticks on the hillside, but less harmless is the water spirit who is said to lure people to their deaths in the pond below the hills. There are also the primitive spirits of the Ancient Picts in the area, and General Tam Dalyell (who founded the Royal Scots Greys in 1681) gallops on his horse over the ruined bridge near Binns Tower and up to the house. In his lifetime he was rumoured to have played cards with the Devil (this story also crops about Lord Crawford in Glamis Castle).

The Devil, never a good sport at the best of times, lost a game and retaliated by throwing a table into the pond. During the summer of 1978 the pond dried up, and a card table was revealed to be stuck in the mud. In another gambling session Old Nick petulantly threatened to blow the house up, but the General retaliated by saying he would build extra thick walls and a turret at each corner to support the walls. The turrets are still to be seen.

HUGHENDEN MANOR
High Wycombe, Buckinghamshire

BENJAMIN DISRAELI (Earl of Beaconsfield) purchased this late-Georgian house in 1848, and his ghost now roams it. He has been seen near the staircase and in his old study. He was once seen by a Ghost Club member Mrs M M Wynn-Williams and another member of the ghosthunting party, John Watson, sighted him going down the staircase. The ex-Prime Minister, who died in 1881, has also been seen at the bottom of the stairs to the cellar.

HUNTER'S TOR
Lustleigh Cleave, Devon

IN 1956 two women out riding here, came across a dozen men on horseback, accompanied by some more on foot and a pack of greyhounds. The men were all in medieval costume. The ladies followed the ghostly party until they were hidden by a stone wall. When the women rode past the wall a few seconds later, the entire medieval party had disappeared. The women were also unable to find any hoofprints in the soft ground, to account for the strange riders.

ICKNIELD WAY
Oxfordshire

THIS ANCIENT roadway may not be an important thoroughfare for us lesser mortals any more, but if rumours and folklore are true, then it is practically congested with spooks of all shapes and sizes. Among those haunting the Icknield Way are Roman Legionaires, phantom black hounds, various spectral coaches and Queen Boadicea's army, who tore along it on their way to St Albans, which they sacked and reduced to a mere shadow of its former self in 61 AD.

Ancient folklore also claimed that the Icknield Way is no less than the road to Hell!

IGHTHAM MOTE
Ivy Hatch, Nr Sevenoaks, Kent

THIS 14TH CENTURY moated manor house was the home of the Catholic Selby family from 1591-1889. In 1605 Dorothy Selby sent a note to Lord Moneagle warning him of the impending Gunpowder Plot. Friends of the conspirators walled her up in the tower as a punishment for grassing on them, and her restless ghost has walked here ever since.

A few years earlier in 1552 the priest to the family of Sir Thomas Browne killed a serving-maid and bricked her up in the tower.

In 1872 some workmen found a sealed door which led to the discovery of a female skeleton, whether she is Dorothy or the serving-maid is uncertain. In spite of an attempted exorcism held at the house, a peculiar chill is still said to linger around the area where the skeleton was found.

INVERARY CASTLE
Strathclyde, Scotland

THE CASTLE here, like so many Celtic homes, seems to have its own 'Messenger of Death' legend. The castle is also famous for containing Rob Roy's dirk-handle and his sporran. The ruins of Rob Roy's house are five miles away at the Falls of Aray. According to legend, prior to the death of a member of the household, a galley containing three standing figures can be seen sailing up Loch Fyne. The boat carries the coat of arms of the Dukes of Argyll. Ravens are also said to fly over at such times. On 10 July 1758 Sir William Hart and three companions were in the grounds of the castle, when they looked up to see a Highland battle taking place above them in the sky. The scene slowly dissolved. The montage was also seen by two Campbell ladies on the road to Kilmalieu. It was later discovered that the Master of Inverawe House had been killed in a battle that day at Ticonderoga. Inside the castle the area near the Green Library is said to be haunted by an inexplicable crashing sound. A former Duke of Argyll once heard this noise for over an hour, which must have been pretty tiresome for him. It is usually only members of the family who are "privileged" to hear this sound, which has been repeated on a regular basis for nearly a 100 years.

There is also, to my mind, the equally irritating sound of a harp twanging away in the area of the Blue Room, even though there is no harp in the castle. The ghostly harpist is said to be a little man who was hanged when Montrose's men were looking for the First Marquess of Argyll. Many people were hanged at the gallows on Foreland Point. The harpist himself is sometimes seen as well as heard, a 'dashing wee fella' dressed in the Campbell tartan. He has been seen by successive Duchesses of Argyll and various lady visitors.

ISLE OF IONA
Strathclyde, Scotland

ST COLUMBA landed on this island some 1400 years ago, whilst on his grand tour of bringing Christianity to the Scots, as well as confronting the Loch Ness Monster! The island is now haunted by ghostly monks. Viking longboats are also said to re-enact past raids here, and ghostly music and bells have been heard.

ISLE OF MULL
Strathclyde, Scotland

MULL has it's own personal Messenger of Death. During the 16th century Chieftain Ewan, riding around the island on the eve of a battle, came across an old woman washing bloodstained shirts in a stream. The Chieftain instantly recognised her as the local harbinger of doom, and purposefully rode into battle the next day, fully anticipating his own demise. He was not to be disappointed. He was decapitated with an axe during the course of the battle. He has now replaced the old woman as the island's messenger of death.

ISLE OF PORTLAND
Dorset

DORSET is another area of Britain that has a shaggy dog story to tell. The phantom hound on the Isle of Portland has a scruffy coat, saucer-sized red eyes, and stands as tall as a man. He is known locally as the 'Tow Dog'. Although he bars the way of people, he does not attack them. Decent of him.

J

JACK AND JILL INN
Leamington Spa, Warwickshire

IN JUNE 1971 the ghost of a former landlord, Graham Boulton, was seen by the then present landlord on the patio roof, which had been the old boy's favourite spot for sitting and enjoying warm summer evenings. A few weeks later a barmaid saw a shadowy figure moving among the beer barrels. The barrels could be seen clearly through the apparition.

JENNY HURN BEND
River Trent, Wildsworth, Humberside

ACCORDING TO LEGEND this stretch of the River Trent seems to be infested with strange creatures. Jenny Hurn Bend is haunted by a small man with a seal's face and long hair, who crosses the bend in a pie-shaped boat. Another inhabitant of the area is a creature with walrus tusks that crawls out of the river to graze in the fields. Many people, including experienced boatmen, tend to avoid the bewitched spot .

KEMSING (CHURCH)
Kent

EVERY YEAR at the end of December, a ghostly knight visits Kemsing Church and kneels in prayer. He is reckoned to be one of the assassins who murdered Thomas á Becket in Canterbury Cathedral.

KENSINGTON PALACE
London

KENSINGTON PALACE is like a sort of granny-flat (or "aunterie" as Prince Charles is rumoured to call it) to Buckingham Palace. It has three ghosts. One is a man in breeches who strolls round the courtyard, another is a lady called Sophia, aunt of Queen Victoria, who sits at a spinning-wheel (a favourite occupation with ghostly ladies it would seem), and King George III who stares at a weather-vane. He died here, after suffering from the mental disease porphyra, on 25 October 1760.

KENSWORTH (CHURCH)
Bedfordshire

THE PATH over Bury Hill to the church is said to be haunted by a witch and a headless milkmaid.

KILLINEVER CHAPEL
Loch Awe, Strathclyde, Scotland

THE CHAPEL boasts of having the handprint of a ghost on the lintel. The story behind its appearance is that a sceptical tailor spent a night in the church to dispel the rumours that had sprung up about a haunting. To prove that he was not intimidated by any restless spirit, he spent his time knitting stockings, and refused to look at the phantom when it did appear. Eventually the tailor couldn't take the pressure anymore and rushed from the chapel with the ghost in hot pursuit. The phantom hit the lintel with his hand as he made an unsuccessful grab at the tailor.

KILWORTHY HOUSE
Tavistock, Devon

ELIZABETH, daughter of Judge John Glanville, was forced into marriage with a Plymouth goldsmith. To show her displeasure at this arrangement, she conspired with her maid and her sailor lover, to have the goldsmith "disposed of". It followed that the Judge had the unenviable task of sentencing his own daughter to death, and the three conspirators all went to the gallows. The Judge was so emotionally wrecked by this experience that his sad ghost has roamed the house ever since.

KIMBOLTON CASTLE
Kimbolton, Cambridgeshire

QUEEN CATHERINE OF ARAGON, one of King Henry VIII's wives that we don't hear an awful lot about in connection with the supernatural, died here in 1536. Her ghost now haunts the gallery.

KING JOHN'S HUNTING LODGE
Axbridge, Somerset

THIS TUDOR merchant's house was restored to much of its former glory in 1971, and is now used as a museum of local history and archaeology. An Elizabethan lady and a tabby cat are said to haunt a panelled room on the first floor. On 22 August 1978 the presence of the Elizabethan lady was recorded in the museum diary, when two people reported seeing a lady in white sitting in the mayoral chair. A medium verified the haunting of the White Lady and claimed, as mediums are wont to do, that the room had a history of violence.

Frances Neele, the vice-chairperson of the museum, was very sceptical about the medium's allegations and said that the mayoral chair was Stuart not Tudor, although frankly as an argument against a supernatural presence this seems quite flimsy, as I have yet to hear of a ghost being fastidious about the furniture! A more substantial phantom though, is the cat, which has been seen entering the panelled room through a closed door. He once caused a considerable stir by entering in the middle of a lecture, then sitting down, curling his tail round his paws, ... and disappearing.

For reasons best known to itself, the spectral feline is more commonly sighted in the evenings, and is often seen skulking near the doorway to the panelled room, at the top of the stairs. The first recorded sighting of the cat occurred at the same time as the "visitation" of the controversial White Lady but she hasn't been seen since.

KINGLEY VALE
Stoughton, West Sussex

THIS STRETCH of the countryside is haunted by ghostly warriors although some say that they could be phantom druids.

KINGS ARMS
Monkton Farleigh, Wiltshire

THE KINGS ARMS has a haunting that must be immensely satisfying if you happen to be in the company of a cynical sceptic. In 1974 a customer was rash enough to announce his own disbelief in the supernatural. His statement was immediately followed by a loud crash upstairs, a flood of water cascading through the ceiling and a heavy freezer was pushed forward onto it's front. On a similar occasion a tray of steaks was thrown across the room. Aside from the touchy poltergeist, people have also heard the disembodied voice of an old lady coming from one room, talking to some invisible children.

On one occasion sometime in the early hours, the pub manager heard someone in heavy boots walking along an upstairs corridor. Several regular customers have also heard the wings of a large bird flapping in the bar. Sudden sharp drops in temperature accompany each incident.

KINGSTHORPE
Northamptonshire

DURING THE WINTER of 1940 George Dobbs set out to walk to the *Fox and Hounds*. On his way he saw a cyclist weaving about in the road and who seemed to be blissfully oblivious to the car close behind him. The car drove on past the cyclist, who immediately afterwards disappeared. George related his strange story to the other customers when he reached the pub. He was astounded when Lid Green, the local gravedigger, informed him that the cyclist sounded like a man he had buried 25 years before. He had been knocked off his bicycle outside the cemetery gates, and his head was torn off in the process. George's phantom cyclist didn't appear to have a head.

KINGTON (CHURCH)
Hereford & Worcester

THOMAS VAUGHAN came from a powerful family in the area, whose ancestral home was Hergest Court. Vaughan is buried at the church with his wife, Ellen Gethrin who according to the church booklet, was known as 'Ellen the Terrible'. For reasons unknown local legend has decreed that Vaughan had also been rather on the unpleasant side in life and a flaming nuisance after death as well.

Some of the wicked misdeeds attributed to him seem to be tenuously linked to black magic. When his ghost became too troublesome 12 priests carrying 12 candles met at the church and tried to entice his spirit into a snuffbox, (perhaps it was the only thing they had handy), but when all the candles went out most of them fled in fear, though one priest stoutly refused to move until the exorcism was complete. Vaughan was buried for a 1000 years at the bottom of Hergest Pool with a big stool placed on top to stop him going for an unwelcome stroll.

All this is very dramatic stuff to be sure, but it would appear that Vaughan was in fact killed at the Battle of Banbury in 1469, and was not really the evil man that history has painted him. Oh dear, another legend bites the dust. But groan not, for the church is also said to be the haunt of a phantom black hound, rumoured to have been Vaughan's pet dog. The dog likes to lurk near a pond on the road from Kington and as such, this spot tends to be avoided by nocturnal travellers.

KINTBURY (CHURCH)
Berkshire

SEVERAL PEOPLE have reported seeing a man wearing a black cloak and a wide-brimmed hat at this site. Generally the phantom faded away as they approached.

KIRKSTALL ABBEY
Leeds, West Yorkshire

THE GATEHOUSE here is now a museum and is said to be haunted by an old abbot. Strange noises have been reported from here at night.

KIT'S COTY HOUSE
Blue Bell Hill, Kent

KIT'S COTY HOUSE is a tomb which dates back to the 5th century, and is said to be where ghostly soldiers re-enact an old battle.

LACOCK ABBEY
Chippenham, Wiltshire

IN 1232 Lacock Abbey was founded by Ela, Countess of Salisbury, and the Abbey was consecrated as an Augustinian convent. It became a private house in 1540. It has a resident ghost, but nobody seems to be certain who it is. Suggestions range from the holy Countess herself, or Rosamund - mistress of King Henry II, or Olive Sharington - daughter of Sir William Sharington, who was given the Abbey by King Henry VIII at the Dissolution.

A photographic expert paid a visit to the Abbey in recent times and noticed a beautiful girl standing on the steps at the west front. She was staring up at the Abbey, whilst the witness took a photograph of her. Afterwards he went to approach the girl, and was about to speak to her when he realised there was nobody there.

On asking round the Abbey and the village, he discovered that the ghost could often be sighted on bright summer days, inside and outside the building. The witness hastily developed his photograph, and found that although he had a beautiful picture of the Abbey the girl was nowhere to be seen.

LAKENHEATH AIR FORCE BASE
Suffolk

EARLY IN 1951 an American security policeman was driving around the base one night when he noticed a man in RAF uniform, hitching a lift. He stopped and the pilot got in. The hiker asked for a cigarette, and the driver passed him a cigarette and lighter. When the driver looked again, his passenger had vanished, leaving only the lighter behind on the seat.

LANCASTER CASTLE
Lancashire

LANCASTER CASTLE was a convenient place for keeping prisoners, including the Pendle witches tried and executed during the early part of the 17th century. The prisoners were usually tortured in Hadrian's Tower, so it is not surprising that part of the wall there is said to drip blood. Ghostly moans and shrieks have also been heard from time to time.

LANHYDROCK HOUSE
Bodmin, Cornwall

LANHYDROCK was originally owned by the Augustinian Priory of St Peters, but was surrendered to King Henry VIII at the Dissolution in 1539. The property passed into the hands of Sir Richard Robartes in 1620, but unfortunately most of the structure was destroyed by fire in 1881, so the present building is mainly late Victorian. Although smoking is strictly banned in the house, an aroma of fresh cigars has often been smelt in the Smoking Room. The

Long Gallery, which is 17th century and survived the fire, is haunted by a ghostly Grey Lady. She has also been sighted in the Drawing Room. An intangible "presence" has also been felt in Her Ladyship's Room.

LANGSTONE ARMS
Chipping Norton, Oxfordshire

THIS PUB achieved fame in the local press during the mid-1960s when an outbreak of paranormal phenomena occurred here. The inexplicable sounds of coughing and shuffling feet seemed to occur every 2-3 weeks on a regular basis. An elderly woman wearing a veil was seen gliding around the passages, and on one occasion she was seen to pass through a glass partition.

Before that in the 1950s a former chef at the inn reported instances of rather intriguing ghostly phenomena. He claimed he had heard a disembodied voice in the cellar, who informed him tartly that "Fred would not do it like that". On another occasion he was entering the kitchen late one night when the same voice told him that his supper was on the table. True enough, when he reached his room he found a meal waiting for him on his bedside table! On 1 January 1954 he was returning from a New Year party when he found a pretty woman standing in the kitchen. When he asked her what she wanted, she replied "a good nights rest like you're going to have". The poor man decided soon after that he had had enough of this well-meaning, but tiresome phantom and left the pub for pastures new. Certainly a very unique haunting. Who was the pretty lady? And just as curious, who was old Fred?

LAUGHTON (CHURCH)
Lincolnshire

TWO WORKMEN were repairing the tower of the church in 1974 when they heard footsteps on the stairway but when one of them went to look there was nobody else in the building.

LEEDS CASTLE
Maidstone, Kent

THIS FAIRYTALE castle, set romantically in the middle of a lake, now plays host to a dizzying calendar of social events all year round, and so it is not surprising that the one phantom linked with the building has quietly retired from the scene in the last 70 years. At one time the ghostly black hound that haunted this site was regarded as a useful prophet of doom. Former owners of the castle, the Wykeham-Martins, claimed that the dog usually vanished in the middle of a room, or through closed doors. In spite of his spooky description he was said to be of a fairly benevolent nature. It was reckoned that he served as a kind of warning of impending disaster and one story certainly reflects this. An old lady sitting in a window watched the phantom hound as he disappeared into a wall. The woman naturally got rather curious, and left her seat to examine the wall but whilst she was doing so the window collapsed inwardly. But for the dog she would have been killed or certainly badly hurt by the falling glass .

LEIGH WOODS
Bristol, Avon

THE WOODS include Nightingale Valley, and the Iron Age fort at Stokeleigh. Isambard Kingdom Brunel, builder of the suspension bridge, and who died in 1859 through overwork and over indulgence in cigars, is said to still walk in the area. More unnerving are the spectral screams and other weird noises that have been heard coming from the woods on dark, winter nights. Dogs have also been known to show extreme terror when in this part of the countryside, which is hardly surprising.

LEISTON (CHURCHYARD)
Suffolk

AT THE TURN of the century the redoubtable Lady Rendlesham and a companion decided to set up a vigil in the churchyard, to watch for the 'Galley Trot' the local phantom black hound. The ladies were not to be disappointed. At midnight the animal suddenly leapt over the churchyard wall and ran down the lane towards Sandhills.

LEITH HALL
Kennethmount, Grampian, Scotland

AMERICAN AUTHORESS Elizabeth Byrd resided here at Leith Hall for five years, and encountered paranormal phenomena so frequently that she wrote a book about it. The house, now under the care of the National Trust, dates back to 1650, and was the home of the Leigh family for 300 years. In July 1966 Elizabeth and her husband, Barrie

Gaunt, moved into the East Wing, and it wasn't long before Gaunt saw a woman in Victorian dress lurking in the Leith Bedroom.

Elizabeth heard footsteps on the third floor, and noticed that the doors had an unnerving habit of slamming shut on their own. Their guests reported feeling distinctly uneasy near the Master Bedroom on the second floor, and Elizabeth suffered from nightmares when she slept in the four-poster bed in the same room. One morning as she was getting up, she saw a man with a bandaged head standing between the dressing-table and the floor of the bed ... he slowly vanished. The witness changed her sleeping arrangements soon after. From a portrait Elizabeth reckoned that the bandaged spectre had been a man called John Leith, who had been shot dead by his wife in 1763.

Other supernatural phenomena recorded at the house includes the sound of ghostly pipes and chanting, the aroma of food and camphor, as well as heavy footsteps and slamming doors. A former inhabitant, Alanna Knight, thought that the nursery area was haunted as well, and logically surmised that the ghost was an old nanny. In 1929 one of the staff employed at the hall, Donnella Gordon, related another story. She said that a maid took her boyfriend off to the Gun Room for some privacy, and they returned as the rest of the staff were having tea. Donnella said that the boy was as white as a sheet, and the girl was practically sick with fear.

The couple related that they had heard someone clanking around in chains in the Music Room directly above them, as well as an eerie groaning noise. This does sound suspiciously like someone having a joke at their expense, but even so the maids had often told how they had felt an "unseen presence" when cleaning the notorious Leith Bedroom, and it would be incredibly narrow-minded to dismiss the haunting of Leith Hall outright.

LETHAM BATTLEFIELD
Tayside, Scotland

THE BATTLE OF NECHTANESMERE was fought here in 685 AD, and in 1950 Miss E Smith saw a complete re-enactment of it as she was driving home one winter's night. Her car had skidded into a ditch and she decided to walk the rest of the way, when she noticed people carrying torches near Letham. Her dog growled at the phantoms, who appeared to be examining the corpses strewn about. Miss Smith said that they wore the clothes of Pictish warriors.

LEVENS HALL
Kendal, Cumbria

MRS BAGOT, mother of the owner of Levens Hall, once spoke on television of a lady in a pink dress and mob cap, one of the resident ghosts at her Tudor home. In 1972 the ghost was sighted by some worthy members of the Women's Institute at the top of the stairs. Another ghost is the Grey Lady, who is said to have been a gypsy woman who was turned away when she came begging at the house in the 17th century. As gypsies are wont to do when cruelly slighted, she cursed the family, and she later died of starvation. In 1971 the phantom gypsy was seen by the 7 year-old daughter of Mrs Bagot. She watched as the ghost walked across a field and then through the garden shed. She was dressed in 17th century servant's garb. The ghostly vagabond was sighted again in 1971, standing on the bridge leading to the house, and was thought to be the culprit who nearly caused a road accident. Also at the Hall is a phantom black dog which rushes downstairs for no apparent reason.

LINLITHGOW PALACE
Central, Scotland

LINLITHGOW PALACE was the birthplace of both Mary Queen of Scots and her father, King James V. The ghost of the King's wife is said to still wait patiently for his return in Queen Margaret's Bower. Another ghostly lady has also been seen near the entrance of the palace. She wears a bluish gown, and walks towards the church where she usually disappears. The best time to spot her apparently is at 9:00 AM, in the months of April and September. A creature of habit obviously.

LITTLE ABBEY HOTEL
Great Missenden, Buckinghamshire

THIS 12TH CENTURY building is now used as a private hospital, but was once part of Missenden Abbey. In 1297 a monk at the Abbey committed suicide because of a local married woman, with whom he had been having a clandestine affair. Many years later when it was used as a prep school, a secret tunnel was found that led to the Great Abbey. To prevent any bright young spark getting excitable ideas about exploring it, it was sealed up. In 1972 a handyman was on the top landing repairing a window, when he noticed a man in a brown habit coming up the stairs.

This same ghostly monk is said to be the one who has an unwelcome habit of keeping people away from the lounge, purely by exerting his eerie presence.

LLYN CERRIG BACH
Valley, Anglesey, Wales

ANCIENT METALWORK was found here, all of which was dated before 60 AD, and the ghosts of Roman soldiers and Druids are said to haunt the area of the lake.

LONGSTONE LIGHTHOUSE
Farne Islands, Northumberland

IN 1976 two lighthouse-keepers appeared on television to relate their intriguing tale of how they believed the lighthouse was haunted by the ghost of Grace Darling. Grace was born at the lighthouse in 1815, and became a national heroine after helping her father rescue nine people from the steamer 'Forfarshire'. She was to die of consumption four years later. The keepers said that they had heard her ghost clomping around the engine room in her clogs. The lighthouse went fully automatic in 1991 and the last lighthouse-keepers were interviewed on Radio 4. When one of them was questioned as to whether the lighthouse was haunted or not, he replied in a very economical fashion, "no!"

LONG STONE
Minchinhampton, Gloucestershire

ANOTHER OF those inimitable phantom black dogs is rumoured to lurk in this area.

LORD CREWE ARMS
Blanchland, Northumberland

THE LORD CREWE ARMS is named after a former Bishop of Durham, and it was originally used as the guest-house to a monastery. The Inn, like all good ones, has a resident ghost, in the guise of Dorothy Foster. The problem is that nobody knows *which* Dorothy Foster. One was the sister of Tom Foster, who plotted a rebellion in 1715, the other was her aunt, who at the age of 21 married the 79 year-old Lord Crewe. In December 1968 a Canadian lady visitor claimed that she felt a "presence" in her room, and felt a thump at the bottom of her bed. This story is marred for me by the fact that the visitor had insisted on being put in this room because of the haunting. I'm probably being unfair, but I'm always wary of the experiences of people who desperately want to see the ghost in question. Nevertheless, on another occasion a chambermaid cleaning this room found that her neatly folded linen had been strewn around the floor, literally whilst her back was turned!

LORTON HALL
Cockermouth, Cumbria

THIS HOUSE is close on a 1000 years old so it is not surprising that it should have a ghost in situ.

The story goes that one of the former inhabitants was a mongoloid daughter of the resident Bragg family, called Elizabeth. She died in the late 18th century, well into her sixties and totally insane. Because of that the local vicar refused to bury her in consecrated ground, and now around the time of the full moon Elizabeth appears very early in the morning, carrying a lighted candle. She usually passes through the dining-room window, originally the front door.

At the end of World War II, some Girl Guides were camping in the grounds when they saw her ghost drift out of the house and across the garden. A more disturbing event was in 1923 when a priest had attempted to carry out an exorcism here; he collapsed and died before it was accomplished. Elizabeth's ghost has also been seen standing in the garden. One woman was so terrified at seeing her that she crashed her car in her haste to get away from the site, although fortunately the accident wasn't fatal.

LOSELEY HOUSE
Guildford, Surrey

LOSELEY HOUSE has been the home of the More-Molyneaux family since the mid-16th century, and Queen Elizabeth I, King James I, Queen Anne and Queen Mary were all guests here at one time or another. Although described in the 'Historic Houses Guide' as having a "friendly atmosphere", it has at various times experienced some rather disturbing supernatural phenomena. On one occasion a lady of the house saw the ghost of a smiling woman standing outside the bathroom door. She later discovered a portrait of the ghost in the attic. Several visitors have reported seeing a woman in brown with dark, staring eyes standing at the bottom of the stairs. The figure generally disappears and is usually accompanied by a drop in temperature.

The Brown Lady was a far from pleasant person when living. About 400 years ago she sadistically murdered her stepson by hacking off one of his legs and letting him bleed to death, just so that her own son would become the sole heir. Her husband retaliated by imprisoning her in a room on the top floor for the rest of her life, which can only have been a sample of what she fully deserved. Horrific screams have been heard from this particular room on a certain night of the year, and an evil presence has been felt in the vicinity.

At one time the daughters of the house spoke of a kindly old lady who would sit silently with them. I cannot imagine in my wildest dreams that this sweet little old lady is the wicked stepmother, unless she has miraculously reformed in the 'After Life'. Even so, this particular ghost would never be spoken of by the adults of the house. At one time a party was held at the house, to which a medium was invited. Strange raps and bangs broke out at this gathering, and the guests were, understandably, far too unnerved to go to bed. The lady of the house pleaded with the guests not to tell the outside world of what had happened, but a guest broke his word and told a relative of the psychic disturbance, who in turn went on to publish the story. On another social occasion a dinner-party was held at the house, and outside staff, in the form of an elderly butler, were brought in to help with the arrangements.

A storm broke out and a bed had to be made up for the butler in the spare room. The following morning the old gentleman calmly reported that a man in fancy dress had kept walking through his room. Dogs are also apt to get rather upset in the Long Gallery. In spite of all that Loseley is still said to retain it's "friendly" atmosphere.

LUDLOW CASTLE
Shropshire

THIS 11TH CENTURY castle was surrendered to Cromwell in 1646, and inevitably now stands as a ruin. It is haunted by a ghostly white Lady and a rather peculiar wheezing noise. The origin behind the White Lady is that she was a woman called Marion de la Bruyere, and she lived there at the time of King Henry II. She used to leave a rope dangling, Rapunzel-fashion, so that her lover could get into the castle to see her. On one fateful occasion the lover was so preoccupied with the task in hand that he left the rope dangling behind him, and as a consequence Welsh brigands hauled themselves up it and stormed the castle. Feeling that she had been deliberately betrayed, Marion took her lover's sword and felled him with it before taking her own life by jumping from the tower. Her ghost roamed what is now called the Hanging Tower for many years after. Unfortunately the supernatural phenomena has decreased until only the wheezing noise remains. This is reckoned to be Marion's lover, eternally gasping his last breath!

During World War II a Liverpudlian family were evacuated to the castle. They reported hearing mysterious raps and bangs, as well as doors opening and closing of their own accord. Officials at the castle still complain from time to time about the wheezing noises in the tower.

LYDFORD GORGE
Devon

THE AREA near the pool, known as Kitty's Steps, is haunted by the phantom of an old woman wearing a red kerchief. Two old ladies visiting the area saw the ghostly old lady with her basket, fall into the water. An old man informed them later that it was the ghost of 'Old Kitty', who had fallen into the pool and drowned one stormy night.

The location near the castle is said to be haunted by a phantom black hound. The gloomy castle itself is haunted by the notorious Judge Jeffries. He used the area as his old courtroom and now he sometimes appears as a black pig, which would be highly appropriate. As a note of interest, the Gorge is also known as The White Lady, in honour of the Pagan Great White Goddess, Diana, Mother of Nature.

As recently as 1968 a young soldier drowned in the water near Kitty's Steps. At the inquest the coroner made the astonishing remark that the soldier could have been so overcome by the eeriness of the place that he threw himself in!

LYME PARK
Disley, Cheshire

SIR PIERS LEIGH VII built Lyme Park, described by the National Trust as the 'Palace on the Edge of the Peaks', in 1541. It was grafted onto an even older building dating back to 1465. One of his ancestors Sir Piers Leigh II, was killed at the Battle of Agincourt in 1415. His grief stricken mistress, known to us only as 'Blanche' committed suicide beside the River Bollin.

Sir Piers was buried on top of a hill, now known as 'Knight's Low' or 'Knight's Sorrow', and 'Blanche' is buried in 'Lady's Grove'. At the time of the full moon, (a popular time for spectral rambles in the countryside it would seem) the phantom funeral cortege of Sir Piers re-enacts it's journey up the hill. A ghostly White lady follows on behind, and from her distinct sobbing this would appear to be the unfortunate 'Blanche'.

Inside the house there is an intriguing room which opens out from the Gallery, and is known as the Ghost Room. A skeleton was once found beneath the floorboards here. Apparently phantom bells can also be heard in this area at night.

LYRIC THEATRE
Shaftesbury Avenue, London

IN NOVEMBER 1983 the story of the haunting of the Lyric Theatre was published in *Psychic News*. The well known medium Leslie Flint gave a detailed account of how it is haunted by a former usherette. It appeared that in March 1970 Flint and a friend, Bram Rogers, paid a social visit to the theatre. Inside was an old usherette of whom they enquired how much the programmes were. She told them, they paid her, and she put the money in a little beaded bag. Once seated they discussed the unusual lady. They remarked on how old fashioned her clothes were. She was thin with her hair in a bun, and wore a black skirt and blouse, adorned with a cameo brooch.

At the interval they made enquiries about the lady. The staff denied all knowledge of her. Some months later the medium was attending a seance when a Cockney voice suddenly appeared on the psychic airwaves. It was the ghostly usherette giving Flint a much-needed reminder of the incident. The chirpy-voiced old girl informed them that her name was Nellie Klute, and during her life she had earned a living selling programmes in several London theatres.

Nellie had lived in Drury Lane, and had been killed during a zeppelin raid in World War I. She was of Jewish extraction and her mother had been employed as a dresser for Grimaldi, the original great clown of the theatre. Nellie had an encyclopaedic knowledge of the old plays and shows, and displayed a rich humour when relating some of the goofs and praftfalls she had seen on stage.

After hearing of countless wailing lady phantoms and sinister male spooks, Nellie sounds a delightfully sane ghost.

LYTCHETT MATRAVERS (CHURCH)
Dorset

ON 30 MARCH 1915 a cleaner sweeping the chancel in the church, saw an old lady in a black poke bonnet go to a pew. The cleaner thought nothing of it and returned to her work but when she looked again, the old lady had gone, and the sexton, who had been outside the church, had seen nobody.

MAGDALEN COLLEGE
Oxford

DURING THE SPRING of 1987 students at the college claimed to have heard and seen a ghost in their rooms. Andrew Green, a parapsychologist, informs me that having investigated the report, he discovered it was a prank by some students.

MANCHESTER AIRPORT
Manchester

DURING 1971 THE GHOST of an old man was sighted at the airport nearly everyday. Other paranormal phenomena recorded here includes strange noises, footsteps, a bloodcurdling scream and the mysterious movement of office furniture.

One night the police were called to an empty freight-handling warehouse where a witness had reported hearing suspicious noises. A policeman and a lorry-driver both saw the ghost in this area and an import clerk sighted him sitting in the store-room. Night staff here have also reported seeing an old man in bare feet walk through an office.

MANOR HOUSE INN
Rilla Mill, Cornwall

DURING THE 1960s the landlord at this pub reported hearing mysterious footsteps in an upstairs room, which had supposedly gone on for many years. Regular customers backed up his story, and mysterious drops in temperature have been felt here as well.

MANOR HOUSE
Sandford Orcas, Sherbourne, Dorset

THIS RATHER forbidding-looking Tudor manor house has been the home of the Medlycott family since 1736. The house has among its motley collection of ghosts a most unpleasant character, a former depraved footman who during his lifetime preyed on serving-maids whose ghost still has an unwelcome habit of appearing now and again, but legend doth say only to nubile young virgins.

In 1966 a daughter of the house tried to spend a night in the Nursery Wing. It wasn't long before she fled screaming back to her own room. She reported that she had heard loud knocks on her door and weird dragging sounds. Another ghost is that of a farmer, who in the 18th century hanged himself from a trapdoor in the house. The trapdoor is now boarded-up but the farmer still walks. The lady of the house saw his ghost, dressed in a white smock, flit past the kitchen window. He can usually be seen in mid-afternoon.

A former footman and housekeeper, employed at the manor, once claimed that the stone carvings of the apes above the porch, appeared to laugh at them in the moonlight. This sounds like the house has a multitude of ways of getting to people psychologically. A Mrs Gates of

Taunton once spent a night in the infamous Nursery Wing where she saw the ghost of a man in evening dress with an evil face. I have a feeling that this was probably the depraved footman, which would scrub out the whimsical notion that only virgins see him, unless Mrs Gates has her own secrets of course. Other supernatural phenomena recorded at this marvellously atmospheric house includes harpsichord music coming from an empty room, a strange haze of blue smoke, disembodied voices heard in the inner courtyard of the Rear Wing, and footsteps pacing empty passages.

A couple who rented the house from the Medlycott family for a while, Colonel and Mrs Claridge, even managed to take a photograph of the suicidal farmer in his white smock. A man from the BBC was doing a programme on the house when he saw the phantom farmer passing the kitchen window. A ghostly old lady has also been seen climbing the stairs, and a strange aroma of tobacco smoke and incense has been smelt here.

Other spectres include a priest, (he was rumoured to have been involved in black magic), who attempts to smother sleeping guests with his cloak, a man-servant who strangled his employer, and a young boy who killed a fellow naval cadet at sea and was then locked in a back room at the house for the rest of his life. His insane screams are still said to ring through the building occasionally. Sandford Orcas Manor House is now open to the public and the owner himself, Sir Mervyn Medlycott, gives personal conducted tours on summer afternoons, which may help to reduce the sinister aspects of the house. He says the house is haunted only by the sound of footsteps in the cellar, and that the rest of the haunting is pure fabrication.

MARGAM ABBEY
West Glamorgan, Wales

THE RUINS of the Abbey are haunted by a ghostly monk, who has been sighted by several visitors.

MARLPITTS HILL
Nr Honiton, Devon

IN 1904 a party of schoolchildren walking in the area, saw a wild looking man in a wide-brimmed hat and a long, mud-spattered brown coat. Although the teacher with them saw nothing, the children described the man's dazed, exhausted, expression which they said had frightened them. It would appear that a man who had lived in a cottage in the area in 1685, had escaped from the Battle of Sedgemoor and was making his way home but just as his wife and children were about to welcome him, a troop of soldiers rode up and ran him through with their swords. The ghost was seen again one bright moonlit night in 1907.

MARSTON MOOR
Long Marston, Nr Wetherby, North Yorkshire

ON 2 JULY 1644 Cromwell defeated the Royalists here in the famous Battle of Marston Moor. Since that time the ghosts of Cavaliers fighting the Roundheads have been heard, and the battle has been seen re-enacted in the sky.

In November 1932 two touring motorists were driving past the area, when they noticed a small group of ragged man. The tourists slowed down and saw that they were dressed as Cavaliers. The phantoms staggered across the road directly in the path of a bus which appeared to drive straight through them. The tourists found no trace of them afterwards. In 1968 another group of tourists saw what they mistook to be tramps, dressed in 17th century clothes, in a ditch. The ghosts vanished. The phantoms were seen again in 1973.

MAYFIELD RAILWAY STATION
Manchester

MAYFIELD STATION appears to have disturbing effects on people. One man hanged himself in the signal box, a station foreman did likewise in the gentlemen's lavatory, and a night-porter fell down a 50ft baggage-hoist shaft and was killed outright. So it is not really surprising that the station is haunted. Footsteps have been heard at night approaching the foreman's office along an empty platform but to which of the three men they belong is not known.

MEAYLL CIRCLE
Cregneish, Isle of Man

THE CIRCLE consists of six T-shaped stone chambers, where burials were carried out in Prehistoric times. A ghostly army of men and horses has been sighted nearby.

MICHELHAM PRIORY
Upper Dicker, East Sussex

THIS TUDOR farm-house was an Augustinian Priory in the 13th century and is now haunted by a Grey Lady, who has been sighted near the 14th century gatehouse. She also has an unnerving habit of visiting anyone sleeping in one of the bedrooms. Usually, she looks down on them briefly, before leaving the room via a closed door.

Mr A C Gottleib, the Director here, recently told of his unusual experience in one of the upper rooms. On entering, the window opposite the doorway gradually opened of its own volition, despite never having been touched for decades and was suffering from very rusty hinges.

Another executive of the Sussex Archaeological Trust, the late Commander Harrison, reported that two visitors had witnessed a ghostly couple running down an invisible staircase.

MIDDLESBOROUGH RAILWAY STATION
Cleveland

ONE END of a platform at this station was once used as a temporary morgue. A man called Archer was employed here as a telegraphist in days gone by, and he made it well known that he hated passing "the dead house" alone. One night, at around 2:00, he saw signalman Fred Nicholson standing on the platform ahead of him but then to his consternation, Nicholson vanished!

He rushed to tell another signalman what he had seen, and his colleague gravely informed him that Nicholson had been killed by a train that very afternoon. At the time Archer had seen him, Nicholson's corpse was laid out in the "dead house", awaiting the attentions of the undertaker.

MINSDEN CHAPEL
Preston, Hertfordshire

AT HALLOWE'EN a ghostly monk is said to appear in the ruins. Bells are rung to herald his appearance.

MONEY TRUMP
Bisley, Gloucestershire

ONE NIGHT two men swore they had seen a group of headless male phantoms at this Prehistoric round barrow.

MUCHALLS CASTLE
Stonehaven, Grampian, Scotland

THIS 17TH CENTURY building is haunted by a young woman dressed in green who has been seen several times during the last 100 years. In the 1970s a visitor spotted her in an upstairs dining-room. She was seen facing a wall, and wore a lime-coloured dress but she vanished as the witness entered the room.

NAGS HEAD
Hackney Road, London

THE NAG'S HEAD has a ghost in its cellars. In 1968 a barman saw an old woman in black, and wearing a shawl, standing in the corner. A few weeks later he went down to the cellar again and saw her once more. Nobody seems to be terribly certain who she can be. Mysterious footsteps have also been heard in an upstairs room.

NAGS HEAD ROAD AREA
Enfield, London

IN 1899 three Ponder's End factory workers were going home when they saw a phantom coach. The driver and another man, leaning out of a window, could be seen. Other witnesses to the spectral vehicle have also reported seeing two women in large hats. On one occasion it even passed right through a house. In 1961 a boy cycling along Bell Lane saw the lights of the coach coming towards him. The apparition drove through him.

It has been described as a black coach, drawn by four horses, and appears to speed along 6ft above the ground.

NAPPA HALL
Wensleydale, North Yorkshire

IN 1878 a guest at the Hall claimed he had seen a positively beautiful phantom, whom he recognised from portraits as being none other than the glamorous, but ill-fated Mary Queen of Scots. He said she was tall, slim and wore a black velvet gown. Mary had visited the Hall whilst she was under house arrest at Castle Bolton nearby.

NASEBY BATTLEFIELD
Northamptonshire

IN 1645 King Charles I suffered defeat at the Battle of Naseby. Whilst he was staying at the *Wheatsheaf Hotel* in Daventry the night before, a friend's ghost, the Earl of Stafford, appeared and gravely advised him against going ahead with the battle.

Unfortunately the King, (a stubborn old devil at the best of times), gave into his General's insistence that the show must go on as planned. For about a century afterwards the battle was seen re-enacted in the sky, which has been the customary aftermath of many famous and bloodthirsty battles. The area around here is still considered to be haunted, and some believe that a controversial plan to construct a road across the south side of the battlefield may resurrect old ghosts. Literally.

NATIONAL MARITIME MUSEUM
Greenwich, London

THE REV R HARDY and his wife visited the museum in 1966 and took photographs of the Tulip Staircase, which was empty at the time – or so he thought! The reverend returned to Canada and developed the photographs. To his surprise two figures, shrouded in white, had appeared on the Tulip Staircase. One of the phantoms sported a large ring on one hand. The reverend contacted the prestigious Ghost Club in London, who examined the film. No defects were found and the Club members interviewed the Reverend and his wife. This resulted in the Club sponsoring an overnight ghost-vigil. They reported hearing footsteps and weeping. Most of the time the ghosts only appear in daylight hours.

NATIONAL WESTMINSTER BANK
Stevenage, Hertfordshire

THIS BUILDING was once known as the *Castle Inn*. In 1724 owner Henry Trigg died, leaving orders that his body was to be lain in a coffin in the loft. In 1850 the owner of the Inn prised open the coffin to find that Trigg's body was still in a state of preservation. Trigg obviously went on to decay, as during World War I some drunken soldiers broke open his coffin, and gave his bones to American soldiers as souvenirs of 'jolly old England'.

In 1970 a workman on the site saw the ghost of Henry Trigg gliding out of the 'Nat West' and into the barn, where it vanished. The phantom has been seen several times by visitors and staff.

NETHERHALL MANSION
Maryport, Cumbria

NETHERHALL MANSION was a rambling, neglected house, that stood empty for its final 20 years with the ground-floor boarded-up. The building has been repeatedly vandalised, and the floors and ceilings have rotted. The last lord of the manor died in 1970, and then the house was left in the custody of a local resident. He reported seeing a Grey Lady on the landing and at a window on the attic floor. During the last few months of the Hall's existence the contents were thrown about and furniture moved around the decaying building, even though a lot of the passages were blocked with rubble preventing vandals from gaining entry. In 1973 it was completely gutted by fire, and many blamed the fire on the Grey Lady. (It's not uncommon for phantom Grey Ladies to be accused of pyromania, see Borley).

Now only the shell of the pele-tower remains.

NEWARK PARK
Wootton-under-Edge, Gloucestershire

AFTER THIS castellated Elizabethan hunting-lodge had been given to the National Trust in 1949, some Ghost Club members decided to spend a night there.

They had been alerted to the house by tales of doors opening and closing at will, strange rustling noises, footsteps along deserted passages, disembodied voices, mysterious lights, bells ringing, thumps and bangs, rattling chains (obviously an aristocrat of a haunted house), eerie drops in temperature – all these had been experienced by people staying at the house during the restoration process. A warden of the house, Bob Parsons, said that one night he had heard footsteps and chains rattling, and his dog was clearly terrified. The Ghost Club members reported hearing rustling at the top of the stairs. When they played back their tape-recording they heard two unknown voices casually discussing the infrared cameras positioned at the top of the stairs. The President of the Ghost Club, Peter Underwood, said he had heard footsteps on the landing. Another investigative party reported hearing knocking, and feeling drops in temperature, and listening to the windows vibrating in a peculiar rattling fashion. Other witnesses have noted the extreme coldness and silence at the house, as well as furniture being moved by an unseen force.

Tappings have also been heard from within a room. One man heard female voices conversing in the downstairs hall, which he believed was deserted at the time. Two men upstairs heard the sound of wheels on the gravel outside, but when they looked out they saw nothing. A ghostly tread on the stairs has been attributed to the Abbot of Kingswood. Presumably the reasoning behind that is because the building materials for the house were partly taken from Kingswood Abbey and village crosses.

NEWSTEAD ABBEY
Linby, Nottinghamshire

NEWSTEAD ABBEY was built as a priory in 1170, and after the Dissolution it became the home of the Byron family. It is haunted by a black friar who is said to portend a disaster when he appears. Lord Byron had the misfortune to see him on the eve of his marriage to Annabella Milbanke, which Byron had very dim views about and even went so far as to describe it as the unhappiest event in his life!

The ghost of the 16th century gentleman, Sir John Byron, tends to sit in front of his portrait reading a book.

The Abbey is also haunted by a White Lady, and Byron's beloved pet dog, 'Boatswain'.

NEW TYNE THEATRE
Westgate Road, Newcastle-upon-Tyne

IN SPITE OF its name the theatre is Victorian, and has been haunted by stage-hand Rob Crowther for nearly a 100 years. Crowther was killed by a cannonball in the 1880s. This was one of eight, used in a thunder-roll machine, and had broken through a safety net and, weighing 36lbs, smashed Crowther's skull. Many people have noticed a drop in temperature here, and a strange man walking around backstage. Several years ago a producer was even threatened with a strike because of Crowther's ghost. In desperation, he sought the advice of a medium, who told him to welcome the ghost by allocating him a seat at the theatre. To make sure this rule is upheld a shrouded dummy is kept in Crowther's seat up in the gods. The ghost has often been seen there.

NUN'S BRIDGE
Huntingdon, Cambridgeshire

HINCHINGBROKE HOUSE here was once a convent, and the ghost of a nun haunts the bridge over Alconbury Brook. In 1965 a couple were driving across the bridge when they saw two ghosts. One was the nun, and they said the other looked like a nurse.

OGMORE CASTLE
Mid Glamorgan, Wales

THERE IS a long-standing rumour here that treasure is hidden in the ruins, and guarded by a ghostly White Lady. The story then continues that she once surreptitiously showed the hoard to a man who spoke to her. She gave him half-a-guinea for his time. Being of a human disposition, the man later returned to the ruins to get at the rest of the treasure but the White Lady caught him red-handed and scratched him with her talons.

The man eventually acquired a wasting disease (a mysterious ailment which was popular with Victorians and could have been absolutely anything), and died. Many believe it was the White Lady's revenge. It is has to be said that Welsh hauntings tend to be bogged down in myth and legend, which makes them hardly worth the effort of investigating.

OKEHAMPTON CASTLE
Devon

LADY HOWARD is said to haunt the castle grounds, under the guise of a black hound. Apparently her 'After Life' task is to pluck one blade of grass nightly, and carry it to her old home in Tavistock. She has to keep up with this interminable task until there is no grass left around the castle. A path near the castle has been named 'Lady Howard's Walk'.

OLDE ROCK HOUSE
Barton-on-Irwell, Lancashire

THE HOUSE is haunted by a gentleman who goes around muttering "now thus, now thus" in a Lancastrian accent. This is said to be a member of the De Trafford family, who escaped persecution from Cromwell's troops by posing as a country bumpkin!

OLDE SILENT INN
Stanbury, West Yorkshire

THIS MOORLAND village inn with the wonderfully sinister name has a rather gentle ghost in the form of a former landlady, who goes around stroking the foreheads of guests while they sleep. One of her habits during her lifetime was to feed the wild cats on the moors, by summoning them first with a bell. Local residents say that her bell can still be heard.

OLD SMUGGLERS INN
Coombe Cellars, Devon

THE OLD SMUGGLERS INN was once known as the *Ferryboat*, and was the romantic assignation point for Lord Nelson and Emma Hamilton. During the 18th century a woman was murdered in one of the bedrooms, and in the 1960s the landlord purchased a drawing of the murder. It was at about this time that the barmaid started complaining of an unseen presence in her room. Around 1970/71 two men went into the loft to fit a television aerial, then one of them returned to the landing to shout instructions. Very soon his colleague came down the ladder. He was in a disturbed state but refused to say what had frightened him and declined to return to the loft. The one and only clue to the mystery is that the area of the loft he was working in is sited directly over the haunted bedroom.

OLD SOAR MANOR
Nr Borough Green, Kent

THE MANOR dates back to the 13th century, and was, rather curiously, given the name 'Soar' - the Norman word for grief. It was owned by the Culpepper family, and is now haunted by an 18th century dairymaid, who committed suicide in the chapel after being made pregnant by the family priest. Mysterious lights have been seen in the deserted building at night, as well as strange music coming from the chapel. The people living in the farmhouse next door reported hearing the music, even when the property was left empty.

In June 1972 a young couple exploring the house told the custodian that they had seen a priest in the chapel, and had felt a sharp drop in temperature. A week later visitors to the house also spoke of an eerie coldness in this area. In June 1973 the custodian found a grey cloak hanging in the chapel, but when she looked for it again it had vanished. A few days later a visitor saw the phantom priest bending over the piscina, which is where the unfortunate dairymaid was said to have drowned herself in the few inches of holy water. Other supernatural phenomena noted at the manor includes a vision of water in an otherwise empty piscina, an unhappy presence felt on a spiral staircase, and light (possibly female) footsteps. Just for good measure, the hauntings always seem to occur in the month of June.

OSTERLEY PARK
Osterley, London

OSTERLEY PARK is an Elizabethan house haunted by a mysterious Woman in White. Two workmen employed at the house saw her on a number of occasions, and always at 4:30 in the afternoon. In 1978 some schoolchildren sighted her in the archway of the main stairs, and in Gobelins Tapestry Room, where she floated out of sight. The teachers with the school-party had the story verified by the attendants.

OXWICH (CHURCH)
West Glamorgan, Wales

EARLY IN THE 19TH CENTURY a boy and his father were walking by the churchyard at midnight (which seems to be rather an odd time for Dad to take his son out for a ramble), when they saw a white horse walking on its hind legs up the church path. It crossed over the stile into the churchyard and vanished. This sounds a fairly typical Welsh legend – full of eyewash. But more interesting is the tale that in the latter part of the century some people saw a white form gliding amongst the tombstones at midnight. In other words a less-embroidered version of the white horse legend, rather like Chinese whispers in reverse. Welsh whispers?

OYSTERMOUTH CASTLE
West Glamorgan, Wales

SEVERAL PEOPLE claim to have seen a phantom White Lady amongst the 11th century ruins here. Her back appears to be bleeding, and she usually stand crying by the tree close to the castle wall.

PASS OF KILLIECRANKIE
Pitlochry, Tayside, Scotland

THIS WAS the site of a mega-battle between King William III's troops and the Jacobite army on 27 July 1689. It is now haunted by a mysterious red light on the anniversary of the battle. A stone marks the spot where Viscount 'Bonnie' Dundee fell, and King William's men retreated. Dundee had a vision of the red light the night before the battle, and saw a man bleeding at the foot of his bed.

The man asked him to follow him, but (wouldn't you know it!?) Dundee woke up, considerably troubled by his dream. His guard reassured him that no one, bleeding or otherwise, had entered his tent during the night. The battle went ahead, and Dundee was shot as the enemy retreated. In more recent times two witnesses have testified to seeing ghostly soldiers running down the hillside, the whole scene bathed in an eerie red glow.

A cyclist once decided to camp at the site, and he was woken by a distant booming sound at 2:00 AM. He was then treated to an entire but ghostly re-enactment of the battle, including a girl robbing the corpses.

PEAROYD BRIDGE
Stocksbridge, South Yorkshire

A MYSTERIOUS hooded figure was seen in this area by two security guards patrolling one night in September 1987. The men drove closer to the figure, and the beam from their car headlights shone right through it. Two nights earlier, one of the guards claimed to have seen three spectral children dancing around an electricity pylon, again, in the middle of the night.

PEDDAR'S WAY
Great Massingham, Norfolk

THIS AREA is haunted by one of those inimitable phantom black hounds. In October 1977 a male hitch-hiker saw the animal, which went to attack him and then abruptly vanished.

Exactly one year later the jinxed hiker had a road accident, which has confirmed the nervous belief of many that the dog is a portender of doom. There has also been the odd sighting of a phantom grey-hound in the area, but the sinister black hound remains the most consistently seen. Early one morning in 1962 a motorist saw the black dog. The animal vanished, and then reappeared on the other side of the car!

PEEL CASTLE
Isle of Man

THE ISLE OF MAN has it's own phantom black hound, known locally as the 'Moddey Dhoo', and he used to frequent Peel Castle. He was such a familiar sight to the soldiers in the guard room, that they would let him sit by their fire. One night a drunken soldier decided to find out once and for all if the dog was really the Devil (as is often rumoured). He volunteered to take the castle keys to the captain of the guard, and stopped off at the dog's lair on the way. The soldiers heard a loud noise, and their drunken colleague rushed to rejoin them. He died three days later, and the dog was never seen again. The passage where the soldier had encountered him was then sealed off.

PENGERSICK CASTLE
Prah Sands, Cornwall

PENGERSICK CASTLE is now merely a fortified tower, but was once part of a 12th century manor house. There is a legend attached to the building claiming that treasure salvaged from a shipwreck is bricked-up inside it. Smugglers also used the secret tunnel leading to the beach. In spite of the dramatic history attached to the area the building has a very poor haunting. Visitors claim to have felt a "presence" here.

PENHOW CASTLE
Gwent, Wales

PENHOW CASTLE is nearly 900 years-old and is the oldest inhabited castle in Wales. It is haunted by the ghost of a young girl wearing a blue/grey apron. She has been seen frantically scurrying about the Great Hall by several visitors.

PEVENSEY CASTLE
East Sussex

THIS CASTLE was once a Roman coastal fort which, in the old days, had the sea rushing right up to the south wall. The ruins now lie about a mile inland. The Normans built a castle inside the Roman wall, which is now reduced to ruins itself, although the dungeons and part of the keep can still be seen. The ghost of one Lady Pelham stalks the walls at dusk, and sounds of a spectral battle have been heard in the area. A phantom army, led by King William Rufus, travels across the marshes and re-enacts an attack on the castle.

PILGRIMS WAY
Kent

THE LANE linking the Pilgrim's Way with Bearsted is haunted by a ghostly rider wearing a wide hat and silver spurs. (I assume he wears something else as well but these are the only items of clothing I've heard about!) He has conversed with people who were convinced that he was real, until he vanished. Sometimes just the sound of the horse's hooves are heard.

On Midsummer's Eve the horseman is said to ride from Pilgrim's Way, via Eastwell Park, and straight into the lake. The stretch of the Way near Trottiscliffe is also said to be haunted by a phantom black hound.

PLAS NEWYDD
Llangollen, Clwyd, Wales

PLAS NEWYDD is world-famous for being the home of the two eccentric old dears of Llangollen, namely Lady Eleanor Butler and her "beloved Sally", Miss Sarah Ponsonby. Together they created their own little retreat from a world which didn't understand them. Visitors to the house have noticed a drop in temperature in the State Bedroom. Some even claim to have seen the little old ladies in their sober clerical-style riding-habits. During their lifetime they made an oath whereby they would not spend a night away from their home, and are said to have kept this up for 50-odd years. It is therefore not surprising that such a strong attachment to a place should carry on after death.

PLAS PREN
Denbigh Moors, Clwyd, Wales

I HAVE TO ADMIT to being surprised to seeing this poor old house being included in Simon Marsden's book *The Haunted Realm*. It looks every inch a gothic nightmare and is in fact known locally as the 'Haunted House' although I think this is rather more due to it's forbidding appearance than reputation. The house is an unforgettable sight as you drive across the Denbigh Moors; an enormous, tumbling ruin stuck high up in the middle of nowhere.

The house was built by Lord Davenport at the turn of the century as a shooting-lodge. This was not a very practical idea as it was so inaccessible that getting such necessities as coal up to it, created no end of problems, and its isolated spot wasn't a great temptation for prospective servants. The house was abandoned in 1925 and has steadily gone to seed ever since. The house is now a sorry sight, groaning under rubble and graffiti, and frequented only by sheep.

Mr Marsden claimed that when he visited the site he felt that "something terrible" had happened there, and on eagerly questioning the locals in the *Sportsman's Arms* at the bottom of the hill, he was told some convoluted tale about a luminous skeleton terrifying a courting couple at the ruins.

PLOUGH INN
Clapham High Street, London

THIS 150 YEAR-OLD pub has a hidden room, which only came to light when the landlord realised that although he could see three windows on the top floor outside the building, he could only find two inside. The entrance to the hidden room was discovered in 1970, and the maverick window has since been blocked-up. The door to the secret chamber is still found open of its own accord occasionally, and this is attributed to the pub's resident ghost, nicknamed 'Sarah'. This lady, like so many ghosts, usually has a disturbing affect on the pub dog. At the time that the room was discovered, the resident barman awoke in the night to find a woman in his room. She had long hair and wore a nightgown, and she stood watching him from a corner. Since then the supernatural phenomena has included cold spots, weird prickly sensations and the creepy feeling of being watched. For some curious reason this haunting (rather mild by some standards) caused one landlord to lose his job.

PLUCKLEY
Kent

PLUCKLEY has earned itself the questionable title of 'Most Haunted Village in England'. In 1975 the ghost of a Woman in White was seen gliding amongst the tombstones, and a phantom white hound has also been seen inside the church.

Pluckley's claim to fame has been treated with scepticism in recent years, and the village does appear to have an insatiable appetite for publicity where the supernatural is concerned. One of the village pubs, the *Black Horse*, has also got in on the act with claims of a haunting. But as far as I can gather, the phenomena is limited to objects disappearing and then returning of their own accord.

There are other villages included in this tome that have just as good as, or better, hauntings than this one. Like a lot of things in rural life, the haunting is not what it was, and in recent years seems to have done a trick worthy of the ooozalum bird!

POLESDEN LACEY
Bookham, Surrey

THE ORIGINAL HOUSE on this site stood from 1632 until the early years of the 19th century. Now all that remains of that building is a terraced wall that was built in 1761. Polesden Lacey has two ghosts, a brown hooded figure that haunts the bridge, and a spectral whirlwind (of all things) on the Nun's Walk.

The figure that haunts the wooden bridge is usually described as wearing a brown-hooded cloak which hides its face. The whirlwind tends to mainly consist of a strange whistling noise. In April 1984 Mr Davis, a member of staff, went on radio to announce that he had had the unenviable experience of finding a dead woman on the sofa in a small room. Other ghostly phenomena includes the sighting of a man in old-fashioned clothes in the billiard room, who vanished, and the very chilling sound of a shrill cry for help. All this phenomena is recorded as happening in the mornings.

POLSTEAD RECTORY
Suffolk

IN APRIL 1978 the Rev. Hayden Foster, accompanied by his wife and son, arrived to take up his post in Polstead (which incidentally is not very far from that supernatural theme park – Borley). All went well for the Rev Foster until the fifth night, when the couple had to move into another bedroom to accommodate guests, who had arrived for the vicar's inauguration ceremony the following day.

At 3:00 AM Mrs Margo Foster awoke to find that the wallpaper had changed to a different design, and appeared to be very old and peeling in many places. As if that wasn't strange enough she went on to hear a horrid screaming, like a childs, and then felt herself being strangled! Villagers fuelled the rumours of a haunting (as they are wont to do) by saying that they had seen monks walking along the road past the rectory gates – their sandals 6ft above the ground. The Rev John Whitmore, Vicar at Polstead from 1795 to 1840, had once performed an exorcism in the house, which doesn't appear to have had much effect. In fact, the belief that exorcisms are an infallible method of disposing of unwelcome spooks has been proved, time and again, to be far from true. The Diocese Bishop, Leslie Brown, naturally grew curious about the haunting after the Rev Foster had fled the coop. The Bishop questioned an earlier Polstead vicar's wife, who informed him in a blase' manner that they had grown quite accustomed to hearing strange footsteps on the stairs. Nevertheless the church decided to put the rectory up for sale.

POSTBRIDGE
Dartmoor, Devon

FLORENCE WARWICK was sitting in her car on the side of the road leading from Postbridge to Two Bridges on Dartmoor. There was something wrong with her vehicle and she was checking the manual, when she happened to look up and saw a pair of disembodied hairy hands on her windscreen! Florence hasn't been the only witness to this peculiar haunting. During the 1920s the spectral hands were busy overturning pony traps, wrenching the handlebars from the grasp of an unsuspecting cyclist, and causing various horses to shie and bolt. On one occasion a doctor and two children were roaring along in a motorbike and sidecar when the engine suddenly detached itself.

An army officer told how a pair of hairy hands covered his on the steering-wheel, and a couple spending the night in their caravan in a layby did not escape the unwelcome attentions of the hairy hands. The woman was woken up by a strange scratching sound outside. She also felt an eerie chill, on looking up she saw a pair of hairy hands covering the window above her husband's bunk. She said that on making the sign of the cross the hands vanished.

It is quite common for road accidents to be blamed on the paranormal, which makes it all very thrilling but they are nigh on impossible to prove. In 1960 a motorist was found dead beneath the wreckage of his car. On examination there was found to be no possible mechanical fault with the vehicle, and the accident has largely been attributed to the hairy hands. A hiker walking along the road at dusk suddenly felt gripped with an inexplicable feeling of sheer panic, which wouldn't be hard to understand on finding himself along that particular stretch of road at such an atmospheric time of day. The only possible clue to the mystery of this most unusual haunting possibly lies in the fact that there was once a Bronze Age village along this road.

POULTON ROAD
Bebington, Merseyside

POULTON ROAD is haunted by a nun, who was apparently killed on her way to the nunnery. In August 1970 a man driving here at night saw a girl in his headlights. She vanished completely when he stopped the car.

POUNDSTOCK (CHURCH)
Cornwall

ON 2 MARCH 1971 Ivor Potter spoke to the ghost of a priest in the church porch here. The priest generally appears in solid form, and has been known to stand next to the vicar during funeral services.

POWIS CASTLE
Welshpool, Powys, Wales

KNOWN AS the 'Red Castle', because it is made of red sandstone, Powis Castle was the home of the Princes of Upper Powys, until the line died out in the 16th century. In 1784 an heiress of the Herbert family married Edward

Clive, the first Earl of Powys, and there is now a Clive of India museum on the site.

The ghost story associated with the castle was made public by a Weslyan Methodist, Rev John Hampson, who claimed to have spoken with an old inhabitant of the castle, who had once conversed with the ghost in person. The story has now gone down in local folklore, and it does sound a bit like something out of a Grimm's Fairy Tale at times. Here it is in the abridged version.

Let us go back, dear reader, to the winter of 1780, when a poor woman of the area worked as a freelance hemp spinner. She would tour houses with her trade, and stay under the roof of her employers whilst her work was in progress. She went to Powis Castle, touting for business, and was invited in and shown to her quarters, a comfortable ground-floor room, but which unbeknown to her was haunted. Also unbeknown to her, was the fact that she was to be an unwitting guinea-pig in an experiment on the haunting being carried out by the steward and his wife.

The woman was sitting quietly reading the Bible, in her plush new quarters when the figure of an opulently-dressed gentleman entered the room. He stood staring out of the window, and then after a fairly lengthy sojourn, he noiselessly left. The woman grew nervous and started to pray, which had the effect of making the apparition return. He walked stealthily all around the room, and then left again. On the third visit (aren't you glad I didn't write out the *full* version?) the ghost walked fairly close to her. The woman plucked up the courage to ask him what he wanted. He told her to follow him, and led her into a small room. He drew out a box hidden beneath the floorboards, and unlocked it with a key that was hidden in a crevice in the wall.

He instructed her to send both the key and the box to the Earl, who was in London at the time, and then he vanished. The woman shouted for the steward and his wife. The couple relieved her of the box, and the woman went to bed. The Earl received the box and, obviously gratified by its mysterious contents, made sure that the spinner was provided for, for the rest of her born days. This is a rotten story, irritating because after all that, the punchline is denied us. What was in the wretched box that was so damned important?

Unfortunately the ghost still walks at the castle, and is now joined by a spectral lady in white who lurks in one of the bedrooms, and a man on horseback in the garden. However, the present Earl regards the haunting to be extinct, but as recently as 1981 it was believed that the ghost of the second Marquess of Powys haunted the Duke's Bedroom.

PRIEST'S HOUSE
Muchelny, Somerset

THE NAME of this late medieval building dates from when the house was the residence of priests who served the parish church. Former tenants have related intriguing stories of monks, buried treasure, a strange lady and a banging door. There is considerable scepticism thrown on these stories though, because one former tenant who believed fervently in the insubstantial legends about the house, was a bit of a one for the drink.

PRIORY GATEHOUSE
Cartmel, Cumbria

THIS BUILDING is said to be haunted by ghostly monks who once guided people across the sands. There have also been reports of the cries of people who were trapped and killed in the quicksand. The ghost of a middle-aged man in a waistcoat, breeches and tall hat, walks the lanes around the priory.

PRINCE OF WALES INN
Kenfig, Mid Glamorgan, Wales

THE PRINCE OF WALES INN once played host to a new idea in psychic investigation. In 1982 the landlord reported hearing ghostly voices and organ music. This prompted John Marke and Allan Jenkins to carry out a psychic experiment for him. The two men connected electrodes to the stone wall of the main bar late one night and left tape recorders running in the locked room for four hours. When the tape was played back it revealed voices, organ music and a clock ticking – which was odd as there was no clock in the room at that time. The voices appeared to be talking in a very old form of Welsh. Somehow these sounds of former inhabitants had managed to get trapped in the stone walls of the building for hundreds of years. This is definitely one of the most fascinating pub hauntings that I have come across.

PUNCH BOWL INN
Hurst Green, Nr Clitheroe, Lancashire

THE HIGHWAYMAN Ned King was captured here during a shoot-out in the barn, and his ghost is said to roam this area. The barn is now the inn's restaurant, and King was hanged from a gibbet near the main door. His ghost gallops on horseback across the fields. A priest tried to exorcise the pub in 1942, but phenomena such as bottles falling off shelves has continued. Guy Lyon Playfair (author of *The Haunted Pub Guide*) remarks that he thinks it might be the people at the inn who need exorcising.

PUTTENDEN MANOR
Nr Lingfield, Surrey

A FORMER OWNER of this 15th century house, Sir George Sondes, became Earl of Feversham in 1676. He was killed by his younger brother in a fit of jealousy, and his grief-stricken widow planted two ash trees in the grounds in remembrance of him. The male line of the family petered out, and a curse seemed to be on every family who settled there for the next 150 years. In 1901 Mark Napier purchased it, and started on extensive renovation work. Perhaps as a consequence the house is now said to have a much friendlier atmosphere, although workmen, who were once sleeping in the Master Bedroom, complained about heavy footsteps keeping them awake. A mysterious aroma of pipe tobacco has also been smelt here.

QUARR ABBEY
Quarr Hill, Isle of Wight

THE RUINS, if popular legend is to be believed, are thought to be haunted by King Henry II's wife, the formidable Eleanor of Aquitaine. She is said to be buried here in a gold coffin ... but another lovely slice of mythology has to bite the dust. The truth is that Eleanor never came anywhere near the island, in life or death! The Abbey ruins are thus haunted by an unknown lady phantom.

RAILWAY HOTEL
Waterfoot, Lancashire

THE HOTEL is still thus named, even though the station is
no longer here. The resident ghost has been affectionately
nicknamed "Jane", and has been known to perform such
ghostly feats as walking through walls, drifting across
bedroom floors and playfully removing bedclothes.
Successive landlords and their spouses have been addressed
by a disembodied voice in the tap-room. The only clue to
Jane's identity might lie in a bricked-up room at the top of
the building, but the present landlord apparently doesn't
like to discuss his spectral guest .

RAINHAM HALL
Essex

THE CURRENT owners have resided here since 1973, and
their ghost appears to be a certain Edwardian gentleman
called Colonel Mulliner. He seems to be a very friendly
ghost who generally has the consideration to limit his
appearances to daylight hours. In 1968 the Colonel was
seen by a carpenter working at the house.

RAMSEY ISLAND
Off St David's Head, Dyfed, Wales

IN THE 6TH CENTURY St Justinian was murdered by his own followers. His ghost is now said to walk through the main building on the island, and across the sea to his chapel. Mysterious disembodied footsteps have been attributed to him.

RAY ISLAND
Essex

A ROMAN CENTURION haunts Ray Island on spring nights. Mrs Jane Pullen claimed to have had the dubious pleasure of his company for a couple of miles when she was walking here.

During the 1920s her grandson, Ivan Pullen, decided to camp in the area for a couple of nights. He said that he heard heavy footsteps walk around his tent, at one point they even seemed to enter it. When he cautiously peered out he saw nothing. He later emphatically remarked that nothing would induce him to spend another night there.

RAYNHAM HALL
Nr Fakenham, Norfolk

THE PHANTOM Lady in Brown that haunts Raynham Hall is quite a celebrity in the world of the paranormal. She has been written about in scores of books on the subject of the supernatural. She is Dorothy Walpole, sister of the Prime Minister, Sir Robert Walpole. The story goes that Dorothy fell in love with her childhood sweetheart, Charles Townsend, but the romance was cruelly crushed before it had a chance to turn into marriage. Charles, who later comes across as a bit of a heartless swine, sought comfort with a baron's daughter. In the meantime Dorothy buried her sorrow and went to Paris to sow *her* wild oats, chiefly with the notorious lothario Lord Wharton. In 1711 Charles's rich wife died, and Dorothy sped back to join him. After a respectful interval they married and were blissfully happy for a while - that is, until Charles learnt of his wife's indiscretions in Paris. His male ego couldn't bear such an affront and poor Dorothy was confined to her rooms and allowed no visitors. In 1726 she died, which set off a riot of rumours that she had been murdered.

In 1786 King George III paid a visit to the house. His stay was cut short when he awoke in the night to find Dorothy's ghost standing by his bed. The King roused the entire house with his fury and departed immediately. The Townsends were appalled at having offended their monarch and instructed the male servants to mount a round-the-clock watch for the phantom.

Dorothy didn't disappoint them. She walked right through one unfortunate individual, who said he had felt a piercing icy blast. Dorothy was inexhaustible over Christmas 1835, causing several guests to depart the house in a hurry on seeing her. This was not surprising. The aspect of her that terrified them the most was the fact that she had no eyes! On another occasion the writer Captain Marryat, and a companion, sighted her in an upstairs corridor. Dorothy smiled at the normally bluff captain, who panicked and fired at her with his gun. The bullets went right through her and were embedded in the door opposite. On 19 September 1936 Dorothy made the appearance that was to ensure her a permanent place in supernatural debating circles. The photographer Indra Shira arrived to take pictures of the house for a magazine. His assistant saw a strange cloud of vapour appear on the staircase and Mr

Shira hastily snapped at it for posterity. When the photograph was developed it revealed the blurred outline of a woman dressed in a white gown and bridal veil. This photograph has been reproduced in numerous books on the paranormal and it has been hotly debated. Arthur C Clarke (who can be very tiresome in his quest to pooh-pooh the paranormal), claims the photo is a fake, and is the result of double-exposure. I suppose anything is possible, and photographs of ghosts are fairly dodgy to substantiate as the 'Real Thing'. Even so, the picture does send a certain questioning shiver down the spine when you look at it.

Just as intriguing is the issue of Dorothy's portrait. By daylight it appears fairly normal, but viewed by candlelight Dorothy appears to take on a rather malevolent expression, as the flesh seems to disappear and only her skull remains.

RENISHAW HALL
Derbyshire

DAME EDITH SITWELL couldn't wait to get away from her gloomy 17th century ancestral home when she was young, which is understandable as I shouldn't think a bleak, cold house with a depressing ghost is a marvellous environment for a budding genius. Her father, Sir George Sitwell, ordered that a ground floor room and a first floor bedroom were to be demolished. In the process the builders discovered a coffin dating back to the early days of the house's history. The coffin had been secreted between the joists of the bedroom floorboards. It contained no body, but marks inside the coffin indicated that once there had been. In 1885 a Miss Tait, a guest at the house, was woken by someone kissing her three times. She was rather disconcerted when she discovered that the room was empty, and refused to sleep there again. Several years later Lady Sitwell was entertaining in the upstairs drawing-room when she saw a ghostly servant-girl, standing in the passage just outside the open door. Her hands were clasped in front of her. She vanished at the top of the stairs. Lady Sitwell later remarked that the ghost had cast no shadow, and appeared to be full of sadness.

Had the girl been the occupant of the makeshift coffin? Answer comes there none, but it does open up the possibility that there may be a 400 year-old unsolved murder hanging around the house.

RHUDDLAN
Clwyd, Wales

IN JULY 1953 a man returning home from the pub (which unfortunately is a dubious start) saw dozens of ghostly monks blocking his way. He dived into a hedge so that they could pass. Several years later a Norman graveyard was found nearby.

RICHMOND CASTLE
North Yorkshire

OH DEAR, oh dear – another 'Underground Tunnel/ Disappearing Ghostly Drummer Mystery'. The underground tunnel in question is said to run to Easby Abbey, a mile away. A drummer boy was sent to explore it and (inevitably) he was never seen again. His ghostly drumbeats can still be heard.

RING O'BELLS
Middleton, Manchester

THIS PUB is haunted by a Civil War Cavalier. After mysterious footsteps were heard in the cellar, the flagstones were pulled up to reveal weapons dating back to that era, as well as old bones.

The ghost has a habit of heartily slapping customers on the shoulder, and his laughter booms out from nowhere. Cavalier soldiers are said to still meet in the snug at night, and the area around the Cavalier's seat is marked by a drop in temperature.

ROAD BETWEEN
BATH & WARMINSTER
Wiltshire

AS SEBASTIAN Cliffe approached a bend at Limpley Stoke, all his dashboard gauges stopped functioning and he felt a strange chill. Then a ghostly face appeared at his windscreen. As it faded, his gauges began to work again.

ROAD BETWEEN BUCKTON &
FENWICK
Northumberland

A CLUMP OF TREES in this area is haunted by a figure in a dark cloak who vanishes. The story behind it is that in 1685 Sir John Cochrane was sentenced to death for supporting the Duke of Argyll. His daughter Griselle decided that somehow or other she was going to stop his execution from taking place. She disguised herself as a highwayman and held up the mail-coach carrying her father's death warrant. The delay in execution thus enabled Sir John's friends to arrange a pardon for him. Griselle now haunts the woods in her disguise.

ROAD BETWEEN
MARLBOROUGH & HUNGERFORD
Wiltshire

ONE AUTUMN NIGHT in 1956 four people were driving home from the cinema when they unexpectedly met the ghost of a boy's grieving father. Back in 1879 little Alfie Watts worked for a carter. One day Alfie tragically met an early death when he was crushed under the wheels of a cart.

A memorial was erected to him on the roadside by the villagers. Frederick Moss and his friends described the ghost in the middle of the road, as tall and thin, wearing a long brown coat, standing with his back to his son's memorial. Moss got out of the car to investigate the strange character, but he had completely vanished. He even searched the roadside with a torch but found nothing. Moss's wife, a local woman, on being told of the incident said that it sounded suspiciously like Henry Pounds Watts, who had died in 1907. The appearance of Alfie's father that October night coincided with a plan to widen the road, thus destroying his son's memorial. The theory is that Henry was quite concerned about this, and this provoked him to manifest himself. The road was widened, but Alfie's little cross was lovingly replaced nearby.

ROAD BETWEEN THE MOUNT
& BARFORD BRIDGE
Rushton, Northamptonshire

ALONG THIS PART of the A6003 which runs from Corby to
Kettering, lies an ancient burial-mound. The area was
excavated in 1964 and skeletons were uncovered in the
process. Numerous witnesses have since seen a monk
crossing the road with "something" in his arms.

ROAD BETWEEN NUNNEY &
CRITCHILL
Somerset

THIS STRETCH of highway is said to be haunted by a
phantom hitchhiker. The ghost has been described as
looking between 30/40 and wears a checked sports jacket.
He has a habit of stopping cars and asking to be dropped at
Nunney Catch, but as the unsuspecting motorist reaches
the village his passenger disappears. Three reports of this
roadside menace have been passed onto the Frome police.

ROAD SOUTH
Great Snoring, Norfolk

BEFORE WORLD WAR II a motorist driving along this road
inadvertently drove right through a phantom white hound.
The driver was so stunned by this experience that he
abandoned his car.

ROBIN HOOD'S GRAVE
Llansannan, Clwyd, Wales

THERE ARE MANY that say that this damaged tumulis is
haunted, and people have made a point of avoiding it at
night. Whether this local rumour has any foundation I
cannot say, simply because everything about this site seems
uncertain, even as to the justification of its name which is
very arguable to say the least. Robin Hood has as many
graves dotted around the British Isles as King Arthur.

ROCHESTER CASTLE
Kent

ROCHESTER CASTLE was built in 1098, but its haunting
dates back from Good Friday 1264, when Simon de
Montfort, Earl of Leicester, besieged it. The castle was
valiantly defended by Crusader Ralph de Capo and his
fiancee, Lady Blanche de Warenne. Ralph left the castle to
pursue the rebels, amongst whom had been a suitor of Lady
Blanche's, namely Sir Gilbert Clare who seized the
opportunity to enter the castle behind Ralph's back. Ralph
had cause to look back at the castle, and was horrified to
see his lady love struggling with Sir Gilbert on the
battlements. Ralph recklessly shot an arrow, which
accidentally pierced Lady Blanche. Her ghost now roams
the battlements on the anniversary of her death, with the
arrow still embedded in her chest! Her footsteps have been
heard in the area as well. Another theory on the tragic
eternal triangle is that she committed suicide by jumping
off the Round Tower, which doesn't account for the arrow
protruding from her chest though.

ROYAL HOTEL
Hoylake, Cheshire

THE HOTEL was built in 1797. In 1943 a female member of staff reported seeing a strange man dressed in tweeds, walking down the passage to the ballroom. Twice he vanished, and every movement he made was noiseless. A barman saw him pass from the billiards room and vanish in the passage.

A mysterious opening and closing of doors has also been observed, as well as disembodied footsteps. Small objects are apt to disappear, seemingly of their own accord. The ghost is said to be a man who drowned in the Irish Sea. His body was washed ashore, but the owners of the hotel uncharitably tossed him back! He has been making a point of returning ever since.

RUFFORD ABBEY
Nottinghamshire

DURING THE SPRING OF 1942 the ghost of a monk carrying a crucifix was seen by a soldier on guard duty. The ruins are also said to be haunted by a monk with a skull for a face.

RUFFORD OLD HALL
Nr Ormskirk, Lancashire

THIS 15TH CENTURY HOUSE is haunted by a Grey Lady, a man in Elizabethan costume and many believe none other than Queen Elizabeth I herself. The ghostly young man has been sighted standing beside a fireplace in the Great Hall. Gloriana herself has been seen twice in the dining-room, and on each occasion she vanished. The Grey Lady has been spotted near the main entrance, in the grounds and on the drive leading up to the church. She was even on one occasion seen enjoying a piano recital in a ground-floor room!

The Grey Lady is believed to be Elizabeth Hesketh. Her husband disappeared during a war with the Scots soon after their marriage. She was sighted as recently as 1981 by the administrator late one night. Notable occasions in the history of the house include a visit by William Shakespeare in 1584, and a secret room that was found in 1949 which was believed to be where Catholic priests were hidden. However, there is no evidence to suggest that Good Queen Bess ever visited the house, and so I can only assume that the opulent spectre in the dining-room is probably another eminent lady of that era.

RUINED CHAPEL
St Davids, Dyfed, Wales

GHOSTLY hymn-singing has been heard in these ruins, on the nights before and after the 1st of March – St David's Day.

ST ALBANS ABBEY
Hertfordshire

PHANTOM MONKS have been heard singing matins here at
2:00 AM.

ST ANDREWS CATHEDRAL
Fife, Scotland

THE CATHEDRAL is now sadly in ruins, but the Round
Tower is said to be haunted by a Woman in White, or Grey
(there seems to be a difference of opinion as to what she
wears). She has been seen very little in recent times, but
she was spotted by a couple in 1975, who thought that she
was real. She moved towards them, wearing a veil, and
then promptly vanished.

ST ANNE'S CASTLE
Great Leighs, Essex

THIS PUB lays claim to being the oldest in England, which
as I have already pointed out (*Ferry Boat Inn*) is an
arguable statement. There have also been 100 signed

statements from witnesses swearing that the inn is haunted. A visitor who was sleeping in one of the bedrooms was woken by shouts. When he jumped out of bed the noises stopped, but not surprisingly he had no rest for the rest of the night. A girl who was allocated the same room, (on a different occasion), spent the entire night huddled at the window. A mysterious black shape which frequents the room has been seen by many witnesses. Other supernatural phenomena includes bangs and thumps, furniture being moved, cold blasts of air, curtains torn down, bedclothes ripped off, clothes thrown around and general chaos whenever the ghost is present. A brewer's delivery-man refused to go into the cellar after seeing something very unpleasant down there, and a girl saw something so nasty in the downstairs bar that she passed out on the spot. Both have refused to impart what it was that they saw.

A child is alleged to have been killed here, and the inn was once a retreat of monks, Royalists and highwaymen. Any one of whom could cause the mayhem described above.

ST BENET'S ABBEY
Ludham, Norfolk

THE RUINS are said to be haunted by a monk called Ethelwold. He was hanged above the gateway for letting in King William the Conqueror's army.

ST CUTHBERT'S CAVE
Hazelrigg, Northumberland

LEGEND STATES that St Cuthbert's body was rested here while it was being transported to Durham Cathedral. It is haunted, not by the lad himself, but by an eccentric character entitled the 'Hazelrigg Dunny'. This ghost was said to have buried some treasure here and then forgot precisely whereabouts it was. He sometimes takes the form of a dun-coloured horse.

ST DUNSTAN'S
East Acton, London

ST DUNSTAN'S is haunted by monks, who file in procession up the centre aisle. During the 1930s the curate claimed to have seen them, and in 1944 the vicar confirmed that ghosts were active in his church. He himself had seen them on many evenings, and even claimed to have spoken with one of them. He said that he had seen no less than six hooded monks walking towards him, and that the ghosts had then passed right through him. The church was built a mere century ago, but in the Middle Ages a Chapter of St Bartholomew was sited near here.

ST JAMES' PALACE
London

THE GHOST at this royal residence is a decidedly grisly spectacle – a man sits propped up in bed with his throat cut. The haunting is the aftermath of what nearly became a very big scandal of its time. On 31 May 1810 a man called Sellis, who was the Italian valet to the Duke of Cumberland, was found murdered in his bed. Rumour claimed that the culprit was the Duke himself, who denied it vigorously and claimed that Sellis had tried to kill him, and when foiled in the attempt had taken his own life. The Duke escaped any charges but suspicion still hangs over him.

ST JAMES'S PARK
London

THE BARRACKS of the Coldstream Guards were sited here during the 1870s. At the same time there were lurid tales of the ghost of a headless woman, who was said to walk from Cockpit Steps, in Birdcage Walk, and towards the lake. One guardsman made a solemn statement that he had seen the ghost rise up in front of him at 1:30 one morning. He said she had worn a red-striped gown and vanished as he watched. Another guardsman reported shrieks from the empty Armoury House at night. He said the voices were shouting "bring a light!" He shouted back and then heard the sounds of sash windows being flung open. When a search of the building was made, nothing was found. The records were then searched and provided the story behind the haunting. In 1784 a sergeant of the Guards had killed his wife decapitated her and finished his grisly task by tossing her corpse into the lake. She was later identified by her distinctive dress. She is still to be seen, with blood spurting from her neck. In 1975 a London taxi-driver said he had seen her stepping out in front of his cab as she glided across Cockspur Street and vanished.

ST JOHN'S CHURCH
Boughton, Northamptonshire

THE CHURCH is haunted by a ghost colourfully called 'Captain Slash'. This 19th century gang-leader haunts the ruins at Christmas time.

ST MARY'S CHURCH
Beaminster, Dorset

THERE APPEARS to be a depressingly high number of ghosts caused by murder including that of children. One of these in 1728, was a local schoolboy called John Daniels who was strangled in the village. His murderer was never brought to justice, and his ghost still roams around the church.

ST MARY'S CHURCH
Deerhurst, Gloucestershire

IN 1965 a couple arrived to look round the church. The man went into the building whilst his wife waited in the car, watching a lady in Edwardian costume who was standing on the path. The man returned after some 15 minutes and announced that he didn't like the atmosphere in the church. He didn't see the ghostly lady on the path.

ST MARY'S CHURCH
Reigate, Surrey

DURING THE SPACE of a few days in 1975 a witness heard ghostly singing coming from the locked church, and saw a woman walking down the path towards the building, who vanished when only a few feet from the witness. The bemused spectator returned to the church a few months later, and saw the same ghostly lady in the long white dress.

ST MICHAEL'S ISLAND
Langness, Isle of Man

THE 12TH CENTURY ruins on this island were once the burial-place of people who were drowned at sea. Their lost souls have been seen sitting on the graves and walking up from the shore.

The church itself is haunted by pirate raiders, who had been imprisoned here for murdering the priest and stealing his treasure. The unscrupulous killers drowned when they tried to set sail. There is a legend that if you knock on the outside of the church you will hear their screams and curses.

ST MICHAEL'S MOUNT
Marazion, Cornwall

THE 14TH CENTURY castle on this island contains a haunted four poster bed, which itself dates from the 17th century. A strange atmosphere has been felt around this unsavoury item of furniture, and there is a disturbing rumour that no child has ever been able to survive a night in it. The other curious case of the Unknown here is the ghost of a rather bewildered figure who wanders around the priory church.

ST OSYTH'S PRIORY
St Osyth, Essex

THE GREAT GATE HOUSE was originally a nunnery founded by St Osyth herself. Like most saints she was alleged to have met a very grisly end – decapitated by the invading Danes in 653 AD. Again, like most saints, colourful myths and legends have grown up about her death. She is said to have carried her head to the door of St Peter and St Paul's Church, and then promptly expired on the spot. Osyth walks again one night every year, carrying her head of course.

In more recent times the Priory was used as a convalescent home, and the patients reported seeing a ghostly monk here. A spectre in white robes has also been seen near the ruin but 'tis not the headless one.

ST PETER'S CHURCH
Preston Park, Brighton, East Sussex

DURING THE 1970s a couple were walking in the churchyard when they saw and spoke to a lady in Medieval costume. They had no idea that she was a ghost and assumed that she was wearing the costume for a historical pageant. They were curious that she hadn't bothered to answer them, and also that they couldn't hear her footsteps. On looking round they saw her fade away by a large tomb.

SALISBURY HALL
St Albans, Hertfordshire

KING CHARLES II bought the house as a present for his mistress Nell Gwynne in 1668. Nellie's ghost was once seen on the staircase by the grandfather of Winston Churchill. Another ghost has been known to walk with heavy footsteps outside a bedroom door. In the children's bedroom, situated directly over the Entrance Hall, some children claimed to have been disturbed by a strange figure standing by their bed. The governess verified the story and added that she herself had seen something that she described as "terrifying" emerge from the wall by the fireplace.

SALLY-IN-THE-WOOD
Avon

THE GHOST of an old gypsy woman has been known to stagger across a bend in the Bath to Bradford-on-Avon road in this area. The site is also a notorious accident black spot.

SALMESBURY HALL
Preston, Lancashire

SALMESBURY HALL holds a tragedy regarding two star-crossed lovers in its 600 year-old history. One of the lovers was of the Roman Catholic faith, and the other was a Protestant. They knew they were not going to be given permission to marry each other so they decided to elope. But they never had a chance to carry out their wish. The young man together with a friend helping him to carry out his plan, were murdered on their way to the Hall by his prospective brother-in-law. Their bodies were buried near the chapel at the Hall. His lover, Lady Dorothy, was packed off to a convent abroad, where she died insane. During the 19th century, whilst the road was being rebuilt, three skeletons were discovered.

A ghostly Lady in White now passes along the corridors and gallery of the house, and into the grounds. Once while a play about the tragic lovers was being performed at the Hall, the phantom White Lady was observed crossing the grounds. She was also sighted in the grounds by two soldiers during World War II On another occasion the caretaker's daughter awoke to find the resident ghost leaning over her bed.

Ghost-hunters visiting the house have reported hearing weeping, the rustle of long skirts, and seeing a chair rocking of its own accord. A mysterious Grey Lady haunts the A677 road outside the Hall, and has been known to cause a few stirs of her own. During the 1970s a bus stopped on the road because the driver mistook the phantom for a passenger! At 4:30 one morning in 1981 a greengrocer was driving past the Hall, when he had to brake sharply to avoid ploughing straight into her. Not that I expect it would have mattered if he had.

SALTNEY JUNCTION
RAILWAY STATION
Nr Chester, Cheshire

IN THE so-called 'Good Old Days' a 'knocker-up' would be employed by the railway authorities to go around in the early morning tapping with a long pole on the bedroom windows, to make sure employees got to work on time. One morning the knocker-up saw the light of a bicycle-lamp heading in his direction. To his consternation the phantom cyclist and his machine both vanished. This ghost is said to have been a railway worker who hanged himself at the station. He has always been seen very early in the morning, and usually in winter.

SANDRINGHAM HOUSE
Norfolk

NO BRITISH stately home would be complete without a ghost but Sandringham, holiday home of the Royal Family, has a Christmas poltergeist as well as, it seems, a ghost. Supernatural phenomena of a physical nature on Christmas Eve, usually centres around the second floor servant's quarters. This includes Christmas cards being flung about, sheets being torn off beds, and the maids reporting a presence which tends to breathe heavily at them! Prince Christopher of Greece once saw the ghost of a mysterious masked woman sitting in one of the guest rooms. He later saw a portrait of her at Houghton Hall nearby, and recognised her as Dorothy Walpole! Not the Brown Lady of Raynham Hall? This means her ghost must visit Sandringham as the pretty, merry young lady she once was, and not the dowdy, cantankerous trouble-maker that she appears as at Raynham Hall.

SANDWOOD COTTAGE
Cape Wrath, Highlands, Scotland

SANDWOOD COTTAGE is extremely remote and is reckoned to be the most northerly-situated haunted house in Britain. It is haunted by the ghost of a tall man dressed as a sailor, who has been seen several times around the cottage ruins.

SAWSTON HALL
Cambridge, Cambridgeshire

ON 8 JULY 1553 Princess Mary Tudor was sleeping in the Tapestry Room when she was urgently woken by her host, John Huddleston. He warned her that due to the death of her brother, King Edward VI, the Duke of Northumberland had staged a coup to prevent Mary and her Catholic ideas from ascending the throne. The Princess was smuggled out of the house disguised as a milkmaid and watched from a safe vantage point as the Duke's soldiers set fire to the house. When Mary became Queen on 19 July, she remembered the allegiance of the Huddlestons, and repaid them by helping them to rebuild their house. Work was eventually completed in 1584. Her ghost has been seen in the Tapestry Room, which survived the fire, and also around the grounds. The playing of her virginal has also been heard.

SAVOY BINGO HALL
Folkestone, Kent

In 1870 an old cottage stood on this site, and in 1918 a theatre was opened here. The building was wrecked by fire in 1928, and re-opened during the 1930s. In World War II a young boy was killed when an extractor fan fell from the ceiling during bomb repairs.

In 1972 members of staff reported seeing a female phantom on the stairs, in the staff-room and walking through closed foyer doors. In May of that year a psychic investigator arrived on the scene. He reported the sinister feeling of being watched by unseen eyes, and observed as a row of seats snapped down, one after the other. Two nights later a sharp drop in temperature was felt, and a woman in 1930s clothes was seen standing in the centre of the aisle. It was noticed before she vanished, that she appeared to have a "weepy eye".

A week later several people decided to stay overnight in the theatre on a ghost-watching vigil. They reported that a colleague's walking-stick had appeared to rise up by itself. Other recorded phenomena was the sighting of a black, shapeless mass which appeared on stage and moved towards the balcony before vanishing, as well as voices heard from the balcony, and another sighting of the female phantom as she walked across the centre aisle before vanishing. The sister of the young boy who had been killed in the theatre during the War, was shown a photograph of the ghost. She confirmed that it was her mother, and that she had been afflicted with a weepy eye.

SCARBOROUGH CASTLE
North Yorkshire

THE CASTLE is haunted by a silent and shadowy figure who is thought to be the ghost of Piers Gaveston, the favourite of the homosexual king, Edward II, who bestowed the title Earl of Cornwall on his beloved friend. Gaveston created a wave of controversy wherever he went, and eventually he had to surrender the castle to the barons on condition that he was allowed a fair appraisal of his alleged misdemeanours. Up until then he had bravely resisted surrender until hunger had driven him to give in. But the dastardly Warwick broke his word and had Gaveston beheaded outside the castle walls.

His restless spirit now haunts the ruins. There have also been reports of a headless ghost, which could be Gaveston, who tends to try to drive over the battlement edge any unsuspecting person who happens to be lingering at the castle after dark. Perhaps he keeps hoping that one of them might be a descendant of Warwick!

SCHIEHALLION
Tayside, Scotland

AT THE EAST END of Rannock Moor strange beings are believed to roam. Evil spirits haunt the hills, and if that isn't enough there is also the shadowy figure of a phantom hound.

SCOTNEY CASTLE
Lamberhurst, Kent

FOR MANY YEARS Elizabeth Durrell kept this moated 14th-century castle locked-up. In 1720 her son Arthur died, but as his coffin was being lowered into the ground, a cloaked figure said to a mourner "that is me they think they are burying". During the 19th century sexton John Bailey found Arthur's coffin resting in Scotney Chapel, but inside were only heavy stones. It was true that Arthur hadn't died when he was "buried". He used his pretended death to cover up a smuggling racket that he operated, using secret hiding-places at the castle to carry out his errant deeds.

On one occasion Arthur threw a Revenue Officer into the moat, where the wretched man drowned. The murdered civil servant is now said to rise from the stagnant water, walk to the great door and hammer on it with his fists. When the door is opened he disappears. Very tiresome of him. Unfortunately this story is as unlikely as it sounds. There is a strong chance that it may have been entirely concocted by a local waiter, when working as a part-time guide for the then owner, Mr Hussey.

SEATON DELAVAL HALL
Whitley Bay, Northumberland

THIS HOUSE, designed by Sir John Vanbrugh in optical illusion style (it looks much bigger than it really is), was completed in 1728. The ghost of a Grey Lady has been seen at a window in the West Wing ever since.

SECOND-HAND CITY
West Kensington, London

THIS GLORIFIED flea-market was once a Methodist chapel. In 1966 an old prostitute, Annie Doonan, was found battered to death in the basement.

Annie had disappeared at Christmas 1965, when she was seen leaving the *Old Oak Inn* at 10:30 PM, accompanied by a young man. Both were a bit worse the wear for liquor. Annie wasn't seen again until her corpse was discovered in the basement here. The culprit was soon arrested, and he confessed that he had killed her accidentally in a quarrel over her "fee". He was sentenced to life imprisonment.

After the chapel had become a bric-a-brac market, reports of a haunting began to appear in the newspapers. A man working in the Antiques Section claimed that he had seen a pinkish shape in a long hooded robe hanging in mid-air. An upholsterer working late watched as a phantom glided past the chairs he was mending. He vowed never to work late again! A witness passing the building at 3:00 in the morning reported that all the lights were on, but when the staff arrived a few hours later they found everything in darkness. Witnesses are quick to assert that the ghost seems a very contented one, and has often been seen gliding down to the basement, usually disappearing near the fireplace or sitting next to the fire. It has also been several times around some Victorian chairs in the store-room. Other reported phenomena includes footsteps heard in the empty building and objects mysteriously moved. No-one is willing to state who the ghost is, but it sounds very unlikely that such a happy soul is poor old Annie, who ended her days in such a humiliating way.

269

SEDGEMOOR BATTLEFIELD
Westonzoyland, Somerset

THE FAMOUS Battle of Sedgemoor took place here in 1685, and like most old battle-sites a haunting is now associated with it. On one occasion a couple nearly ran into some strange men carrying staves and pikes. There have been numerous sightings of these characters.

SELBORNE
Hampshire

SELBORNE VILLAGE was the home of Gilbert White, the naturalist, and it also seems to have more than its fair share of supernatural phenomena. The steep hill known as 'The Hanger' is the favourite spot of some mysterious phantoms. The Priory here was dissolved in 1484, but ghostly monks have been seen in the vicinity of the building and along the lane ever since. A phantom hound lurks at the 15th century farm. The vanishing dog can usually be seen at around 9:00 in the evening. In 1976 a monk was seen by three people walking along the lane. The ghost of Gilbert White himself has also been sighted in his old garden and up on 'The Hanger'.

SHAFTESBURY ABBEY
Dorset

IN THE RUINS of this Saxon abbey is a horde of treasure (or so legend has it anyway), buried here by a monk. His ghost now walks in the ruins and has been seen disappearing into a wall.

SHAKESPEARE HOTEL
Fountain Street, Piccadilly, Manchester

THE HOTEL is haunted by a servant-girl, who was killed in the 19th century when her clothing caught fire in the kitchen. She has frequently been seen near the stairs. Other supernatural phenomena recorded here, includes the movement of an empty rocking-chair and the gas cookers activating themselves. In recent times a member of staff left the job after seeing the servant-girl's apparition on two separate occasions.

Former landlord Harold Bailey once remarked that the bar was afflicted with various cold spots, and his dog and cat both ran out of the building the day he moved in, and refused to return.

SHAUGH BRIDGE
Plymouth, Devon

THE WILD HUNT are said to have been heard here. This is a pack of ghostly hounds who, when heard (they are never seen), usually portend a death or disaster of some kind or another.

SHAW'S CORNER
Ayot St Lawrence, Hertfordshire

THIS APPEARS to be a very insubstantial rumour that Lawrence of Arabia haunts the home of George Bernard Shaw. This is usually based on the connection that he was a friend of Shaw's. This haunting appears to be more a case of wishful thinking though I'm afraid.

SHEPPEY'S RESTAURANT
Shepherd Street, Mayfair, London

THE RESTAURANT has stood for more than 300 years, and part of it was once a theatre. During the 18th century the ground floor was used as a coffee-house, whilst the upper floors were lodging-rooms for highwaymen. It was also the home of Regency dandy Beau Brummell. The resident ghost could either be the obsessively fussy dresser himself (who died in an asylum abroad) or a highwayman. He appears to have a mischievious disposition. Cleaners working here in the early morning have felt their bottoms being pinched and their dresses tugged! He is described as being tall and thin, and usually wears a black coat. But his features are always in shadow. Various attempts to exorcise him have all failed.

SHUTE BARTON
Axminster, Devon

THE RESIDENT Grey Lady at this Medieval house dates from the Civil War, when Shute Barton was a Royalist stronghold. Lady de la Pole was captured by the Roundheads in a grove of trees near the house. They hanged her from a tree, and this area is now known as The Lady Walk. At one time the house was utilised as a girl's school, and reports of the Grey Lady continued to be made. A young teacher sighted her walking amongst the trees.

Lady de la Pole has also been seen by a pupil, and the staff's pet dog would bark inexplicably when near the Lady Walk. Other phenomena includes the mysterious movement of objects, including furniture and a heavy piano, all without making a single sound. Doors lock and unlock themselves, lights switch themselves on and off, and a phantom white cat walks through walls. In April 1979 two National Trust members saw the Grey Lady walking through the trees. She vanished.

SILVERWOOD COLLIERY
Rotherham, South Yorkshire

IT WAS DEEP DOWN in the mines here that miner Stephen Dimbledy saw a ghost. He said that the figure of a fairly solid form appeared out of nowhere. It seemed like an ordinary person until he shone his torch onto the face, and found there were no features. Understandably he turned and ran, vowing never to go back down the mine.

SISSINGHURST CASTLE
Kent

NOWADAYS THE CASTLE is chiefly famous for being where the odd couple Harold Nicolson and Vita Sackville-West made their home. In earlier times a priest had been walled-up in the castle, and his ghost is said to walk in the gardens. Visitors have reported hearing disembodied footsteps walking beside them. Another ghost is thought to be Sir Harold himself. He had a habit of clicking his teeth on his tongue, and this noise has been heard in the castle since his death.

SIZERGH CASTLE
Kendal, Cumbria

SIZERGH CASTLE was owned by the Strickland family from 1239 until 1950, when it was passed to the National Trust. Queen Catherine Parr haunts the tapestried room in the tower that she slept in, and her presence has been detected here but the room above Catherine's is also haunted, by the cries of a woman. This unfortunate lady was confined in here whilst her husband was away fighting in the Border Wars, and she slowly went insane. In another room the floorboards have often been found inexplicably pulled up.

SKULL HOUSE
Appley Bridge, Wigan, Lancashire

THIS RATHER unsavoury-sounding residence comes complete with a priest's hole, and leaded windows decorated with skulls. The skull itself rests on a beam in the living-room, and as is to be expected forms yet another Screaming Skull Legend. The skull is said to be what remains of a monk, who would vanish up the chimney to his secret room directly above whenever danger was at hand. Unfortunately he wasn't clever enough to outwit Cromwell's troops, who lit a fire in the grate, thus forcing the monk to show his face. He was then decapitated by them.

But that isn't the only theory behind the grisly memento (there always seems to be two possible stories behind a Screaming Skull Legend). Another idea is that the skull was once a knight, who was knocking around in the days of King Arthur, until he was killed on the banks of the River Douglas. Naturally medical evidence disagrees with both theories and asserts that the skull is that of a woman. There is really no need to go into any more detail because all Screaming Skull Legends appear to be the same. This one was once thrown into the river, but needless to say it found its way back to the house again.

SLIEU WHALLIAN
St Johns, Isle of Man

WITCHES were tortured to death on this hill, by being rolled downhill in a barrel full of spikes. The area is now haunted by the agonised cries of a murdered witch, usually heard in a howling wind.

SNOWSHILL MANOR
Broadway, Gloucestershire

A FORMER OWNER of this Tudor manorhouse turned a top-floor room into a special place where he could practice his magical skills, even painting a pentagram on the floor. Whether due to the amateur wizard or not, the house certainly has an effect on many who visit it. Some people have even adamantly refused to cross the threshold and enter the building.

Another legend of the manor dates back to St Valentine's Eve 1604, when Anne Parsons was forcibly married to a fortune-hunter in the notorious top-floor room, but she refused to spend the night in it.

During the 19th century a farm worker, Richard Carter, was riding along the lane, when he suddenly found he was being accompanied by the ghost of his dead employer, Charles Marshall! An intriguing epilogue to this episode is that the ghost went on to meet Carter in the chaff-house at midnight, entrusting him with a message for his widow.

In more recent times, in 1981 to be exact, a cleaner, Mrs

West, reported hearing mysterious footsteps at the house. A monk also haunts the manor, usually by skulking on the stairs and in the lane. The explanation for his presence is that a Priory stood here in Medieval times.

SOUTHER FELL
Mungrisdale, Cumbria

ON MIDSUMMER'S EVE 1735 a phantom army was seen on the mountain. It was seen again in 1745, but no trace of the soldiers or horses was ever found.

SOUTH EFFORD HOUSE
Aveton Gifford, Devon

ACCORDING TO old village gossip, the one-time owner of this house, a retired naval officer, was completely mad. He was one of those overly-sensitive bad-tempered old devils who can frequently be found in small villages. One of his unsociable traits was to lean out of the windows yelling at affectionate courting couples as they passed the house. When he eventually lay dying he went to his Maker shouting vehement curses at the villagers. There was to be no peace for anyone after he'd gone either, as apparently his vitriolic curses can still be heard ringing around the house.

His ghost certainly has no chance of becoming lonely. South Efford House is also haunted by the spectre of a manservant who hanged himself over one of the stairways. His swinging corpse has occasionally been sighted by extra-perceptive visitors.

The third and final ghost only appears in daylight hours. He is said to have been a ferryman who got very upset when a former owner blocked up the doorway which opened onto the steps leading down to the river. The ghost of the ferryman has been sighted heading purposefully to the blocked doorway, armed with a crowbar!

SPEKE HALL
Liverpool, Merseyside

IN 1731 a lady called Mary Norreys inherited this Elizabethan dwelling. Her luck changed when she had the misfortune to marry the gambling no-good scoundrel, Lord Sidney Beauclerk in 1736. He bankrupted them very early on in the marriage, and Mary reacted by tossing their baby son into the moat and then, for good measure, ran and drowned herself. She is now said to haunt the Tapestry Room. Now the sad story of Mary Beauclerk is all good dramatic stuff, but the true facts seem to reveal that Mary didn't depart this mortal coil until 1766 – some 30 years after her marriage to the no-good bounder. Her only child, a boy called Topham, survived into adulthood and inherited the house from her. He didn't die until 1780.

Even so, Mary is still said to haunt the house, and a Miss Adelaide Watt, who lived here, reckoned that she had seen Mary's ghost strolling into a wall in the Tapestry Room. The ghost even put in an appearance at one of Miss Watt's dinner-parties, and the guests spoke to her before she then did her party-piece of vanishing into a wall. A room was added to the house in 1598, in which a White Lady has remained since the 19th century. Other phenomena includes strange footsteps in empty passages, voices from equally deserted rooms and a cradle rocked by invisible hands.

SPRINGHILL
Moneymore, Co Londonderry, Northern Ireland

THE HON. ANDREW STUART once claimed that he had had the exasperating experience of having his belongings mysteriously moved at this 17th century house. It is just one example of a strange but extremely intriguing haunting. A governess sitting in one room overheard two children in the next, calmly discussing a woman standing by the fireplace (curious how children seem so much more casual with ghosts than adults do).

During the late 19th century a Miss Wilson stayed at the house. She was sitting reading in the Cedar Room until very late, after her hostess had gone to bed and suddenly realised that her hostess had left her diary behind and decided to take it up to her. In the moonlight she saw a tall woman standing at the top of the stairs. Miss Wilson watched as the phantom went to a door, threw her hands up in despair and then vanished. On another occasion a different guest, Miss Hamilton, stayed in the room the ghost had so mysteriously reacted to. The next morning she informed her hostess that she had been lying in bed, minding her own business, when suddenly the room had become full of excited servants! The door opened and a light shone in, which appeared to quell the emotional rabble. Miss Hamilton's hostess said that this door was now papered over.

A later owner was more curious. She had the door re-opened, to find a bricked-up window and fireplace. It also contained a pair of gloves and a bag of bullets! A former National Trust guardian, Teddy Butler, reported seeing a Woman in Black at the bottom of the stairs and hearing marching footsteps. He said that during his period of administration, 1964-1977, he and his wife often heard the heavy footsteps on the stairs and landing. One March

278

afternoon at 4:00 he had collided with a woman going through the back door. She vanished. He described her as small, thickset, with grey hair. She is believed to be the ghostly wife of a Colonel Conyngham, who served in the Crimea. The miniature portrait of her vanished a few years ago, and was then mysteriously returned in a brown paper cover! Then it vanished again, and it hasn't been seen since.

STAINMOOR PASS
Cumbria

IN 1937 a lorry-driver was snowbound on the Pass, so he decided to while away the time by going for a walk. He reported seeing a headless woman riding a white horse across the moor. The story behind her is that 900 years ago a Saxon Chieftain lived on the edge of the moor. There was a running feud going on between him and a Norman gentleman over hunting land.

The Saxon grew impatient with his enemy and took the daughter of the Norman as hostage. He then discovered that he rather liked his attractive prisoner and wanted her as his wife. The girl was eventually rescued by the Normans, but as they bore her back across the moors the enraged Saxon pursued them. When he caught up with them he severed her head with his sword.

STANBRIDGE
Bedfordshire

THE STORY of the Stanbridge phantom hitch-hiker is a favourite with many writers on the paranormal, and I don't see why I should be an exception. In October 1979 Roy Fulton was driving home from a darts match, when he saw a young man hitching a lift near the first group of houses in the village, so he decided to do the decent thing and let him on-board. He was curious that his passenger didn't say a word, he merely pointed towards Totternhoe when questioned as to where he wanted to go. After a couple of miles he vanished – without even getting out of the van!

Fulton reported that the man had looked about 20 years of age and wore a rather old-fashioned suit. The story of Fulton's experience on that dark, foggy night is still a reliable one to scare lone motorists with.

STIRLING CASTLE
Central Region, Scotland

THE CASTLE is chiefly famous for being the site of the coronation of Mary Queen of Scots in 1543. It also has a rather good haunting. A woman in a long, pink dress walks from the castle to the church, and a sinister Green Lady roams the castle itself. The latter phantom seems to be a portender of doom, as her appearances always precede a disaster. Mysterious footsteps have also been heard in the area known as the Governor's Block. In the 1820s a sentry was found dead here with a look of horror on his face.

STOKE (CHURCH)
Devon

IN 1973 the vicar reported seeing a figure in a monk's habit in the churchyard. He stood on the grass to wait for him, and was rather disconcerted when he vanished. Other witnesses have also sighted the ghostly monk.

STOURHEAD
Stourton, Mere, Wiltshire

THE PRESENT 17TH CENTURY building supercedes an earlier house that was pulled down by Henry Hoare, and stood between the present house and the road from Zeale to Kilmington. The earlier house had a history of violence and murder, as well as a ghost that refused to go away when the house was demolished. The 8th Lord Stoughton, Charles, was hanged for murder in Salisbury market-place in 1557. Due to his elevated position in the community he was entitled to be strung up with a silken rope, instead of a hempen rope!

His Lordship's ghost, and those of his victims, now apparently roam the fields and roads near Stourhead House and Kilmington Church. Lord Stourton has sometimes been seen riding a horse, followed by people in 16th century costume. They all gallop towards Kilmington, where they disappear into the door of the church. The house itself attracts many strange rumours and legends, and children are loath to play near there. Visitors have reported seeing people in old-fashioned costume, and have spoken of a strange atmosphere in the building. Others have claimed to have seen men in period costume fighting each other without making any sound, whilst some people have only heard the fight, but have not actually seen anything.

SUDELEY CASTLE
Winchcombe, Gloucestershire

QUEEN CATHERINE PARR was certainly a lady who travelled around a lot, numerous old houses up and down England were once her home, and this 12th century castle is no exception. For once though, she doesn't haunt this one.

The ghost here is identified as a former housekeeper called Janet. She has been sighted in the Main Bedroom, the Needlework Bedroom, and departing from the Rupert Room.

SUNDERLAND EMPIRE
Tyne & Wear

THE FOUNDATION STONE of the theatre was laid by veteran comedienne Vesta Tilley on 29 September 1906, and it possesses two ghosts. Sometime in the early 1950s an Assistant Stage Manager, Molly Moxelle, walked out of her digs and never returned. No trace of her was ever found. A Dress Circle Barmaid, Kitty Naylor, often reported hearing mysterious footsteps walking down the stairs to the bar. They would habitually cross the front of the bar and then return upstairs. This was said to be the same route that 'Disappearing Molly' had taken every evening, when she did her rounds to check that all was in order. Another former employee of the theatre haunts the dressing-room area. Mrs Johnstone was the theatre violinist, and she collapsed one evening in the orchestra pit, dying later in her dressing-room. In the late 1970s the Manager, Ron Jameson, watched a lady in a long dress walk up the aisle at the edge of the Dress Circle. She vanished. Her dress was thought to be similar to one worn by the unfortunate Mrs Johnstone.

SUN INN
Chipping, Lancashire

IF ALL LEGENDS around ghost stories were true, then I wouldn't be surprised if the countryside used to be littered with the corpses of jilted young ladies!

Lizzie Dean was a serving-wench at this pub in the mid-19th century. After being rejected by her lover she hanged herself in the attic. She left a note stipulating that she had to be buried in the path leading to St Bartholomew's Church, so that when her ex-lover walked over her grave every Sunday he would be reminded of her. Lizzie's ghost rested in peace until alterations were made to the area at the end of the 19th century and Lizzie's grave was moved into a new position, underneath a yew tree. But Lizzie didn't think much of this new arrangement and her ghost took to frequenting the pub again. She became such a regular visitor that landlord Ted Oakes even went on television to talk about his own resident ghost. On one occasion he related how he was sweeping the hall when the telephone rang but on returning to the hall he found that unseen hands had finished the job for him and replaced the broom against a different wall to the one he had left it on. One night, after closing-time, he watched Lizzie walk across the bar and through a piano. A year later Ted had a hatch-way knocked though a wall, which revealed a hitherto undiscovered door that had once led to another room. This was where Lizzie's ghost had been heading when he had seen her.

SWANTON NOVERS RECTORY
Norfolk

A MOST UNUSUAL haunting occurred here in August 1919 when oil, water, meths and sandalwood oil spurted profusely from the walls and ceiling.

SYDERSTONE RECTORY
Norfolk

WHAT A GODSEND to the avid ghost-hunter these East Anglian rectories are! This one suffered a protracted outburst of poltergeist activity, which finally ended its 40-year reign of terror in 1833. Recorded phenomena here included groans, doors slamming, running footsteps in the passages, and knocking.

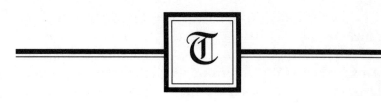

TALBOT INN
Oundle, Northamptonshire

WHEN KING JAMES I (or VI depending on your side of Hadrian's Wall) took over the English throne, he demanded that Fotheringay, where his mother Mary Queen of Scots had been beheaded, be completely destroyed. The landlord of the *Talbot Inn*, William Whitwell, purchased some of the fixtures and fittings, including the staircase. The unsuspecting licensee didn't realise that Mary's ghost was part of the deal. Sounds of a woman sobbing or singing (nobody seems quite sure which) have been heard from Rooms 5 and 6. Because the phenomena usually occurs around 8 February, the date of Mary's execution, the noises have usually been attributed to her.

A woman in a buff-coloured dress has been sighted in the building. A barmaid, sleeping in Room 5, woke in the early hours to see a clammy mist pervading the room. She also had the weird sensation of being forcibly held down by an unseen presence. Another former employee, a Mrs Beesley, saw an apparition outside the front door that so unnerved her, that her husband had to escort her into the building from then on.

Guests who are foolish enough to question the Scottish Queen's presence may suddenly find her portrait crashing onto the bar-room floor! A local press reporter once spent a night in another haunted room at the inn, Room 7, and took a photograph at the stroke of midnight. It came out blank, which is not surprising as ghosts seem to have an aversion to having their picture, or one of their boudoir, taken, (show-offs like Dorothy Walpole, Raynham Hall, are the exception rather than the rule).

If Mary is behind all the supernatural phenomena at the *Talbot Inn*, then unlike most decapitated ladies, she seems to have miraculously kept her head!

TALLEY
Dyfed, Wales

DURING THE 1970s ghostly monks were heard chanting in the ruins of Talley Abbey. An underground passage links the old Abbey to Talley Manor House, which is thought to be haunted by a cloaked man, possibly yet another monk.

TAMWORTH CASTLE
Staffordshire

THE GRAND-DAUGHTER of King Alfred the Great, Editha, has been seen in her nun's habit climbing the stairs leading into the Tower Room, and ghostly sighs and moans attributed to her have even been recorded on tape. A phantom lady has also been seen in the Tower Room and on the terrace.

TARRANT HINTON
Dorset

MAJOR BLANDFORD, worthy member of the British Army, had an illegal penchant for poaching. On 16 December 1780 he and some male companions were stalking deer in the grounds of Cranborne Chase, when they were caught by the gamekeepers. In the ensuing fracas the men were wounded, and one of the gamekeepers died during a fierce gun battle across Chettle Common.

Blandford lost his hand in the process but managed to flee to London, where he died. His severed hand was buried in Pimperne Churchyard. Local legend doth say that it sometimes appears in search of its arm!

TATTON PARK
Knutsford, Cheshire

IN AUGUST 1981 the Director of Tatton Park, Commander Peter Neate, was plagued by ghostly interference with his television set. This always seemed to happen on the dot of 9:20 in the evening. The television aerial would also fall out, and a candle once fell off its holder and onto his plate. A ghost in casual wear, i.e a sports jacket and flannel trousers, has also been seen by the Commander going into the bathroom!

TEMPLE NEWSHAM HOUSE
Leeds, West Yorkshire

THIS 17TH CENTURY house is haunted by an old lady in blue. In 1908 Lord Halifax reported seeing her walking across his bedroom. He said that she wore a shawl around her shoulders. Another ghost is a small boy who has an unnerving habit of suddenly stepping out of cupboards. Weird screams have also been heard here.

TESTWOOD HOUSE
Totton, Southampton, Hampshire

NOW KNOWN by the excruciating name of "Rumasa" (Testwood House sounds much more distinguished), this was one of King Henry VIII's hunting-lodges. Strange footsteps have been heard in the passages here. On one occasion two teenagers saw a tall man trying to open the front door, but when they called out to him he vanished.

The cook also reported seeing a man wearing a top-hat in the driveway. The same phantom has also been seen standing by the gate. A more disturbing experience was when the caretaker and his son heard the front door rattling violently, but no-one was there. The boy then saw a face at the window which slowly faded. In 1972 the secretary working in the building saw the elusive top-hatted gentleman in the downstairs reception room.

THEATRE ROYAL
Bath, Avon

THE BATH THEATRE ROYAL is haunted by the ghost of an 18th century actress, whose husband killed her lover in a duel. Grief-stricken, she hanged herself in her dressing-room. Her name unknown, she has gone down in posterity as yet another of Britain's mysterious Grey Ladies. On 23 August 1975 she appeared, sitting alone in a box, during a performance of *The Dame of Sark*, starring Dame Anna Neagle. The staff at the theatre have also noticed a strong aroma of jasmine from time to time.

In June 1963 one of the props for a production included a clock. To everyone's exasperation whenever the hands reached 12:30 during rehearsals it would chime three times. The stagehands decided that they had better remove the chime mechanism before the first performance! Another manifestation is a ghostly butterfly that tends to appear on stage during the pantomime season. This gentle spook has even been recorded on film by a local newspaper.

In 1954 an actor went into the empty theatre, but whilst on the stage he was disturbed to hear strange footsteps overhead. He decided to exit the building, and as he was leaving, via the stage door, a disembodied voice politely bade him "goodnight sir". Out of curiosity he went back to the stage and encountered a mysterious man in a long cape. The figure walked through a wall, and a door was heard slamming.

THEATRE ROYAL
Bow, London

WHEN THE THEATRE WORKSHOP was first established here the staff had to sleep in the dressing-rooms. The unpaid trusty old caretaker, George, slept in the boiler-room. In 1968 Old George died, leaving only a tin box of tips he had collected during his work at the theatre, secreted in a hiding-place. His last request when he died was that the box should be left in the care of the theatre ghost!

This phantom has been described as small, tubby and dressed in brown. People have claimed to have felt his friendly presence late at night. This ghost is believed to have been one Frederick Fredericks, who built the theatre in 1880. The ghost generally makes a nightly appearance to make sure that his carved initials stay in place in the centre of the proscenium arch.

THEATRE ROYAL
Bristol, Avon

THIS THEATRE, which was built in 1766, lays claim to being the oldest one still standing in Great Britain. The great tragic actress Sarah Siddons played here for four years from 1778 onwards, and her dressing-room remains intact. The actress Yvonne Mitchell was appearing here in *Macbeth*, when she saw a tall figure wearing a draped-style of costume (a vogue of dressing favoured by Miss Siddons apparently), standing in the scenery dock. The figure vanished. Miss Siddons's favourite role had been that of 'Lady Macbeth'.

THEATRE ROYAL
Drury Lane, London

AROUND 50 cleaners claim to have seen a ghostly man wandering around the Dress Circle in this theatre. He appears to be an 18th century dandy, and a visit from him usually portends a good run for the present show. There is usually an association between him and a skeleton that was uncovered by workmen inside a wall in the mid-19th century. The skeleton had a dagger in its ribs. Another ghost is that of the great clown, Joe Grimaldi, who died in 1837 with a wish that he should be buried near the theatre.

During the 1780s Grimaldi began his 45-year career here, and since his death, his ghost in full clownish make-up, has been seen staring into the Auditorium. His face also has an unnerving habit of being seen to peer out from among the audience and stare at the actors on the stage during a performance. Yet another ghost is Dan Leno who often appeared in pantomime here. The poor man went insane and died at the ludicrously young age of 43.

Stanley Lupino once claimed to have seen Leno's ghost, sleeping on a couch in one of the dressing-rooms. He also heard a curtain move, and saw a shadowy figure cross the room and go through the door. The Stage Door Keeper hadn't seen anything, but another actor saw it later and fainted from the shock. The American actress Betty Jo Jones was appearing here in a comedy when she felt unseen hands guide her across the stage, so that the audience could hear her better. Whenever a scene went well she felt someone give her a pat on the back. Another recipient of this ghost's goodwill was Doreen Duke, who was auditioning here for *The King and I*. She felt unseen hands on her shoulders giving her encouragement, and on leaving the stage she too was credited with a pat on the back. A ghostly Man in Grey never makes a point of appearing later than 6:00 in the evening, and is thought to be associated with a skeleton that was found buried at the corner of Russell Street and Drury Lane.

THEATRE ROYAL
Margate, Kent

THIS THEATRE is, like so many nowadays, currently utilised as a bingo-hall, but was built back in 1787. One of the ghosts is believed to have been an actor who threw himself from a stage box after being sacked. The box then suffered having his gloomy figure sitting at the back of it and was understandably shunned by the patrons, until the management had to concede and have it taken out.

During the 1890s Sarah Thorne, an ardent theatre lover, died. One of her after-death visits to her beloved theatre in 1963 caused two rehearsing chorus girls to faint when she joined them on the stage. In 1972 she caused a painter to run out of the building late at night. All this must be terribly demoralising for the poor phantom. She sometimes appears as a ball of light, and in such form has been sighted on the stage, in the auditorium, and in the dressing-room corridors. During the 1960s another painter reported hearing footsteps, thumps, a door banging loudly, and seeing the ball of light moving across the stage. Other phenomena reported here includes the emergency doors being bolted, the emergency lights turned out, the main lighting activating itself in the auditorium in the middle of the night, scenery props mysteriously moved, lights burning in the toilets, strange shuffling and thudding noises, and sudden blasts of ice-cold air.

THEATRE ROYAL & OPERA HOUSE
Northampton, Northamptonshire

THIS THEATRE has a ghost that floats along the passages, over a doorstep (which is an old gravestone) and into the carpenter's shop. The phantom was sighted by a scenic designer in December 1957. The witness reported hearing strange footsteps in the carpenter's shop, and then seeing a shabbily-dressed little old lady who ignored the witness's salutation, and carried on walking out into Swan Street. One Christmas Eve assistant John Lane found the atmosphere so oppressively eerie that he fled the building. He claimed that he felt he was being watched.

During the summer of 1958 Brian Douglas, stage carpenter and theatre photographer, saw the little old lady cross the passage from the workshop. In July 1960 a painter looked up and saw her standing on the fourth step up to the gallery. Various reports of sightings of the little old lady all confirm that she doesn't remain usually for longer than a minute. Chief electrician, Patrick George, saw two strange people sitting in the prompt box, who then vanished. In August 1960 two members of the Tape and Cine Club staged an all-night ghost-vigil, but naturally saw nothing. In January 1978, two budding ghost-hunters, James Graham and Paul Merrick, also decided to stage an all-night vigil, but again, nothing was forthcoming. They did mention an inexplicable feeling of being watched though, especially in the vicinity of the carpenter's shop. The ghost appears to have been an old lady who leased part of her garden to the theatre, so that they could build a carpenter's shop there. She insisted though on a right of way with a door opening into the shop.

THEATRE ROYAL
Winchester, Hampshire

THIS THEATRE'S chequered history goes as follows. In 1880 it was built as a market hotel. On 24 August 1914 it opened as a theatre. From 1922-1974 it was used as a cinema, but re-opened as a theatre in 1981.

One of its resident ghosts is John Simpkins, the builder. The second ghost is a lime-boy, who operated the spotlights. On one occasion a dancer fainted on-stage, after seeing a soldier who had been killed the day before in World War I, standing in the wings.

THEATRE ROYAL
York, North Yorkshire

YORK'S THEATRE ROYAL has one of those redoubtable Grey Ladies as its ghost. Actress Julie Dawn Cole saw her whilst rehearsing on stage one Christmas. She described her as wearing a hooded cloak, although her outline appeared to be intangible. Miss Cole added that the ghost's appearance had left her with a warm, happy feeling. The theatre was opened in 1740 on the site of St Leonard's Hospital (which knocks Bristol's claim to being the oldest theatre into a cocked hat). The ghost is believed to be a nun who was walled-up alive in the hospital for breaking her vows, but as the ghost appears to be a contented spirit, I would argue that the nun was probably willing to be bricked-up to show her true faith – a not uncommon wish of Roman Catholic nuns during the Middle Ages.

The Grey Lady has been seen by a former Lord Mayor, and has often been sighted in a small room near the dress circle. Many people in the theatre express a feeling that they are being watched by unseen eyes, and a drop in temperature has also been noticed. One actress saw her leaning over the edge of a stage box. In the autumn of 1975 a rehearsal was in progress, when the cast saw a strange light in the dress circle. The glow took on the top-half appearance of a nun, and lasted for a few seconds.

In 1965 some members of the cast set out to lay the ghost. In the small room near the dress circle they heard footsteps, and they saw a hooded woman enter through the closed door. A female witness screamed and the nun vanished.

THORINGTON HALL
Stoke-by-Nayland, Suffolk

A NEW STAIRCASE was put into this house in 1650, and since then the spectre of a little girl has been sighted on the dark landing. She is thought to have a possible connection with the Umfrevilles family who once lived here. A little girl in a brown dress has also been seen in an upstairs passage, and heavy footsteps have been heard (not the little girl's I should think!)

In 1937 a woman's shoe was found behind the

plasterwork in the living-room. This was believed to have been put there as a charm to ward away ghosts. The trouble is, it doesn't seem to have worked. Another peculiar incident was when some American tourists were being shown around the house a few years ago, and the bone of a pelvis suddenly fell from a cupboard in front of them!

THROWLEY HALL
Manifold Valley, Staffordshire

NOW IN RUINS, Throwley Hall was once the home of Oliver Cromwell's family. During Ollie's lifetime, a coachman was taking six members of the family to Ashbourne. He deposited them there and returned to the house. As he was about to set out to fetch them in the evening a torrential storm blew up. Nevertheless the dogged servant set out to pick them up. On their way back a sudden clap of thunder startled the horses, who bolted and pulled their cargo into the river. All were killed. A phantom coach-and-horses are now said to charge along what was once the drive of the house. During the past 30 years numerous people claim to have heard the phenomenon.

TINTAGEL
Cornwall

STRONGLY RUMOURED to be the birthplace of the legendary King Arthur, this enchanting (but very commercial) place also has other stories to tell. At midnight on Midsummer's Eve (always a strangely ethereal time) in 1965, Michael Williams and three other witnesses saw a mysterious light in the chapel windows here, even though the building was locked and bolted.

Williams's dog refused to go along the path to Barras Head, and has since refused to do so on numerous occasions. Merlin's ghost is also said to lurk in the cave named after him.

TINTERN ABBEY
Gwent, Wales

THE ABBEY RUINS here have an underground passage which leads from the Abbey to Trellech, three miles away. A ghostly monk has been seen kneeling near one of the west arches. He usually vanishes when people approach him.

TOBY INN
Edgeworth, Manchester

THIS BUILDING – described in the 1990 edition of the "Good Pub Guide" as "friendly and isolated" – has been plagued by a profusion of thumps in the night. During the mid-1970s the landlord claimed that he actually had a photograph of the ghostly presence. The photo, which was taken by a customer, apparently shows a leering man standing at the back of the bar. The customers have also sighted strange figures. One landlord had a heart-attack near the spot where the leering man had stood.

TOP RANK BINGO HALL
Sutton, Surrey

THIS BUILDING was opened in the mid-1930s, and converted into a bingo hall during the 1950s. There have been three tragic deaths here. A nightwatchman had a heart-attack whilst on duty, and a workman and a boilerman were killed during the conversion process. A mysterious Man in Grey has been sighted by cleaning staff, always between 6:00 and 7:00 in the morning. During the 1950s local residents often complained of organ music coming from the building in the early hours of the morning, which was rather unusual as the organ had been removed several years before!

In 1972 the building was completely re-wired, and the electricians had to work through the night. One of the men turned to find the grey ghost standing in the doorway. The apparition slowly vanished in front of him.

TOWER CINEMA
Peckham, London

ONE SATURDAY evening at midnight, manager Bernard Mathmore and projectionist Jerry Adams, were preparing to leave and started to walk towards the rear exit, when they realised that They Weren't Alone. They were in fact accompanied by a man walking 10ft off the ground. The figure seemed to glow and walked slowly across the stage and through a bricked-up recess in which the cinema organ had been housed. In 1953 two upholsterers were working late when they too saw the ghost, and one of them adamantly refused to return to work there. In 1954 the ghost was seen again by a construction worker. Cement bags were found torn open during renovation work, and water dripped from the ceiling in dry weather. A map dating back to 1819 revealed that the cinema stands on the site of an old chapel, the floor of which was situated 10ft above the cinema auditorium.

TOWER OF LONDON
Tower Hill, London

THIS AMAZING set of buildings which have played host to some incredible historic events dates back more than a 1000 years. Naturally because of its bloodstained history it houses legions of legendary ghosts. The earliest recorded spectral sighting was of Sir Thomas á Becket in 1241. More recent ghostly sightings include a long-haired lady seen in the Bloody Tower in 1970, and in 1977 a yeoman saw a man wearing a 1940s suit near the Traitor's Gate.

Anne Askew was tortured on the rack in the White Tower and her screams can still be heard. In 1954 a puff of smoke was seen to come out of a cannon, it formed into a cube and moved towards a watching officer. It dangled on the steps before vanishing when an alarm bell rang. In 1817 The Keeper of The Crown Jewels and his wife were sitting in the Martin Tower, when they saw a strange cylindrical object hover near the ceiling. When it touched the lady, The Keeper threw a chair at it and it vanished. Some soldiers once saw an axe fly around Tower Green by itself. The ghost of Anne Boleyn has been sighted on autumn evenings in the upper room of the Martin Tower, where she was imprisoned before her execution. The Martin Tower was also used as an animal menagerie until 1834 and in 1815 a sentry saw a huge bear near the door of the Martin Tower. The terrified soldier thrust his bayonet at the animal, and was so disturbed when it went right through the spectral beast, that he died of shock two days later.

A ghostly figure in white also wanders around the Martin Tower. In 1973 the occupants smelt a strange horsey smell, which is explained by the fact that the Earl of Northumberland used to exercise his horses on each side of the Tower. His ghost was sighted by sentries in the 19th century. An earlier Earl of Northumberland was killed in the Bloody Tower, and his ghost walks there on a nightly basis.

The two little princes were brutally murdered in the Bloody Tower as well, some say by King Richard III himself, and their pathetic little ghosts have been seen wandering about ever since. A nightguardsman saw a headless white female form here which vanished. The lady was seen by another guardsman in 1933. It is not really surprising that a guard's officer always claimed that he felt an unpleasant atmosphere in the vicinity of the Bloody Tower! In 1978 two sentries were patrolling this particular building when they felt a chilling blast of cold air. In January 1966 a young soldier, on guard near Traitor's Gate, heard the sound of marching feet. He raised his rifle ready for action. The sound now came from the Tower archway, but when he shouted a warning, there was no reply. He repeated this, and then felt a sharp drop in temperature. The soldier walked through the archway and couldn't see the sentry who was usually on duty outside the Bloody Tower. Another sentry soon joined him and said that he had heard the strange sound as well. On talking to their sergeant they found that he was already familiar with the 'Legend of the Marching Feet' and the resident Tower Warder also knew of it.

In 1967 the same soldier was on night-duty outside the Bloody Tower when he saw a mysterious light in the White Tower. It disappeared 20 minutes later, and was then seen passing from window to window. Many reckon that this light means that Anne Boleyn is having one of her restless prowls (one of her *many* restless prowls!) Sir Walter Raleigh haunts the walk that is named after him. In 1970 a visitor saw a woman at the window of the Bloody Tower. She vanished but was seen again by the same witness a few weeks later.

The Queen's House is haunted by a Grey Lady, and a

man in Medieval dress has been seen climbing the stairs there. In 1978 a visitor staying in the building heard chanting at night, as well as screeches and groans. Perhaps it is not so surprising then that many people feel that a certain room in this building has a horrible atmosphere. A mysterious scented aroma has also been noticed here, and two children related the horrifying story of how they felt they were being suffocated as they slept here.

Perhaps the most famous of all the ghost stories of the Tower concerns a guardsman who in 1864 saw a figure float out of a doorway towards him. He ran it through with his bayonet and then fainted. He was had up for a court-martial, but other soldiers backed his story by claiming that they had also seen the apparition, and he was acquitted. Another sentry saw the floating phantom one midnight, and reported that she was headless. It is inevitable then that the ghost is rumoured to be none other than poor old Anne Boleyn, who seems to lead an exhausting 'After Life' existence. She was executed at the tower on 19 May 1536, just one of many very famous captives in this ancient prison.

TOWN OF RAMSGATE
Wapping, London

ANOTHER PERSON who doesn't seem to do very much resting in peace is Judge Jeffries, although with his conscience I can't say I'm surprised. He haunts this pub, the front of which only dates from the 1930s, but the main structure goes back some 300 years. In 1688 the Judge was arrested on Wapping Stairs. *But* there is a difference of opinion as to the identity of this ghost. Some say it is a cavalier, others say it is a man in a nightshirt! Witnesses include such worthy characters as the Thames River Police.

TRAWSFYNYDD
Gwynedd, Wales

A PHANTOM COACH and horses was seen here on 30 December 1979.

TREASURER'S HOUSE
York, North Yorkshire

A REAL MIXTURE of vintages this building – the structure is mainly 17th and 18th century, with 13th century work in the undercroft, and Roman remains in the cellars. One of the Aislabie family has said to have haunted the house for more than 300 years. The story behind it is that in January 1674 a guest at the house, Miss Mary Mallorie, attended a ball at the Duke of Buckingham's house in Skeldersgate. The following morning Sir George Aislabie thought that Mary's fiancé, Jonathan Jennings, had insulted her honour and challenged him to a duel.

Sir George was fatally wounded in the fight, and his ghost has haunted the house ever since. Several people claim to have suddenly experienced a feeling of personal danger as they pass a certain door. A similar feeling has been attributed to the first-floor Tapestry Room. A former owner undertook extensive renovations of this room in 1897, and people haven't felt very happy about staying in it ever since. The room has always felt to be much colder than the rest of the house. Perhaps the room can also have an unhealthy effect on people; one woman killed her rotter of a husband in there!

During the 1950s a plumber's apprentice, Harry Martindale, was working in the cellars installing piping for the central heating. He heard the sound of a trumpet, which seemed to come nearer and nearer. Suddenly a huge horse came through the wall bearing a soldier in Roman costume! He was followed by an entire army on foot. They appeared to be walking in a dispirited manner and took absolutely no notice of poor Harry. He was later to describe them in great detail, and said they hadn't appeared to have a banner of any kind.

TRERICE
St Newlyn East, Cornwall

THIS MANOR HOUSE was built by Sir John Arundell in 1571 on the site of an even older property. An administrator of the building, Dr Walker, reported hearing doors mysteriously opening and closing of their own accord. There is also a Grey Lady that walks in the North Wing of the house, sometimes venturing along the Gallery and down the stone circular stairway.

An inexplicable aroma of lilacs has been noticed in the Library. This room also caused one visitor to shie from entering it, simply because the atmosphere was too forbidding. Workmen in the North Wing once reported hearing two doors opening and the swishing sound of a garment, as well as a strange fragrance.

TROUT HOTEL
Lostwithiel, Cornwall

AN OUTBREAK of poltergeist activity occurred here in 1987.

TUNSTEAD FARM
Tunstead Milton, Derbyshire

IF I SAY that Tunstead Farm is the home of a skull called "Dickie", then it will become obvious that this is another Screaming Skull Legend. Navvies digging in the soil of the farm to make the rail link between Buxton and Stockport, were hindered by the earth continuously caving in on them. "Dickie" seems to have earned the blame for this, and the bridge over the railway is now known as "Dickie's Bridge". "Dickie" is unusual in that, unlike most screaming skulls, he also earns his keep as a kind of spectral burglar alarm. On one occasion a thief broke into the farm, but "Dickie" caused such horrific thuds and crashes that the burglar was caught red-handed, as well as being terrified out of his wits I don't doubt! Whenever an animal fell ill in the fields, "Dickie" would tap three times on the farmer's window to alert him (don't question how he achieves all this). If anyone should be so ungrateful as to dispose of the cranium, then a strange moaning will issue through every keyhole in the house.

"Dickie" doesn't like strangers either, and if one should appear at the farm then he will start wailing and banging in protest. Once three Irish labourers were sleeping in the barn when they were woken by the clashing of hay-ricks and pitchforks. The skull was once stolen and taken to Disley, causing screams and thumps to erupt in both places. "Dickie" was in fact reckoned to have been a woman who was murdered at the farm, and "She-Dickie" can also have a fairly sinister effect on the occupants of the farm when she appears in phantom form.

During the 1880s Farmer Lomas was nursing his sick baby daughter in the kitchen, when he heard someone coming downstairs. A female figure slipped between him and the fireplace, and then bent low over the cradle.

Farmer Lomas thought it was one of the servants, and told her not to disturb the baby. The figure vanished. The baby died a few minutes later. The moral of this story is that if "She-Dickie" had been left to tend the baby, the little girl might have lived.

TURTON TOWER
Blackburn, Lancashire

IN 1066 King William the Conqueror bequeathed the land to a gentleman named De Orell, in thanks for a few favours granted. De Orell built a strong house here as a kind of fortress. From the 13th century until 1420 the Lathom family held the manor, finally passing it to the Orells, descendants of the original owner. The Tower is now haunted by a lady who walks in the corridors. She is generally detected by the sound of rustling silk.

A phantom Woman in Black has been sighted going up the stairs to the top floor. Other phenomena recorded here includes a wooden cradle being rocked by invisible hands, bangings, screechings and knockings. An heirloom called the 'Timberbottom Skulls' are kept in a glass case at the Tower. These, one female and one male, were fished out of Bradshaw Brook in 1751. One appeared to have been killed by a blow from a sharp instrument, and so, as you might expect, the Tower also pays host to a Screaming Skull Legend.

In 1882 the skulls were obtained by an old lady who asserted that they had been thieves. The legend behind them was that in the latter part of the 17th century the family went away for a while, and the house was left in the care of a manservant. The building was broken into and the loyal servant decapitated two of the thieves with a sword. The other robbers fled, thoughtfully taking their colleagues's corpses with them, but leaving the heads behind. Another more plausible story for the skulls is that a farmer killed his wife, and then committed suicide, though how the corpses became separated from the heads is still a mystery.

TWM BARLWM
Risca, Gwent, Wales

THE REMAINS of a castle mound and a fort on this mountain show that it was once occupied. Many people have heard organ music on the summit.

UNIVERSITY COLLEGE
Gower Street, London

THE NATURAL SCIENTIST, Jeremy Bentham, haunts the main corridors here. He died in 1832, bequeathing his body to the University for medical science. The University re-erected his skeleton into a lifelike figure, and then seated him in a chair complete with gloves and cane. Bentham was not mummified to his exact wishes, however, and so his restless spirit now prowls the University, rapping on doors and windows. A maths teacher once heard the tapping of his cane in a passage, and on looking out he saw Bentham's ghost. The phantom flung himself at the teacher, and passed right through him. A flapping of wings and the inexplicable removal of books has been reported in one room.

UPPARK
South Harting, West Sussex

THE BUILDER of this 17th century house, Lord Grey of Werke, ran off with his fiancée's sister, Lady Henrietta Berkeley, in 1682. He returned to the house several years later and died there in 1701. The estate was passed to his daughter, and her

306

grandson sold it to Matthew Fetherstonhaugh in 1747. In 1780 Sir Harry Featherstonhaugh scandalised everyone by bringing home a 15 year-old girl that he had picked up in a seedy drinking club in London. The girl was eventually thrown out by Sir Harry, but went on to become Lady Emma Hamilton. The Prince Regent was a frequent visitor at the house between 1785 and 1810. In 1825 the old reprobate, (Sir Harry that is), married his head dairymaid, Mary Anne Bullock, and died at the ripe old age of 92. He has haunted the Red Room ever since. He often appears underneath his portrait, which was painted in 1776 and hangs over the fireplace. His ghost has a finickity habit of turning the antique firescreen round. Other reported phenomena here includes the mysterious opening and closing of windows. One of the administrators of the property, John Eyre, conducted several "scientific" experiments involving the firescreen and the ghost of Sir Harry. What they were supposed to prove – other than the existence of Sir Harry's ghost – I do not know.

VINE STREET POLICE STATION
Westminster, London

YOU WON'T be surprised to learn that this police station is haunted by a policeman. About 100 years ago Sergeant Goddard hanged himself in one of the cells here. His ghost has been seen since, usually in the corridors, opening locked cell doors and sometimes rifling through documents.

THE VOLUNTEER
Baker Street, London

BUILT OVER the site of two old farms, this pub is haunted by one Rupert Nevill. He was a Royalist during the Civil War, and fought at the Battle of Naseby. In 1654 his entire family were killed in a fire that demolished their farm. The pub was built on the site in 1794. In 1963 alterations were carried out which seemed to start off a spate of supernatural activity. Lights were inexplicably switched on and off, footsteps were heard, a ghostly apparition was seen, and the landlord himself was in the cellars one day when he saw a figure in 17th century costume.

Guy Lyon Playfair, author of the *Haunted Pub Guide*, asserts that there must be more than one ghost at this pub, or how could a ghost walk around a building that didn't exist in his own time? A fascinating point, and one which, as he rightly says, brings up the question of can ghosts move into our time? Most ghosts appear unaware of those still living – the walking through people trick illustrates this. But as the case of Elm Vicarage points out, ghosts have been known to have conversations with living people, in which they fully recognise that they are dead. Just one of the many fascinating and controversial arguments involving the supernatural.

WALBERSWICK
Suffolk

DURING THE MID-1930s writer George Orwell saw a ghostly
man in the chancel of the church in this village. This
phantom was also seen by a workman 50 years later. A
woman was blackberry picking out on Walberswick
Common when she felt a sharp drop in temperature, and
heard the sound of galloping hooves. Another woman
standing on top of Squire's Hill saw a man who vanished as
she watched him. Her dog began to act strangely and
refused to go any further. Two ladies have also reported
seeing a phantom hound on the common, and this leads us
to the most fascinating haunting associated with the area.

The East Anglian name for their local phantom hound
is 'Black Shuck', from the Saxon word 'Scucca' meaning
Devil. Some call him the 'Galley Trot'. During World War
II an American airman and his wife rented a hut on the
edge of Walberswick Marsh. They were disturbed by a
violent pounding on the door, and the airman reported
seeing a huge beast through the window. The couple
barricaded themselves in by putting furniture against the
door but the phantom hound retaliated by hurling itself
against each wall and then jumping onto the roof. At dawn
the couple tentatively peered outside. The beast had

vanished, leaving no trace of his memorable visit. His appearances have sometimes come complete with a glowing light, and many locals consider him to be an omen of death. He is also said to haunt Overstrand Churchyard.

WALLINGTON HOUSE
Cambo, Northumberland

AUGUSTUS HARE, Victorian ghost-collector, visited this house in 1862, and it is to him that we owe much of the details of this rather uncanny haunting. The phenomena that he said was attributed to this 17th century house included running footsteps in the passages, the flapping of wings against the windows, bodyless people who are said to unpack and put things away all night, and other invisible beings who breathe over unsuspecting sleepers.

The Hall was built in 1688 on the site of an even earlier property, and in 1777 passed into the hands of the rather disconcerting Trevelyan family. When Hare visited them he was put into a room that he vehemently described as "quite horrid". In fact his quarters so unnerved him that he pushed a heavy dressing-table against the door to stop anything undesirable from getting in. From his vivid descriptions of the Trevelyan family, I can assume he included them in the Unwelcome Intruder category. Sir Walter Trevelyan was said never to laugh (ever), Lady Trevelyan didn't care tuppence about the running of her chaotic home and spent most of her time describing the "extraordinary feel" that permeated her house. The household was completed by a Mr Wooster who had appeared as a guest four years before and had never left. This gentleman liked to unnerve people by rolling his eyes until one could see only the whites. Mr Hare described the Trevelyan family as being rather strange and humourless.

311

Now add to this building a reputed monster whom Eric Maple described as flapping against the window and having asthmatic breathing, and the whole place sounds like something out of *"The Munsters"*!

WANDLEBURY HILLFORT
Stapleford, Cambridgeshire

A PHANTOM BLACK HOUND is believed to run over the Gog Magog Hills on winter nights. Another spectral beast was seen about 60 years ago on the road south of this earthwork. He was described as being about the size of a small donkey.

WAPPING OLD STAIRS
London

IN 1701 THE INFAMOUS pirate Captain William Kidd was hanged here for killing one of his crew. As was the tradition in those days his corpse was left to hang for a while. Several days later a shadowy figure was spotted emerging from the waters of Execution Dock. Other sightings have confirmed his presence here.

WARBLETON PRIORY FARM
Rushlake Green, East Sussex

THE FARM was built on the site of an old priory. When the walls of the priory were knocked down a workman found two skulls in the walls, and thus yet another Screaming Skull Legend was born. The first skull was buried, but the following morning it reappeared on the doorstep. It was put

312

on the crossbeams of the house and then placed on a Bible. The second skull turned up in a neighbouring farmhouse, and the surprised farmer buried it. To his dismay a whirlwind blew up, and the farmer returned it to Warbleton Priory Farm.

If the skulls should be threatened with a new home the cows would dry-up. One tenant was so enraptured with his grisly souvenir that he tried to take it with him when he moved (well there's no accounting for taste). Needless to say anarchy broke out. Screams and knockings racked the house and horses reared-up. The skulls are said to be that of a murderer and his victim, and there is rumoured to be a permanent bloodstain in an upper room. At the full moon it is said that hands can be seen at a top window. The skulls were stolen in 1905, and surprisingly all havoc ceased! Nothing was heard of them again until 1963, when one appeared to be up for sale in *The Times*' but by 1977 they had both returned to the farm and displayed in a case in what was then an exclusive hotel.

WARDLEY HALL
Swinton, Manchester

THE SKULL that is reverently preserved in a niche above the staircase here has a typically long and complicated story behind it. Roger Downes was sacked from the court of King Charles II for some unknown misdemeanor (although I suppose it must have been pretty dire for Old Rowley to have got rid of him). Downes thoroughly drowned his sorrows, and then rashly announced that he would kill the first person he encountered. He fatally stabbed a poor tailor, but was, rather surprisingly, pardoned for this offence.

He was next heard of again when he was involved in a riot on London Bridge, which resulted in his death when he was decapitated by a watchman. His body was thrown into the Thames and his skull was sent home to his sister Maria. In 1780 the Downes family vault was opened in Wigan Church, and Roger's body was found to be wholly intact, complete with head!

So who does the skull belong to then? Wardley Hall was purchased by the Downes family in 1600. During the days of Roman Catholic persecution, Francis Downes sheltered a Catholic priest called Edward Barlow. Around Easter 1640 Barlow was arrested by a Protestant gang, and taken before a magistrate. He was executed in Lancaster, and Francis took the skull of his dear friend back to the house. Naturally, removal of Barlow's skull from the house can bring on violent storms. Over the years the skull has been burned, hacked to pieces and thrown into the river. It has always returned intact.

WARWICK CASTLE
Warwickshire

KING WILLIAM the Conqueror built the first motte and bailey castle here in 1068. In 1604 Sir Fulke Greville was granted the property, and spent an enormous amount of money restoring it. He now haunts his old rooms in the Water Gate Tower. Strange footsteps have also been heard in the Japanese Corridor.

WASHINGTON OLD HALL
Tyne & Wear

THIS 17TH CENTURY house was built over the site of an even earlier building, which from 1183-1613 was the home of George Washington's ancestors. It was donated to the

USA in 1975 on a 25-year lease as a bicentennial present. The ghost of a lady in grey has been seen gliding along an upstairs passage. Some witnesses claim there is a strong likeness between her and a portrait in the hall.

WATLING STREET
between Hinckley & Nuneaton, Warwickshire

DICK TURPIN is a very busy boy in the 'After Life'. He haunts this old Roman road, wearing a dashing jacket with red sleeves.

WATTON ABBEY
Driffield, Humberside

IN JUNE 1956 seven workmen were helping with the sale of the furniture and camping on the ground floor of the house. During the night a gale blew up, and at 1:00 AM the tolling of a bell was heard. The workmen were rather disconcerted by this as the bell itself had been removed several years before! In fact, one of the men even jumped out of the window in fright. The auctioneer's foreman fired a shot skywards, and the bell stopped. The men decided to spend the rest of the night in the marquee in the grounds. They claimed that they thought their sleep had been disturbed by the work of the most famous of the Abbey's resident ghosts, a nun called Elfrida.

Elfrida had been victimised by her Abbess who was jealous of her youth, so the youngster ran away, but was seduced by a man, who then deserted her because he decided he'd rather be a monk. Pregnant, Elfrida returned to the Abbey to beg repentance and the old cat of an Abbess had the girl sentenced to death.

Before sentence could be carried out though, the other nuns decided that Elfrida should suffer a bit more first. Her veil was torn off, she was stripped naked and then manacled to the floor in the dungeon. She was whipped until she bled and then kept tied up in the cellar for a while, on a diet of bread and water. The nuns, (who really should have worked out the excess energy caused by their sexual frustration in some more productive way), then decided to have a go at Elfrida's cowardly lover as well. They kidnapped him, took him to a remote part of the convent and tortured him while Elfrida had to watch. A week later Elfrida's son was born and taken away from her. She died soon after.

Elfrida's ghost has been sighted over many years. Another ghost is that of a lady who was beheaded in the Civil War. Armies of Roundhead soldiers had marched over the area, though the owner of the Abbey had been a Royalist. He hid his wife and child in the house and then ran for his life. The Roundheads broke into the house and found the innocent victims. The child was bashed to death against the wall and the woman was decapitated. Her ghost is now thought to be searching for her child. The Civil War certainly ranks as an episode in our history that we have very little to be proud of, but this doesn't deter the current tenants of the Abbey, who are members of 'The Sealed Knot', a society revelling in the re-creation of the English Civil War.

Less disturbing ghosts at the Abbey are a little man in a brown suit, who has been sighted in the garden, and a relaxed cavalier who leans nonchalantly against a nonexistent fireplace in one of the bedrooms.

WEATHERCOCK LANE
Aspley Guise, Bedfordshire

THE GHOST of Dick Turpin is said to ride along this lane (is every male spectre on a horse thought to be him? One witness watched him enter the courtyard of the manor house in this area, where he faded into the wall. This vision was accompanied by the sound of horse's hooves.

WEAVER'S RESTAURANT
Haworth, West Yorkshire

THE GHOST of Emily Bronte not only haunts her beloved moors, she is also said to put in an appearance here on the anniversary of her death – 19 December. In 1966 the owner saw a woman in a crinoline and carrying a basket climbing up the area where the old staircase had been. She was recognised from her portrait in the old parsonage.

WESTHAM (CHURCH)
East Sussex

WESTHAM CHURCH stands not far from Pevensey Castle, and in 1978 a visitor saw a ghost here. A man in a modern suit was walking along the path leading from the church door. The witness spoke to him and the man vanished. He has been seen by other visitors as well.

WEST KENNET LONG BARROW
Wiltshire

THE GHOST of a priest is said to enter the burial chamber at sunrise on Midsummer's Day. He is usually followed by a phantom white hound.

WESTMINSTER ABBEY
London

THE PRESENT Abbey on this site was started during the reign of King Henry VIII, and the west front was completed in 1734. Night-time visitors and cleaning staff have often reported seeing a ghostly monk wafting around. Nobody seems to be terribly certain who he is, and unfortunately he hasn't been seen since the 1930s. In 1932 it was observed by one witness that his feet were several inches off the floor. In 1900 he paid a lengthy visit, wandering around the place for 25 minutes before vanishing. Another ghost is that of John Bradshaw, who signed the death warrant of King Charles I. Bradshaw haunts the Deanery. A soldier in World War I uniform has been seen standing near the tomb of the Unknown Warrior. This mysterious man was given a state funeral in the Abbey on 11 November 1920, to commemorate all the needless waste of human life during the 'Great' War.

WESTWOOD MANOR
Bradford-on-Avon, Wiltshire

A PREVIOUS OWNER, E G Lister, swore blind that one bedroom in this 15th century manor was definitely haunted. He himself had seen a ghostly lady there on several occasions, and also reported hearing mysterious footsteps. One of the upstairs bedrooms has bed-hangings which originally came from Littlecote and were said to have been around when Will Darrell murdered a baby. Another owner, Denys Sutton, claimed that he sometimes slept very badly in this particular bedroom.

On one occasion a Danish ambassador's wife entered the bedroom and asserted immediately that there was a ghost lurking in there. Another ghost, Sutton claimed, is one of the headless kind. This silent phantom wanders about the house, and was also seen by Sutton's predecessor. Sutton's children also reported being scared stiff at the house.

WEST WYCOMBE
Buckinghamshire

THE VILLAGE of West Wycombe was once the stamping-ground of Sir Francis Dashwood, creator of the infamous Hell Fire Club. This was founded in 1755, and met at Medmenham Abbey, six miles away from West Wycombe Park. Its purpose seemed to be for the enjoyment of wild drunken debauchery rather than anything Satanic. Paul Whitehead, a former steward of the club, died in 1774, and his ghost was sighted in the grounds of West Wycombe Park in 1781. It disappeared for good after the death of Sir Francis later that same year. Nevertheless a guest at the house during the 1930s was sitting alone in the dining-room after dinner when the room suddenly went icy-cold, and an unearthly silence was noticed. To his astonishment he was then joined at the table by 11 ghostly figures!

Noel Coward was once playing the piano in the saloon when he looked up and saw a ghostly monk, who promptly vanished. A clairvoyant, Tom Corbett, saw the ghost of a beautiful woman in the Music Room in 1962.

The village pub, the '*George and Dragon*', is haunted by a White Lady. This is believed to be the ghost of 'Sukie', a serving-wench employed at the Inn 200 years ago, and who has been seen on dark nights. In 1967 an American author who was staying at the pub felt cold fingers touch his face whilst he was in bed, and he saw a shape near the door. The room had suddenly gone extremely cold. A Mrs Boon saw the girl sat in a bedroom, gazing miserably into a mirror. The phantom vanished. In 1933 the *Journal of the Royal Society of Arts* claimed that the staircase is *the* haunted spot. It related that the footsteps heard on the stairs were those of a man supposed to have been murdered at the Inn. A psychic guest at the pub also claimed that the stairs were haunted, and said that a terrible quarrel had taken place on them with tragic results. The *Good Pub Guide* says that there is poltergeist phenomena at the pub nowadays, but reassures prospective customers that it is not of an especially violent nature.

WHALLEY ABBEY
Clitheroe, Lancashire

A WOMAN ONCE TOLD of hearing ghostly singing coming from the ruined nave here, and a reporter from the *Daily Express* had the same experience. Two students saw a procession of monks which vanished. The Pope gave monks the licence to appropriate Whalley Church in 1289. In 1296 Abbot Gregory and his monks set up residence here. The last Abbot, John Paslew, was executed for treason at Lancaster in 1537 and in 1553 the Abbey was bought by John Braddyll and Richard Asheton. They divided the property between them. In 1923 the ruins and the house were acquired by the Church, and are now used as a training centre.

Other phenomena recorded here includes doors closing, footsteps heard on the stone floors of the passages, a blue light floating across the grounds, the sound of chanting, a nun sighted in the East Wing, and visitors have felt someone sitting on their bed during the night. Modern-day ghost-hunter Terence Whittaker once spent the night here, and related how he heard a door slam violently in the small hours, then came a knock on his door and footsteps in the passage outside.

WHITBY ABBEY
North Yorkshire

THE ABBEY was founded in 655 AD, and the main ghost here is that of St Hilda, daughter of the founder. Her figure can be seen at the windows dressed in a shroud. Bram Stoker mentioned St Hilda's ghost in his classic horror story "*Dracula*", when Mina writes excitedly in her diary of a ghostly figure in white that is said to haunt the Abbey.

The Abbey also has a bricked-up nun in the form of Constance de Beverley. Constance broke her vows by falling in love with a knight called Marmion (himself immortalised in Sir Walter Scott's work of the same name), and was interned in the dungeon for her sins. She now sits in a distressing state on the steps leading down to her prison.

A coach pulled by four headless horses has also been seen going into the Abbey. Incidentally, any person wishing to go treasure-hunting in the ruins may feel a tap on the shoulder, and on turning is likely to see a white figure with no head. Sometimes at dawn on the old Christmas Day (about 6th January) a ghostly choir can be heard in the ruins.

WHITE CROSS
Leven, Humberside

THE ROAD HERE is haunted by a headless woman who would creep up on highwaymen and slap their ears. The area is generally avoided by local people at night.

WHITE HART INN
Calamore Green, Walsall, Staffordshire

THIS PUB is said to have a haunted attic where a baby's mummified arm was once found. The arm, which is now in the keeping of Walsall Central Library, was found in 1870 along with a 17th century sword. There are rumours that it all has vague connections with a girl who committed suicide here. In 1955 the landlord heard cries coming from the attic. On further investigation he found the imprint of a baby's hand in the dust on a table. One former landlady woke up in the night to find a white form standing by her bed. A relief manager informed the local press that he had heard mysterious footsteps in one room. The pub dog (these animals always seem to have a rough time of it whenever an Inn is haunted) was "disturbed by something" in the building. Some members of a psychic research team spent a night in the attic, and as per usual saw nothing, but they did note a severe drop in temperature. The baby's arm is said to be a hospital specimen injected with preservative. There are also vague mumblings about witchcraft in connection with the attic.

WHITE HART
Oxford, Oxfordshire

THIS 15TH CENTURY coaching house has a resident ghost glamourously nicknamed 'Rosalind'. She has usually been seen wearing a veil and sobbing next to the spiral staircase in the brewery room. She is said to have been a girl who hanged herself here because of unrequited love. Other reported phenomena includes the tipping over of a barrel of sherry, glasses swept from the shelves, and the handbell used for ringing time was once flung to the floor by an invisible presence. 'Rosalind' has obviously got a nasty temper on her.

THE WICKED LADY
Nomansland Common, St Albans, Hertfordshire

LIKE THE FAMOUS Margaret Lockwood film, this watering-hole is named after Britain's only well-known female highway-robber. Lady Katharine Ferrars was a spoilt aristocrat who took to highway robbery at night to recoup her gambling debts. She was fatally shot on the common here. 'The Wicked Lady' is supposedly where she had her illicit rendezvous with her highwayman lover. In December 1970 the landlord was walking his dog on the common one night when he heard the thunder of invisible hooves close to him. His dog was visibly terrified.

WICKEN FEN
Cambridgeshire

TOM FULLER, whose family has lived in Wicken for centuries, said that his dogs always attacked something invisible when on these 700 acres of nature reserve. His grandfather, Joseph Fuller, once met a vague ghostly form as he was driving home at twilight. Nervously he struck out at it with his whip, which went right through the apparition. The fenland is also the home of evil spirits, recognised as mysterious lights, and known as 'The Lantern Men'. A fisherman once claimed that he was chased by one of these eerie creatures. In terror he threw himself onto the ground, and the light passed over him. These "spirits" are now believed to be balls of methane thrown up by the marshes.

Ghostly Roman soldiers have been known to loom up out of nowhere and then disappear again. Just for good measure there is also a phantom black hound who disappears into the mist. This big-eyed animal is said to be an omen of death. A ghostly witch is also known to lurk along the pathways, and chanting monks have been heard at a nearby farm called 'Spinney Abbey' which stands on the site of an old priory.

WIG & PEN CLUB
The Strand, London

THE CLUB, which is chiefly for lawyers and journalists, was built on some Roman remains, and was one of the few buildings to survive the 1666 Great Fire. In its time the building has been used for a number of purposes, including a keeper's cottage.

A proprietor sleeping on the premises often heard

mysterious footsteps at 2:00 in the morning, coming from the ground floor. The story goes that in the mid-1850s a solicitor was found dead in his office on this floor. The restless ghost is thought to be him. It has also been heard on Saturday afternoons.

WILLINGTON MILL
Northumberland

WHEN JOSEPH PROCTOR and his Quaker family moved into their new home in 1835, they were not to know of the terrifying supernatural experiences they were going to endure. The house was reputedly built on the site of an old cottage where a terrible crime had been committed several years before. When ghost-hunter W T Stead researched the haunting in the 1890s he found 40 people who had been witnesses to the paranormal phenomena here. The hauntings began in January 1835 when the nursemaid who was in the second-floor nursery, heard heavy footsteps in the disused room directly above. This went on for several nights. The servants and family sprinkled meal on the floor but no footprints were revealed. One morning the entire household were saying prayers in the parlour when they heard footsteps coming down the stairs and along the passage. When the front door was heard opening, Mr Proctor rushed into the hall. The disembodied footsteps carried on down the garden path. It is not surprising that Mrs Proctor fainted, and the family then had trouble persuading servants to stay at the house. Other reported phenomena included doors opening, the sound of thumps, blows, laboured breathing, the tiny footsteps of a child, chairs being moved and a rustling noise like a silk dress.

On Whit Monday the maid, Mary Young, was washing dishes in the kitchen, when she saw the ghost of a lady in a lavender silk dress walking upstairs. Two of Mrs Proctor's sisters came to stay and were allocated a four-poster bed. On their first night they felt the bed being lifted up. On another night it was shaken violently, the curtains were lifted up and then let down again. Both women saw a female phantom drift out of the wall and lean over them. The ladies refused to spend any more nights in the bed.

Neighbours of the Proctors, the Mann family, were walking past the house one night when they saw the figure of a priest at a second-floor window. During the summer of 1840 Edward Drury and a male companion were invited by the Proctors to spend a night on a ghost-vigil in the Blue Room on the second-floor. The friend went to sleep in a chair. At 12:50 AM Edward Drury saw a woman in grey step out of a closet, and move as though in pain towards the chair where his friend slept. Drury was later carried downstairs hysterically shrieking "keep her off!" One of the daughters of the house saw a woman sitting on her mother's bed. She related calmly that the lady hadn't appeared to have any eyes. Another child was in bed when he saw a strange man enter his room, raise the window, lower it and then quietly leave. The long-suffering Proctor family vacated their not-so des. res. in 1847. Even after the house deteriorated into a slum, strange things were still heard and seen from time to time.

WINCHCOMBE (CEMETERY)
Gloucestershire

A PHANTOM MONK has been seen walking 2ft above ground-level along the road. Ghostly music and chanting have been heard from the site of the church at night.

WINDERMERE
Cumbria

FERRY NAB is haunted by a white horse and a phantom boat, and an eerie moaning sound has been heard from the lake. One particular ghost to be strictly avoided in this area is the 'Crier of Claife'. Its presence is detected by shouts, screams and weird howling noises. In recent times some hounds on a fox-hunt refused to pass the area. A schoolmaster set out from Colthouse one night, determined to lay the ghost. He was never seen again.

WINDSOR CASTLE
Berkshire

BUILT BY King William the Conqueror, this royal residence has a very prolific haunting. The cloisters of the Deanery are haunted by King Henry VIII. His weary groans and dragging footsteps have been heard in the passages here. In 1977 the royal lecher was sighted by two soldiers on the battlements but the bloated phantom faded into a wall. With such a man wandering the castle it is not surprising that Anne Boleyn puts in the odd appearance now and again. She has been seen at a window in the Dean's Cloister and the writer, Hector Bolitho, once reported hearing mysterious footsteps in the passage in the old Deanery.

A ghostly little boy was seen in a bedroom at the castle 40 years ago, complaining that he "didn't want to go riding today". King Charles I visits the Canon's House from time to time, and has also been seen standing by a table in the library whilst Queen Elizabeth I haunts the Royal Library, and was once seen by Princess Margaret. Lieutenant Carr Glynn saw a Woman in Black in the Royal Library in 1897, and from his description, she was assumed to be Good Queen Bess.

King George III has been seen at a window in one of the rooms below the Royal Library, where he was confined during his mental deterioration and has also been heard muttering "what? what?" – his favourite catchphrase. A phantom groom and horse vanish into a wall in the Horseshoe Cloisters. Footsteps have been heard walking up the stairs in the Mary Tudor Tower, and a wall between two of the bedrooms here, is said to move in the night. Sir George Villiers makes a habit of appearing in one of the bedrooms. Sentries on the Long Walk have been known to declare that some of the marble statues appear to move. The ghost of Herne the Hunter is also said to walk about here and he was seen by a guardsman as recently as 1976. Another soldier saw the ghost of a colleague who had shot himself on the Long Walk a few weeks earlier. Children playing in the Norman Tower once saw the ghost of a man in what was once a prison and an invisible presence has been known to brush past people in the North Tower and the statues in the gardens at the back of the castle near the private quarters are said to multiply from 12 to 13 during the night.

During the early 1970s a sentry is stated to have had a long conversation with a policeman, who had died of a heart-attack 30-40 years before. William of Wykeham, an architect in the 14th century, is said to stand on the Round Tower at night. A Woman in White is said to appear daily in the Horseshoe Cloisters on the stroke of 6:00 PM.

THE WINNATS
Castleton, Derbyshire

DURING THE middle of the 18th century this area was considered to be the Gretna Green of England. Legend goes that rich girl Clara fell in love with poor boy Allan, and they rode off to Winnats Pass to get married. They were thwarted in their plans when they were held up and robbed of £200 by five drunken miners from Castleton. Allan was killed with an axe whilst the bride-to-be was brutally raped and then murdered. Their bodies were tossed into sacks and hastily buried. The spot of their unmarked grave is now haunted by bloodcurdling noises, such as thuds, screams and dragging sounds. Some ten years later miners were digging in a mineshaft when they found the remains of the two pathetic lovers. The tragic couple are still to be seen wandering about the area, hand-in-hand. Of the murderers, one died shortly after the killings, another fell from a wall, another was killed by a falling boulder, one hanged himself and the remaining miner went mad.

WINSFORD HILL
Exmoor, Somerset

A PHANTOM BLACK HOUND with glowing eyes has been sighted here. If he is seen, the traveller is advised to wait politely for him to vanish before continuing.

WISTMAN'S WOOD
Dartmoor, Devon

A HOUND OF the 'Yeth' (or Wild Hunt) haunts this cluster of stunted oaks, and is thought to be the prototype on which Sir Arthur Conan Doyle based his marvellous thriller *The Hound of the Baskervilles*. A funeral procession of monks in white robes has also been seen here. The name of the wood comes from the old local word 'whist' meaning 'eerie'. This title was earned by the appearance of the deformed trees and their creaky swaying in the wind.

WOBURN ABBEY
Bedfordshire

ACCORDING TO a book on sale at the gift shop here the present occupier, Lord Tavistock, is very dismissive about his resident ghost. But that doesn't seem to have any effect on the persistent rumours of various hauntings. One of the hauntings centered around the old Duke's television room. On numerous occasions the door handle would turn, the door open, a slight pause, and then the door at the opposite end of the room would open. The doors have since been removed and the room is now used as an open passage. On three occasions zillionaire Paul Getty had his bedroom doors flung open, followed by footsteps pattering around his room. The Duke and the Duchess of Bedford, when they were still in residence, occasionally felt someone touching their faces with wet hands as they lay in bed. The old Duke believed that the summer house is haunted by his unhappy grandmother. This fascinating lady was nicknamed 'The Flying Duchess', because of her penchant for piloting her own planes. She disappeared back in the 1930s when she took off in her plane to view the flooding in the fenlands.

A manservant to the 7th Duke was killed in the Masquerade Room. His body was hidden for a while in the cupboards, before being pushed out of the window, then dragged to the lake and thrown in. He now haunts a corridor on the first floor, and the dogs react to his presence by howling. The dogs also respond to an invisible being who lurks in the staff quarters in the North Wing. Doors there open by themselves, and the rooms are often icy cold. A cleaning lady and a workman saw the ghost of a monk walking about under the Abbey during excavation work, which is logical as that particular area had once been a burial ground for monks.

Several people claim to have seen a man in a top hat on the second floor of the Antiques Centre. Ten women on different occasions have been groped by an invisible hand in the Sculpture Gallery, whether this is the cheeky work of the ghostly monk who has been seen standing between the entrance pillars I do not know! The last Abbot of Woburn had spoken out against King Henry VIII's marriage to dear old Anne Boleyn. The Abbot paid for his indiscretion with his life. He was hanged from the oak tree at the south front of the house. In March 1971 a figure in a brown habit was seen standing between the entrance pillars to the Sculpture Gallery, and then vanished. A cold blast has been felt whenever the ghost appears. I find it hard to believe that he has turned into a dirty old fumbler in the 'After Life' though!

A female medium once claimed that there were no less than nine ghosts in the old Duchess's bathroom. Apart from making things rather crowded, the Duchess never saw any of them. The communicating doors between the Green Bedroom and the Rose Bedroom have often opened of their own accord. In the same rooms a cold, wet hand passes over unwitting guests in bed.

10 WOODHOUSE SQUARE
Leeds, West Yorkshire

THE TOP FLOOR APARTMENT in this house was used in times gone by as a nursery. After the conversion the occupant Peter Turner, returned home to find a friend outside the flat, too terrified to go back in for he had heard strange noises and felt eerie sensations.

Other supernatural phenomena included the door of a large cupboard swinging open, despite being securely fastened, footsteps crossing a room and then the living room door swinging open. Peter's wife said that the door of the kitchen cupboard would open of its own accord. She also heard shuffling feet, and felt someone standing behind her. During the night they often heard their sofa being dragged across the living room floor. When they went to look, nothing would have been moved. The ghostly furniture moving continued, until one night there was a loud crash. Though they found nothing amiss, their neighbours on the floor below, put in a complaint about the Turner's nocturnal sofa dragging! The haunting is said to be caused by a Victorian lady who constantly searches for her two children, who both died in the nursery.

WYCOLLER HALL
Nr Haworth, West Yorkshire

IT IS ALLEGED that Charlotte Bronte used this house as the setting for Mr Rochester's pad, Thornfield Hall, in *Jane Eyre*, just one of the legends it has attracted. The lanes around the isolated house are said to be haunted by ghostly horsemen and their pack of hounds. The ruined house has stood empty for well over 100 years, but for decades was the home of the Cunliffe family. They lost a lot of their money for supporting the Royalists during the Civil War. The last Cunliffe died in 1820, and the property has deteriorated ever since.

Once a year a phantom horseman makes a visit, wearing a Tudor or Stuart costume. Just as a point of added interest for those planning their holidays, mild weather always accompanies his visit but the snag is I don't know exactly when it is. He rides across the bridge, halts at the door, dismounts and goes inside. Screams and moans then issue out of the building. The ghost reappears and leaves. The story goes that a former Cunliffe lady was murdered in her bedroom, and the ghost is thought to be her dastardly killer. Before her death she had predicted the extinction of the family line. Another more eccentric theory to the haunting is that the ghost is a former squire, Simon Cunliffe. Whilst out hunting he pursued the fox into his house and up the stairs. When he rode into his wife's bedroom, she died of shock.

YORK ARMS
High Petergate, York, North Yorkshire

THIS TOWN CENTRE PUB which stands only yards away from the Minster, has a Grey Lady among its residents. She is thought to have connections with the Theatre Royal, which is also haunted by a Grey Lady. Whether they are one and the same is a matter for speculation. Reported phenomena here includes objects moved around, an old pair of bellows being unhooked from the wall and tossed gently to the floor (this was witnessed by several customers), cutlery and cassettes thrown about, and doors opening and shutting themselves. An ornament on an upstairs window ledge slid about of its own accord. A window crashed shut and a family portrait fell to the floor. On one occasion the invisible phantom opened the bathroom door whilst the landlord was in the tub!

YORK VILLA
Bath, Avon

NOW A BUS COMPANY'S social club, it is haunted by a young boy, a Grey Lady, and a man in a long cloak. They have all been seen upstairs. The building was once the home of the mistress of Frederick Duke of York, son of King George III. He jilted her and returned to London. She followed him, leaving her two children in the care of her staff. Unfortunately she hadn't paid them for some while, and they left in high dudgeon. One old servant had a fit of conscience and returned several days later to find that the children had starved to death but the footsteps heard climbing the stairs, are said to be his.

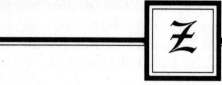

ZENNOR
Cornwall

THE GHOSTLY VOICE heard singing from the sea at Pendour Cove has been attributed to a mermaid, according to legend anyway. Also, if you touch the Witch's Rock twice at midnight, you are safeguarded against misfortune.

𝔅𝔦𝔟𝔩𝔦𝔬𝔤𝔯𝔞𝔭𝔥𝔶

The Good Pub Guide
Edited by Alisdair Aird
Hodder & Stoughton, 1990

*Historic Houses Castles and
Gardens*
Edited by Sheila Alcock
British Leisure Publications, 1990

The World's Greatest Ghosts
by Nigel Blundell and Roger Boar
Octopus Books Ltd, 1984

Atlas of Magical Britain
by Janet and Colin Bord
Sidgwick & Jackson, 1990

Modern Mysteries of the World
by Janet and Colin Bord
Grafton Books, 1990

Great Unsolved Mysteries
Edited by John Canning
Weidenfeld & Nicolson, 1990

Mysteries of the Unexplained
Reader's Digest
The Reader's Digest Association,
1982

The Hound of the Baskervilles
by Sir Arthur Conan Doyle
Foreword by John Fowles
Pan Books, 1975

The Celtic Church Speaks Today
by A W Jackson
World Fellowship Press, 1968

Theatre Ghosts
by Roy Harley Lewis
David & Charles, 1988

The Haunted Realm
by Simon Marsden
Webb & Bower, 1987

The Haunted Pub Guide
by Guy Lyon Playfair
Harrap, 1985

Ghosts of Devon
by Peter Underwood
Bossiney Books, 1982

This Haunted Isle
by Peter Underwood
Javelin Books, 1986

England's Ghostly Heritage
by T W Whitaker
Hale, 1989

Ghosts of Old England
by T W Whitaker
Hale, 1987

Index

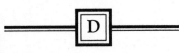

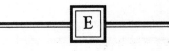

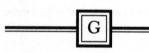
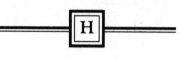

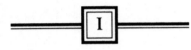
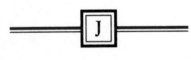
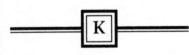

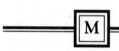

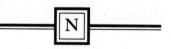

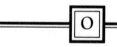

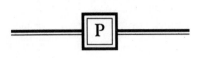
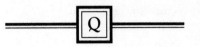
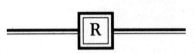
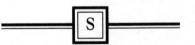

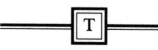

Uplyme, 73
Upper Dicker, 216-7
Uttoxeter, 42

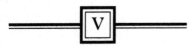

Valley, Anglesey, 204

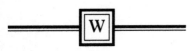

Walberswick, 310-11
Walsall, 322
Waltham Abbey, 37
Wapping, London, 300, 312
Warminster, 250
Warwick, 314
Warwickshire, 35, 40-41, 106-7,
    120, 135-6, 140-41, 144, 189,
    314, 315
Washington, 314-15
Waterfoot, 245
Wellington (Somerset), 34-5
Welshpool, 239-41
West Clandon, 113-14
West Glamorgan, 44, 215, 228-9
West Kennet, 318
West Kensington, London, 269
West Midlands, 49-50
West Sussex, 44-5, 84-5, 120-21,
    193, 306-7
West Wycombe, 319-20
West Yorkshire, 78, 112-13, 139-
    40, 169, 173, 195, 226, 287-8,
    317, 331-2, 332-3

Westerham, 107
Westham, 317
Westminster, London, 308
Westonzoyland, 270
Wetherby, 215-16
Whalley, 320-21
Whitby, 321
White Cross, 322
Whitley Bay, 268
Wicken, 324
Wigan, 274-5
Wight, Isle of, 244
Wildsworth, 189
Willington, 325-6
Wiltshire, 33, 48, 112, 132, 179,
    196, 250, 251, 281, 318-19
Winchcombe, 281-2, 326
Winchester, 104, 293
Windermere, 100-101, 327
Windsor, 327-8
Winsford, 329
Winslow, 114-15
Wisbech, 142-3
Woburn, 330-31
Woodstock, 55
Wool, 115, 177
Wootton-under-Edge, 222-3

Yelverton, 94-5
York, 36, 43, 116, 181, 293-4,
    301-2, 334

Zennor, 336